FOUR EXISTENTIALIST THEOLOGIANS

By Will Herberg

JUDAISM AND MODERN MAN

PROTESTANT-CATHOLIC-JEW

THE WRITINGS OF MARTIN BUBER

FOUR EXISTENTIALIST THEOLOGIANS

❋ ❋ ❋ ❋

A Reader from the Works of
Jacques Maritain,
Nicolas Berdyaev,
Martin Buber,
and
Paul Tillich

❋ ❋ ❋ ❋

Selected and with an Introduction

and Biographical Notes by

Will Herberg

❋ ❋ ❋ ❋

GREENWOOD PRESS, PUBLISHERS
WESTPORT, CONNECTICUT

Library of Congress Cataloging in Publication Data

Herberg, Will, ed.
    Four existentialist theologians.

    Reprint of the ed. published by Doubleday, Garden
City, N. Y.
    1. Religion--Philosophy. 2. Existentialism. I. Ti-
tle.
[BL51.H469   1975]   200'.1   75-17472
ISBN 0-8371-8303-0

Originally published in 1958 by Doubleday & Company, Inc.,
Garden City, N.Y.

Reprinted with the permission of Doubleday & Company Inc.

Reprinted in 1975 by Greenwood Press,
a division of Williamhouse-Regency Inc.

Library of Congress Catalog Card Number 75-17472

ISBN 0-8371-8303-0

Printed in the United States of America

PREFACE

It is the purpose of this book to present, within the confines of a single volume, representative selections from the writings of four of the most significant religious thinkers of our time—Jacques Maritain, Nicolas Berdyaev, Martin Buber, and Paul Tillich—each reflecting the response of a major religious tradition to the perennial problems of human existence. All schemes of selection are unsatisfactory, yet some scheme is obviously necessary if a work of this kind is to be produced. My guiding principle has been to choose for presentation that which would best serve to bring out both the unity and the diversity in the thought of these four men. Other factors, such as availability and freshness of material, have entered into consideration, but the principle just indicated has always been kept in mind. The interpretive essay prefixed to the volume is designed to serve the same purpose, that of introducing the thinking of the four philosopher-theologians and indicating why they belong together, however different they may be in background or in the direction they have chosen to follow.

Since with every one of these men life and thought have been truly inseparable, each profoundly influencing the other, brief introductions have been included supplying something of the information necessary for a proper understanding of the historical and biographical context in which the thought we are concerned with took shape and form. Short bibliographies have also been appended. The selections have been reproduced as they appear in the books from which they were taken; hence the variations in typographical style and translation.

Much of the best creative thinking these days is being done in theology and religious philosophy. It is my hope that this volume will reveal some of the sources of this thinking as well as its relevance to the problems and perplexities of our time.

Will Herberg

November 1957

CONTENTS

FOUR EXISTENTIALIST THEOLOGIANS

General Introduction

It is, perhaps, not the least paradoxical aspect of a movement that makes so much of paradox as does the contemporary revival in theology that among its earliest protagonists were men who, in the stricter sense, were not theologians at all, but religious philosophers. In his influential survey, *Contemporary Continental Theology*, published in 1938, Walter Marshall Horton opens with a chapter on "The Rediscovery of Orthodox Theology," in which the central figure is Nicolas Berdyaev, and then goes on to "The Revival of Catholic Theology," in which it is Jacques Maritain who is given major attention. Martin Buber, though a Jew and therefore not really in the scope of Horton's survey, receives repeated mention; indeed, his *I and Thou* is hailed as the work in which the characteristic note of "the creative religious thought of the period since the [first world] war" is "most explicitly" expressed.[1] Now it cannot be without significance that all three of these figures are laymen and philosophers rather than theologians and clerics. Even Paul Tillich, the fourth of the men presented in this volume, though he is an ordained minister

[1] Walter Marshall Horton, *Contemporary Continental Theology* (Harper, 1938), p. 218.

and thinks of himself as primarily a theologian,[2] emphasizes that his main interest has always fallen in that disputed
area between theology and philosophy in which both the
"philosophy of religion" and the "theology of culture"
would seem to belong.[3]

The essentially lay and philosophical direction of their
thinking is a real bond uniting these four pioneers of the
theological revival. Their common ground, however, is not
confined to this initial orientation; it extends to certain fundamental assumptions and attitudes that in a real sense
underlie their more explicit teachings. Though each speaks
out of his own tradition—Maritain out of Roman Catholicism, Berdyaev out of Eastern Orthodoxy, Buber out of
Judaism, and Tillich out of Protestantism—they all raise
very much the same problems and stress very much the
same themes. Yet because they do speak out of different
traditions and operate with different philosophical categories, they deal with these problems and develop these
themes in significantly different ways. Both what is common to all and what is distinctive to each must enter
into any adequate understanding of the four philosopher-
theologians.

What are the common themes that give unity to the
thinking of men so diverse in outlook and tradition as Maritain, Berdyaev, Buber, and Tillich? Essentially, they may
be reduced to five heads.

1. *Ontology.* All four of these men develop their thought
in philosophic form. They do not present it as the elaboration of revealed truth, but as, in some sense, the conclusions of philosophical reflection and analysis. What they

[2] Paul Tillich, "Autobiographical Reflections," in Kegley,
Charles W., and Robert W. Bretall, eds., *The Theology of Paul
Tillich* (Macmillan, 1952), p. 10.
[3] Paul Tillich, "Autobiographical Reflections," in Kegley,
Charles W., and Robert W. Bretall, eds., *op. cit.*, pp. 9–10, 13–
14, 16.

have to say indubitably possesses theological relevance, and indeed we may suspect the operation of unexpressed theological presuppositions; yet it is not in an authoritative Scripture and tradition that their teachings seek their explicit sanction. Their teachings make their claim to validity primarily on their appeal to human reason and experience, however differently these terms are understood. More particularly, they all base their systems on an analysis of true being; their philosophical approach is therefore basically ontological. Maritain, Berdyaev, and Tillich have much to say about being and non-being, and they say it in quite explicit terms; in Buber, the ontological question appears in rather unusual form, but it is equally central. All of the four philosopher-theologians are ontologists in their point of departure, rather than theologians.

2. *Existentialism.* Even more obvious is the existentialist bent of their thinking. It is probably impossible to achieve a single unequivocal definition of this much used, much disputed term; but most generally we can describe thinking as existentialist if it makes existence rather than essence the starting point of its ontological reflections. In the sense this term has acquired since Kierkegaard, it is human existence, the "human situation," that is the starting point; existential thinking then becomes (to employ some of Kierkegaard's own expressions) the thinking of the existing subject about his existence as he "exists" his existence. Its notes are experiential concreteness, personal concern and commitment, the uniqueness of the existing individual, the primacy of enacted being (existence) over the mere concept of being. In this rather broad signification, the term is obviously open to many versions and interpretations, and these it has received in the course of recent decades. The four men we are considering have on repeated occasions referred to their thinking as existentialist in its emphasis on existence and personal involvement, but they have not all or always meant the same thing. By and large, we may

recognize the Kierkegaardian strain in Berdyaev, Buber, and Tillich, although it may be derived from other and more indirect sources. Maritain has also made a point of defining his way of thinking as existentialist; indeed, he has insisted that Thomism, properly understood, is the "only authentic existentialism."[4] But, true to his Thomist tradition, he has meant something rather different by the term: his ontological emphasis is not on the "human situation" or the "human predicament," nor for that matter on anything specifically human at all, but on the act of existence as the enactment of being. Nevertheless, it is not too difficult to recognize an "existentialist" temper in his thinking that brings him close to the men of the other three traditions; and in particular contexts, especially when dealing with men and society, the affinity becomes much more clear and intimate.

3. *Personalism.* This affinity is perhaps most obvious in the strong personalistic emphasis that permeates their philosophies. Roman Catholic, Eastern Orthodox, Jew, and Protestant are at one in insisting on the primacy of the person, on his uniqueness and integrity, in the varying relations of life; and each makes this affirmation a cornerstone of his social philosophy. They likewise agree in seeing true personal being fulfilled, not in isolation, but in community; and they all understand community in the same personalistic way, as involving mutual relation of man with man, rather than a system of external institutions in which the self is diminished and distorted. This personalism is not something superadded to their ontological and existentialist orientation, but flows directly from it. Their ontology—this is true even of Maritain, for all the "objectivist" bias of his Thomism—is strongly personalistic, and their existentialism, of course, even more so. The three—ontology, existentialism,

[4] Jacques Maritain, *Existence and the Existent* (Pantheon, 1948), p. 1.

and personalism—fall together into a coherent whole, as three facets of the same fundamental outlook.

4. *Social concern.* In terms of their common personalism, each of these four thinkers has developed a social concern that is most characteristic of the fundamental outlook they share. Unlike the theologians of Barthian and quasi-Barthian tendency, these men have been very conscious of the social relevance of their teaching, and have developed this aspect to major proportions in their writings. One might even say that at a certain point this social concern becomes their primary interest, never to be really subordinated despite the many and diverse directions of their work. And, as might be expected, the social thinking developed on the basis of their personalist and existentialist ontologies has been thoroughly radical in its uncompromising criticism of the depersonalization and the dehumanization resulting from modern mass society. Maritain's "Christian democracy," Berdyaev's "personalist socialism," Buber's "true community," and Tillich's "religious socialism" exhibit a remarkable agreement in fundamentals, however much they may vary in detailed development.

5. *Apologetic-cultural interest.* Again in marked contrast to the Barthian and quasi-Barthian schools, which cannot see the legitimacy of anything but the proclamation and the explication of the Word, all of the four men we are considering exhibit an ardent concern to establish the relevance of their faith to the intellectual and cultural life of the time. In other words, they display a serious apologetic interest. It is not simply that they desire to make their faith or their religious philosophy appealing to those outside its circle; their concern runs much deeper. They are themselves passionately interested in art, science, and other fields of culture as the creative work of the human spirit, and they are firmly convinced that unless this creative work is somehow related to the ultimate source of being, it is bound to fall into perversity and frustration. They also feel

that the culture of an age reflects the spiritual forces at work within it in a way that is both profound and revealing. If the secular culture has much to gain from the theocentric reference of which theology speaks, theology itself has much to gain from the insights of the thought and culture of the time. Indeed, without some real relation to the life of the time, without some real relevance to its social and cultural concerns, theology runs the danger of degenerating into an abstract, academic discipline cultivated as an academic specialty, instead of being, as it ought to be, in at least one of its aspects, a depth understanding of human existence in its ultimate dimension. To different degrees, all of the four men we are considering are apologetic theologians and "theologians of culture"[5]—Maritain, with his writings on philosophy, poetry, art, psychology, and politics; Berdyaev, with his interest in the creative act in art, literature, and social life; Buber, with his work in psychology, pedagogy, and sociology; Tillich, with his efforts to achieve a "correlation" with psychiatry, painting, and philosophy. When they theologize, they theologize in the midst of life, and with relevance to all the issues of life.

In these basic aspects of their thinking—ontological orientation, existentialist and personalist concern, social and cultural relevance—the four representatives of four religious traditions show their underlying unity. Yet this unity, real as it is, should not blind us to the different ways in which these themes are developed in the work of the four men, for it is the diversity of ways, as much as the common point of departure, that defines the significance of their thought.

Without doubt, the different ways Maritain, Berdyaev, Buber, and Tillich have taken reflect differences of personal temper and background, as well as differences in the religious traditions from which they derive. On another though

[5] Paul Tillich, "Autobiographical Reflections," in Kegley, Charles W., and Robert W. Bretall, eds., *op. cit.*, p. 13.

not unrelated level, these different directions of thought may be seen as stemming from fundamental differences in their understanding of being, and therefore in the content and structure of their ontologies.

Perhaps no concept in the entire field of thought is so difficult to define, or even to describe, as this concept of being, and none more subject to varying and ambiguous interpretations. Particularly complex is the relation of being to non-being, for this latter presents itself even more ambiguously than the being of which it is somehow, in some sense, the negation. Some measure of clarity may be introduced by making a fundamental distinction. Going back to Greek usage, we may distinguish between two kinds of non-being—*ouk on* and *mē on,* the non-being that flatly negates being and can have no commerce with it, and the non-being that, as potentiality, enters into a dialectical relation with being as the other pole of a genuine antithesis. Not all writers, it must be admitted, are fully conscious of this distinction, or take the trouble to indicate in what sense they use the term; but a careful scrutiny will generally reveal just what is involved, no matter how undiscriminating the vocabulary. Fortunately, the four men we are considering leave no doubt as to their usage and meaning.

Maritain, Berdyaev, and Tillich deal with being directly, more or less in the classical sense derived from Greek philosophy. But whereas Maritain, true to the scholastic tradition, sees being as the all-in-all and non-being (*ouk on*) as emptiness, vacancy, privation, non-entity, Berdyaev thinks of being as definition (finitude), limitation, restriction, and brands objectivity as unreal ("'Objective' things are devoid of ultimate reality"[6]). True reality he sees in non-being (*mē on*), the creative principle of freedom, which he designates as "meonic freedom." Tillich, true to

[6] Nicolas Berdyaev, *Dream and Reality* (Macmillan, 1951), p. 28.

his dialectic bent, strives to combine being and non-being: being in its self-enclosed isolation, he says, is sterile and inert; it becomes dynamic by taking non-being (*mē on*) into itself. Tillich, therefore, in a sense mediates between Maritain and Berdyaev: he shares the "ontic" allegiance of the former and the "meonic" passion of the latter; but with him they are united in dialectic tension.

Buber's ontology moves in a different direction, for it owes little to Plato. For Buber, true being, which is always primarily personal being, emerges in the "dialogical" relation of man-with-man (the *Zwischenmenschliche*), in the I-Thou relation. "[The Thou] does not help to sustain you in life," he says, "it only helps you to glimpse eternity."[7] Such statements lend themselves to the interpretation that whereas the I-Thou relation gives access to the world of reality, I-It gives access only to the world of appearance, to use the Platonic terminology. This impression is confirmed by Maurice Friedman's comment on Buber's epistemology, which naturally stems from his ontology. "From Buber's basic premise, 'As I become I, I say Thou,'" Friedman states, "it follows that our belief in the reality of the external world comes from our relation to other selves."[8] Thus, Buber's ontology too hinges on the relation of being to non-being, but in Buber both are from the very beginning interpreted in personalist, dialogical terms.

It is characteristic of the fundamentally philosophical bias of their thinking that the central theological affirmations of these four men directly reflect their ontologies. For Maritain, God is the fullness of Being, "Pure Act," that is, the full and perfect actualization of all the potentialities of being. For Berdyaev, on the other hand, God emerges out of the "meonic freedom" of the "Godhead." In his view, God is to be seen rather as pure potentiality, for he regards

[7] Martin Buber, *I and Thou* (Edinburgh: T. and T. Clark, 1937), p. 33.

[8] Maurice S. Friedman, *Martin Buber: The Life of Dialogue* (University of Chicago Press, 1955), p. 164.

actualization as a form of petrification which destroys freedom. For Tillich, God is Being-Itself; indeed, this statement, according to him, is the only non-symbolic thing we can say about God. But this Being-Itself is not Maritain's "Pure Act"; on the contrary, it reveals a complex structure in which actuality and potentiality, being and non-being, are combined so as to render Being-Itself creative and dynamic. For Buber, finally, God is the Eternal Thou whom man meets in the true "life of dialogue."

If we think in terms of the antithesis of being and non-being (interpreted in the meonic sense), it seems clear that it is stress on the role of non-being, or potentiality, that engenders an existentialist approach, in the Kierkegaardian sense at least. It is therefore intelligible that Berdyaev, with his hostility to actualized being and his insistence on meonic freedom, should be, and should proclaim himself to be, intransigently existentialist, and that Maritain, the philosopher of being as actuality, should espouse a form of existentialism that seems to many not to warrant the name. By the same logic, it is to be expected that Tillich, who strives to hold being and non-being together in a dynamic tension, should affirm both the essentialist and the existentialist ways of thinking in proper relation to each other, which indeed is what he does, quite explicitly, in his later writings.[9] Buber, for his part, takes a thoroughly existentialist attitude, though in a way that emphasizes its dialogical (I-Thou) character far more thoroughly than do the others.

Despite these differences, there is, as we have already seen, a remarkable convergence upon a philosophy of personalism. Here it is unquestionably Buber who was the pioneer, for it was Buber who, in a small book of some hundred pages, *Ich und Du* (*I and Thou*), issued in 1923,

---

[9] See, e.g., Paul Tillich, "Existential Analyses and Religious Symbols," in Harold A. Basilius, ed., *Contemporary Problems in Religion* (Wayne University Press, 1956), esp. pp. 38–44.

first formulated this philosophy in pregnant and unforgettable words. The self becomes a person, Buber taught, only
in genuine personal relation to other selves ("Through the
Thou, a man becomes an I"[10]); the person-in-community is
the primary reality, and all authentic being emerges in the
fullness of personal relation ("All real living is meeting"[11]).
It is as a personal relation that the divine-human encounter of faith is to be understood. "A man can have dealings
with God only as a Single One [that is, a person], only as a
man who has become a Single One."[12] The person is primary, though the person emerges only in community.

In Maritain, essentially the same teaching is given a
characteristic Thomist expression. Maritain distinguishes
between person and individual. "The human being is
caught between two poles," he says, "a material pole,
which does not concern him as a true person, but rather
the shadow of personality, or what, in the strictest sense is
called *individuality,* and a spiritual pole which does concern true *personality.*"[13] "Personality," however, "tends by
nature to communion . . . [for] the person requires membership in a society in virtue both of its dignity and its
needs."[14] Yet, in the final analysis, "the human person is ordained to God as to its absolute ultimate end; its direct or-
dination to God transcends every created common good."[15]

The theme is developed in Berdyaev in line with his philosophy of freedom. Man is man by virtue of the creative
non-being that he shares with God; by virtue of this meonic
freedom, he is a person; the actualized being which he
shares with the objective world would make him only an

[10] Martin Buber, *op. cit.,* p. 28.
[11] Martin Buber, *ibid.,* p. 11.
[12] Martin Buber, "The Question to the Single One," *Between Man and Man* (Macmillan, 1948), p. 43.
[13] Jacques Maritain, *The Person and the Common Good* (Scribner's, 1947), p. 23.
[14] Jacques Maritain, *ibid.,* p. 37.
[15] Jacques Maritain, *ibid.,* p. 5.

individual (Berdyaev, on occasion, adopts Maritain's distinction). "The entire world," Berdyaev exclaims, "is nothing in comparison with human personality, with the unique person of man, with his unique fate . . . Man, human personality, is the supreme value, not society, not collective realities."[16] In Berdyaev's teaching, in short, as in Buber's and Maritain's, "the person is an actual spiritual category bound to God; it is the image of God in man . . . It is the ultimate value in ethics, the divine purpose in each concrete human being."[17]

Tillich does not give this personalist teaching the same emphasis, though he fully shares it. He makes the polarity of individualization and participation one of the fundamental ontological elements characterizing the structure of all being, but he emphasizes that it is in man that individuality really comes into its own. "Man . . . is completely individualized . . . The species is dominant in all non-human beings . . . essentially the individual is an exemplar, representing in an individual way the universal characteristics of the species . . . Man is different. Even in collectivistic societies, the individual as the bearer, and in the last analysis the aim, of the collective is significant rather than the species. Even the most despotic state claims to exist for the benefit of its individual subjects."[18] When individualization reaches the perfect form," we call it "person" (this is Tillich's version of Maritain's distinction); but such complete individualization is impossible unless "participation reaches the perfect form which we call 'community.'" "Participation is essential for the individual, not accidental. No individual exists without participation, and no personal

[16] Nicolas Berdyaev, *Slavery and Freedom* (Scribner's, 1944), pp. 20, 28.

[17] Eugène Porret, *La Philosophie Chrétienne en Russie: Nicolas Berdiaeff* (Éditions de la Baconnière, Neuchatel, 1946), p. 128.

[18] Paul Tillich, *Systematic Theology*, Vol. I (University of Chicago Press, 1951), p. 175.

being exists without communal being. The person as a fully developed individual self is impossible without other fully developed selves" with whom it is in relation.[19] The relation with God is pre-eminently a personal relation,[20] although Tillich on occasion speaks of an "absolute faith" in which the "person-to-person relationship to God" is transcended as "one-sided."[21] Thus even Tillich's personalism, strong and well defined though it is, is taken up in his "balancing" dialectic, which is concerned to avoid every appearance of "one-sidedness." Berdyaev, with his passionate extremism of freedom and creativity, and Maritain, with his pervasive emphasis on form, structure, and order, afford illuminating contrasts.

Contrasting developments of the personalist theme are to be found also in the ethical systems of the four men. Maritain's ethic is an ethic of natural law: the good of man is seen as the true requirements of his nature as a personal being revealed by right reason (ethics is thus "right reason in acting"). But the rationalism of such a position is much mitigated by two qualifications—what is "naturally known" is known primarily "not through conceptual knowledge and by way of reasoning . . . [but] through inclination, by way of congeniality or connaturality,"[22] by way of a kind of

[19] Paul Tillich, ibid., Vol. I, p. 176.

[20] "However, there is a difference between the first and the second elements in each polarity with regard to their power of symbolizing the divine life. The elements of individualization, dynamics, and freedom represent the self or subject side of the basic ontological structure within the polarity to which they belong. The elements of participation, form, and destiny represent the world or object side of the basic ontological structure within the polarity to which they belong. Both sides are rooted in the divine life. But the first side [of individualization, dynamics, and freedom] determines the existential relationship between God and man, which is the source of all symbolization" (Paul Tillich, ibid., Vol. I, p. 243).

[21] Paul Tillich, The Courage to Be (Yale University Press, 1952), p. 186.

[22] Jacques Maritain, "Natural Law and Moral Law," in

intuition, in fact; while the actual implications of the natural law emerge only when one takes into account the "existential state of humanity," the "data of ethnology and sociology," and the "history of the human conscience."[23] Berdyaev, on the other hand, vehemently rejects every ethic of law as an ethic of slavery, and calls for the assertion of meonic freedom in the moral life. "You must not act so that the principle of your action could become a universal law," Berdyaev enjoins in direct opposition to Kant's "categorical imperative"; "you must always act individually, and every one must act differently."[24] His ethic is therefore an ethic of creativity that calls for free expression in the various fields of culture as well as in the field of personal relationships.

Tillich strives to hold both sides together, the side of power and creativity (Berdyaev) and the side of law and structure (Maritain). He therefore develops a dialectic of love, power, and justice, in which love, in its freedom, is the "ultimate principle of justice" (law), for a love that "does not include justice is chaotic self-surrender, destroying him who loves as well as him who accepts such love."[25] "Love shows what is just in the concrete situation," but "justice is the form in which the power of being actualizes itself."[26] In this way, both poles are held together in an ontological tension that avoids the "one-sidedness" of unregulated freedom in one direction, and of rigidified law in the other.

Buber's ethic is rooted in the conviction that "real living

Ruth Nanda Anshen, ed., *Moral Principles of Action* (Harper, 1952), p. 102.

[23] Jacques Maritain, *Existence and the Existent*, p. 49; "Natural Law and Moral Law," in Ruth Nanda Anshen, ed., *op. cit.*, p. 105.

[24] Nicolas Berdyaev, *The Destiny of Man* (Scribner's, 1937), p. 137.

[25] Paul Tillich, *Love, Power, and Justice* (Oxford University Press, 1954), pp. 71, 68.

[26] Paul Tillich, *ibid.*, pp. 82, 56.

is meeting,"[27] that is, that authentic existence emerges in the I-Thou. Buber's man is dialogical man, the man "who commits his whole being in God's dialogue with the world and who stands firm throughout this dialogue."[28] It is a dialogue in which "God speaks to every man through the life which he gives him again and again . . . [and in which] man can only answer God with the whole of life, with the way in which he lives his given life."[29] This wholeness of response in the dialogue is the "good" of man. Naturally, Buber, too, is suspicious of the rigidities of law and the heteronomies of normative structures, though he does not write them off so completely as Berdyaev seems to do. "No responsible person remains a stranger to norms," he declares; "but the command inherent in a genuine norm never becomes a maxim and the fulfilment of it never a habit . . . What it [the command] has to tell him is revealed whenever a situation arises which demands of him a solution of which till then he had perhaps no idea . . . [The situation] demands nothing of what is past; it demands presence, responsibility; it demands you."[30] In the last analysis, therefore, Buber's ethic is thoroughly existential and "situational," demanding total personal response in the concrete situation. "Of God's will," he proclaims in a celebrated passage, "we know only the eternal; the temporal we must command for ourselves, ourselves imprint his wordless bidding ever anew on the stuff of reality . . . In genuine life between men, the new world will reveal itself. First, we must act; then we shall receive—from out of our own deed."[31]

27 Martin Buber, *I and Thou*, p. 11.
28 Martin Buber, "Biblical Leadership," *Israel and the World: Essays in a Time of Crisis* (Schocken, 1948), pp. 131–32.
29 Martin Buber, "The Two Foci of the Jewish Soul," *ibid.*, p. 33.
30 Martin Buber, "The Education of Character," *Between Man and Man*, p. 114.
31 Martin Buber, *Der heilige Weg: Ein Antwort an die Juden und die Völker* (Frankfort, 1920), pp. 67–68.

In the realm of social philosophy, it is Jacques Maritain, perhaps, who has worked through his personalist presuppositions most thoroughly and explicitly. In his writings on Christianity, democracy, and the rights of man,[32] produced under the challenge of the Second World War, as well as in his later writings,[33] he has developed a systematic body of social and political teaching rooted in his Thomist metaphysics. Man is both an individual and a person. In the former capacity he is (quoting St. Thomas) "related to the entire community as part to whole." Because he is a person, however, and not merely an individual, "man is not ordained to the body politic according to all that he is and has";[34] he is something more than merely a social and political being, and possesses "natural rights" in accordance with his dual nature as a member of society while yet transcending it. The end, or finality, of society is the common good, but "the adage of the superiority of the common good is understood in its true sense only in the measure that the common good itself implies a reference to the human person."[35] On this basis Maritain has erected an impressive system of "Christian democracy" that has been widely influential, though it has also aroused bitter hostility in ultra-conventional Catholic circles.

Nicolas Berdyaev's ethic of meonic freedom leads him to a social philosophy that in principle disparages all fixed norms and institutions as "objectivizations of the spirit," and yet advocates a form of economic socialism in the interests of freedom. In effect, Berdyaev distinguishes two types of socialism: "collective socialism, which is based on the su-

[32] See especially *The Rights of Man and Natural Law* (1942) and *Christianity and Democracy* (1942).

[33] See especially *The Person and the Common Good* (1947) and *Man and the State* (1951).

[34] Thomas Aquinas, *Summa Theologica*, II–II, 64, 2; I–II, 21, 4, ad 3 (Jacques Maritain, *The Person and the Common Good*, pp. 60, 61 note).

[35] Jacques Maritain, *ibid.*, pp. 19–20.

premacy of society and the state over the personality . . .
[and] personalist socialism, which is founded on the absolute supremacy of the personality, of each personality, over
society and over the state." The former "offers bread and
takes away man's freedom"; the latter "offers bread to all
men while preserving their freedom for them and without
alienating their conscience from them."[36] Personalist socialism is based on the principle that "only economics can be
socialized; the spiritual life cannot, nor can the consciousness or conscience of man." Socialist measures are to be
justified "not on the rights of the state in economic life, but
on the supremacy of the individual economic rights, on the
guarantee of those individual rights. The state has the duty
to guarantee the free development of autonomous life."[37]
Thus, in Berdyaev's mind, the state action necessitated by
socialist economics is transmuted into the freedom of the
autonomous life. The explanation, perhaps, may be found
in Berdyaev's conviction that with the proper ordering of
economic life, the sphere of coercive law will be reduced
to a minimum and the reign of love will supervene, or at
least be approximated. Berdyaev's "personalist socialism" is,
therefore, basically anarchist, as indeed a philosophy of
meonic freedom would require.[38]

Buber's social philosophy is not very far from Berdyaev's,
though he specifically rejects its anarchistic implications.
True community, Buber holds, emerges out of the I-Thou.

[36] Nicolas Berdyaev, *Slavery and Freedom*, p. 210.
[37] Nicolas Berdyaev, *ibid.*, pp. 218, 150–51.
[38] Hence the aptness of Reinhold Niebuhr's criticism. "A part
of the claim [made by Berdyaev] of the superiority of Russian
spirituality over the West is derived from the illusion that it is
possible to dispense with legal safeguards of both order and
freedom so long as perfect love is achieved. This perfect love
is not ever achieved in man's collective relationships; and it
is a utopian illusion to expect such a consummation . . . The
freedom and the community which is implied in the Christian
love commandment must be at least partially secured by law"
("'The Russian Idea,'" *Religion in Life*, Vol. XVIII, no. 2,
Spring 1949).

Just as the individual becomes a person, a "fact of existence," "insofar as he steps into a living relation with other
individuals," so does a social aggregate become a community "insofar as it is built out of living units of relation
. . . Only men who are truly capable of saying Thou to
one another can truly say We with one another."[39] And just
as the I of authentic personality emerges only in the
dialogic "meeting" with God to whom every other Thou
points, so does the authentic We of community come forth
only out of the relation of the individual members of the
group to the transcendent. "The community is built up out
of living mutual relation, but the builder is the living effective Center."[40] It is this radial relation to the living Center
which is God that makes true community.

Both individualism and collectivism violate true community: individualism because it "understands only a part
of man"; collectivism because it "understands man only as
a part."[41] As against both, Buber presents the vision of an
"organic community," of a "community of communities,"
built out of "small and ever smaller communities," the basic
cell of which is the "full cooperative," best exemplified in
the Israeli kibbutz.[42] Thus, Buber's kind of socialism falls
in not only with Berdyaev's "personalist socialism," but also
with the "communitarian" ideas that have played so large
a part in Catholic social radicalism, and in Protestant social
thinking as well. But establishing true community seems to
Buber pre-eminently a Jewish task, which the Jew can
adequately cope with only under conditions of economic
and political autonomy in the land appointed for the work;
this is the ground of Buber's religio-social Zionism.

Paul Tillich's English writings do not contain any exten-

[39] Martin Buber, "What is Man?" *Between Man and Man*,
pp. 203, 176.
[40] Martin Buber, *I and Thou*, p. 45.
[41] Martin Buber, "What is Man?" *op. cit.*, p. 200.
[42] See Martin Buber, *Paths in Utopia* (Macmillan, 1949),
epilogue.

sive discussion of his social philosophy; for that his earlier
German writings must be consulted.[43] In the 1920s, Tillich
was one of the main protagonists of the "religious-socialist"
movement, which played a not insignificant part in the intellectual life of the times. The basic conviction of this movement was that contemporary society had fallen into a dis-
integrating heteronomy, in which it had lost the very
principle of its being; the only salvation for the West was
the replacement of this decadent bourgeois culture by a
new theonomy, which could only take the form of a
religious-socialist *Gestalt* in which all aspects of life and culture would find renewal. The Christian aware of his responsibility must offer himself as a servant of the new
kairos, of the new historical order for which "the time was
at hand." Both religion and society were looking forward
to the coming *kairos,* for in the new *Gestalt* of "religious
socialism" religion would again become the soul of society,
and society would again express the religious "principle"
informing it in all its organic manifestations.

The *kairos* to which the "religious socialists" of Germany
were looking came, but in a perverted and demonic, though
not totally unrecognizable, form; it came as the National-
Socialist revolution. The "religious-socialist" movement did
not long survive. The "religious-socialist" idea, Tillich still
believes, retains its validity; indeed, he insists that "if the
prophetic message is true, there is nothing 'beyond religious
socialism.' "[44] The present period, however, is a "situation

[43] A full listing of these earlier works will be found in Kegley,
Charles W., and Robert W. Bretall, eds., *op. cit.,* pp. 353–62.
Some of the German writings have appeared in English: *The
Religious Situation* (Holt, 1932; Meridian, 1956), *The Interpre-
tation of History* (Scribner's, 1936), and some of the essays in
The Protestant Era (University of Chicago Press, 1948). See
also Paul Tillich, "Beyond Religious Socialism," *The Christian
Century,* June 15, 1949.
[44] Paul Tillich, "Autobiographical Reflections," in Kegley,
Charles W., and Robert W. Bretall, eds., *op. cit.,* p. 13.

of the void," a kind of "negative *kairos*," in which socialist programs seem to have lost their relevance.

Despite their preoccupations with society and culture, the philosophies of Maritain, Berdyaev, Buber, and Tillich are religious philosophies, with a message that reaches down to man's deepest depths and rises to his highest aspirations. Just as, in some form or manner, each begins with an ontology, a doctrine of being, so each ends with a soteriology, a doctrine of redemption. In between, connecting the two, is a doctrine of sin and evil.

For Maritain, with his positive conception of being, evil is necessarily negative, a negation, a privation, a nonentity, without ontological status or substance. The evil of sin "lies in acting without reference to the rule";[45] the "root of evil of action" is, therefore, a "defect," a "failure in being," which is "a voluntary and free defect, since it is the evil of a free action or a free choice which results from it."[46] With remarkable ingenuity, Maritain attempts to show how the positive evil act can emerge out of such nothingness.[47] Emerging out of the abyss of non-being [*ouk on*], sin effects a violation of man's nature, a diminution of his being, and a rupture of his natural as well as supernatural relation to God. Redemption, therefore, means a restoration to God, which also means a restoration of the integrity of human nature, elevated and transfigured by grace. In its ultimate reach this implies the divinization of life, for in

[45] Jacques Maritain, *St. Thomas and the Problem of Evil* (Marquette University Press, 1942), p. 31.

[46] Jacques Maritain, *ibid.*, p. 23.

[47] See the summary of his argument: "Evil lies in acting without reference to the rule; and in this concrete whole, acting without consideration of the rule, there are two moments to be distinguished, not with regard to time, but according to ontological order: *first moment, not considering the rule,* which is a negation, an absence, the lack of a good which is not yet due; and *second moment, acting with that negation,* which from the sole fact that one acts with it becomes a privation, an absence of a due good in the action" (*ibid.*, p. 31).

his redeemed status man is more than merely human. "For St. John of the Cross, as for St. Thomas, and the whole tradition of Christianity," Maritain declares, "the final aim of human life is transformation into God, to become God by participation, which is achieved in heaven by the beatific vision and the love of beatitude, and here on earth by faith and love."[48]

Berdyaev, too, thinks of redemption as divinization. To Berdyaev, the prime evil is the objectivization, externalization, "thingification" (*Verdinglichung*) of the spirit; for him, free spirit is the only true reality and the only true good. The degradation of spirit into objectivity takes place on every level of existence, ontological, social, and psychological. Being is "enslavement," indeed, the "primary slavery of man."[49] So are objectivized social institutions; so are sex and all other human impulses, desires, and interests, when they are expressed in objectivized form. Man, as spirit, is "theandric," a "potential God-man,"[50] for "humanness is divineness";[51] in his fallen, objectivized existence, however, the divine dimension is truncated, if not altogether destroyed, and man becomes a "thing." Redemption means the emancipation of spirit, the reassertion of meonic freedom against an objectivized, but nevertheless unreal world. Berdyaev, in his latter days, saw this redemption as an imminent eschatological consummation. Following in the Joachimite tradition of the "three ages," he proclaimed the third and final age, the "Age of the Spirit," to be close at hand. "A further revelation of the unknown is at hand," he declared, "a revelation . . . of a new man and a new cosmos . . . The religion of the Spirit will be the religion of

[48] Jacques Maritain, *The Degrees of Knowledge* (Scribner's, 1938), pp. 394–95.

[49] Nicolas Berdyaev, *Slavery and Freedom*, pp. 75, 78.

[50] Nicolas Berdyaev, *The Divine and the Human* (Bles, 1949), p. 112.

[51] Nicolas Berdyaev, *ibid.*, p. 125.

man when he has come of age; it will constitute his emergence from childhood and youth . . . In the religion of the Spirit, the religion of freedom, everything will appear in a new light. There will be no authority and no retribution . . . It will have as its basis . . . creative development and transfiguration, assimilation to God,"[52] in other words, the restoration of God-manhood.

Tillich's doctrine of sin, evil, and redemption is linked at every point with his basic ontology. Being-Itself, which is God, possesses three aspects, levels, or dimensions: power, or primal ground; logos, or structure; and life, or creativity. Each harbors the basic polarities of being: individualization-participation, dynamics-form, freedom-destiny. All this appears pre-eminently in human being (Heidegger's *Dasein*), which is the key to being-as-such (*Sein*). Now in man's "essential nature," the polarities of being are creatively and harmoniously united; "under the conditions of existence," however, they are disrupted, thrown into conflict, and driven to assert themselves in a chaotic and destructive manner. Here emerge sin and evil—in the transition from "essential," or potential, to actual being; in the passage from man as "hidden in the creative ground of the divine life, in the creative vision of God," to man who "has left the ground [of the divine life] in order to . . . actualize what he essentially is."[53] For Tillich, in other words, creation and fall are two sides of the same thing, "logically different, [but] ontologically the same."[54] Thus, the actualization of potential being means, for man, estrangement from his own "essential being" and therefore also from the "ground of his being," which is God; in other words, it means sin. "Existence is separation," Tillich tells us, relating sin (*Suende*) to separation (*Sonderung*); "before sin is an act, it is a

[52] Nicolas Berdyaev, *ibid.*, pp. 200, 185.
[53] Paul Tillich, *Systematic Theology*, Vol. I, p. 225.
[54] Paul Tillich, "Reply to Interpretation and Criticism," in Kegley, Charles W., and Robert W. Bretall, eds., *op. cit.*, p. 342.

state,"[55] a state of alienation. Existential alienation permeates being in its fallen (that is, actualized) state. The disruption of the polar unity of being—so that the power of being rises against its own structure and logos, while the structure of being becomes an oppressive heteronomy stifling power and creativity—engenders the demonic forces that ravage the "fallen" world and imperil human life and culture.

In his "essential nature" man unites the finite with infinity, and it is precisely this unity which Tillich calls "Godmanhood."[56] In the "picture of Jesus as the Christ" (to use Tillich's phrase), we see "the paradox of essential Godmanhood manifesting itself [without disruption] under the conditions of existence, which contradicts original Godmanhood."[57] In man, however, this "original Godmanhood" is utterly disrupted, and this is the misery of his "fallen" existence. Redemption consists in the restoration of "original Godmanhood" in the "New Being." This redemption, like revelation, of which it is a counterpart, is "final, complete, and unchangeable with respect to the revealing and saving event [Jesus as the Christ]"; it is, however, merely "preliminary, fragmentary, and changeable with respect to persons who receive [its] saving power."[58] It is no accident that Tillich uses the same "theandric" vocabulary that the ecstatic Berdyaev and the mystic Maritain (for it is in an exalted mystic mood that Maritain speaks of man "becoming" God) employ in their own soteriologies; Tillich, too, thinks of redemption as divinization, restoration to "original Godmanhood" (the very same term as he uses to describe

[55] Paul Tillich, *The Shaking of the Foundations* (Scribner's, 1948), p. 155.

[56] Paul Tillich, "A Reinterpretation of the Doctrine of the Incarnation," *Church Quarterly Review*, Vol. CXLVII, January–March 1949.

[57] Paul Tillich, "A Reinterpretation of the Doctrine of the Incarnation," *op. cit.*

[58] Paul Tillich, *Systematic Theology*, Vol. I, p. 146.

the Incarnation), though he does so in a much more muted and qualified way.

There is no touch of divinization in the thinking of Martin Buber. Buber thinks of the divine-human relation in dialogic terms, as an I-Thou "meeting," in which there is encounter of person with person, but no "essential" participation in the divine being. (Here Buber is, perhaps, closer to radical Protestantism than the Protestant Tillich.) Since Buber's fundamental conviction is that all "real living is meeting,"[59] he (not unlike Berdyaev) sees the primary evil in the depersonalization of life through the predominance of the I-It over the I-Thou. Under the actual conditions of existence, "without It a man cannot live; but he who lives with It alone is not a man."[60] Authentic human existence—the dialogic life—is existence in the I-Thou. But such is the world that one cannot remain permanently in the I-Thou relation. To survive, we need to know, control, and use things, and what is much more tragic, even human beings. In other words, to survive we must engage in depersonalizing and dehumanizing our fellow men, and therefore ourselves as well. Here we have the most poignant expression of the "wrongness," of the "broken" character of existence, which Buber so pointedly calls the "cruel antithecalness of life."

The predominance of the I-It over the I-Thou destroys community, and therefore destroys the authenticity of man's own existence, since the self becomes an I only in relation to a Thou. Man loses his capacity for genuine decision, and therewith his freedom ("Only he who knows relation and knows about the presence of a Thou is capable of decision, [and] he who decides is free"[61]). In self-enclosed isolation, he commits the primal sin and incurs

[59] Martin Buber, *I and Thou*, p. 11.
[60] Martin Buber, *ibid.*, p. 34.
[61] Martin Buber, *ibid.*, p. 51.

the "primal guilt" of "remaining with one self,"[62] in delusive self-sufficiency.

But the evil runs deeper, for in breaking his bond with his neighbor, sinful man breaks it with God as well. "Real relationship with God cannot be achieved on earth if real relationships to the world and mankind are lacking."[63] The self-sufficiency that destroys the I-Thou relation with men is ultimately a self-sufficiency against God, and in this self-sufficiency we cannot fail to detect the "existential lie against being in which man sees himself as self-creator."[64]

If the self-enclosed isolation that ruptures the bond of relation is the root source of the dereliction of man and the misery of his existence, redemption can only mean a "return" to relation. This "return," or "turning" (teshubah), is quite crucial to Buber's religious philosophy. In the "turning," relation is restored, and with it the possibility of a new life in the I-Thou, the possibility of personal authenticity and community, the possibility of "meeting God" with the "wholeness of being." The "turning" is a miracle of grace—"He bestows grace and mercy on whom he wills"[65] —and yet man's deeds count. Without grace there is nothing, and yet man must make the "beginning." Grace concerns us absolutely, yet it can never become the object of our acquiring. Our freedom is real, yet grace is "prevenient": "The person who makes a decision knows that his decision is no self-delusion; the person who has acted knows that he was and is in the hand of God."[66] These multiple

[62] Martin Buber, "What is Man?" *Between Man and Man,* p. 166.

[63] Martin Buber, "The Silent Question," *At the Turning: Three Addresses on Judaism* (Farrar, Straus, and Young, 1952), p. 39.

[64] Maurice S. Friedman, *Martin Buber: The Life of Dialogue,* p. 107.

[65] Martin Buber, *The Prophetic Faith* (Macmillan, 1949), p. 52.

[66] Martin Buber, "The Faith of Judaism," *Israel and the World,* p. 17.

paradoxes are subsumed and expressed, not resolved, in the "turning."

The "turning" is "something that happens in the immediacy of the reality between man and God." It has its "subjective" and psychological aspects, of course, but essentially it is "as little a 'psychic' event as is a man's birth or death; it comes upon the whole person, is carried out by the whole person . . ."[67] All of life, individual and corporate, depends on the "turning" of God to man and man to God—on the "turning" and "re-turning," for the "turning" that redeems is never a secure and final possession on which man can rest. Thus to the very end does Buber remain true to the existential and dialogical temper of his thinking.

Even this cursory presentation of the leading ideas of the four philosopher-theologians will have made it clear how much the thinking of each bears the mark of the key concept that integrates his entire system. With Maritain, the crucial concept is "right reason," or "rule" (logic is "right reason in thinking"; ethics is "right reason in acting"; art is "right reason in making"). With Berdyaev, it is "freedom," or "creativity." With Buber, it is "relation," or "dialogue." With Tillich, it is "Being" and "New Being." Whatever coherence their thinking possesses over the decades of their intellectual life is very largely due to the consistency with which these concepts have operated in the varying contexts of their thought. It is not difficult to detect the basic motif of the philosopher in every aspect of his philosophy.

Nor is it difficult to see how true each remains to his essential tradition, for all the individuality and originality he may display. The sober and methodic rationalism of Catholic scholasticism permeates every page of Maritain's work, as does the ecstatic spirituality of Eastern Orthodoxy the

[67] Martin Buber, "The Faith of Judaism," *Israel and the World*, p. 20.

writings of Berdyaev. Buber's works are drenched with the
religious personalism so characteristic of the Jewish tradition; and Tillich's religio-philosophical speculations fall in
very closely, as he himself has pointed out, with the strain
of ontological mysticism in German Lutheranism. Each of
these men lives and thinks "at the frontier," yet each is a
representative man in a way that more conventional thinkers could never be.

Profoundly representative though these men are, the influence of their thinking has never been limited simply to
their own communions. On the contrary, their audiences
have always consisted of men of all religious persuasions,
and of none. Buber's works first appeared in English under
Protestant auspices, and his basic ideas have become part
and parcel of the newer Protestant theology, and of an important strain in Catholic personalism as well. Maritain is
read, in this country at least, by Protestants and Jews perhaps as much as by Catholics, while Berdyaev's outreach
has been obviously much more among Catholics and Protestants than among the Eastern Orthodox. As for Tillich,
he has become, one might say, the favorite Protestant
thinker among Catholic theologians in this country, and his
popularity among serious Jewish intellectuals is plain at every turn. But even this does not really describe the contemporary appeal of the four men. Their appeal far transcends even their four religious communities taken together,
and extends deep into the so-called "secular" world. In-
creasing numbers of "secular" intellectuals, whose own
conscious religious concern may be peripheral, have found
in these men an illumination of their experience and a deep-
ening of their understanding that have come to them as a
revelation. Philosophers, psychologists, medical men, edu-
cators, historians, artists, writers, literary critics, men in the
most diverse professions and of the most diverse concerns
in life, have come to look to Maritain, Berdyaev, Buber,
and Tillich as to vanguard thinkers in the continuing en-

deavor to find meaning and direction in the crisis of the culture of our time.

In this sense, the four philosopher-theologians are representative in yet another way. They are heralds of the postmodern mind, trail blazers in the great if not always definable movement of thought that is striving to go beyond the confident positivism, naturalism, and scientism that are the hallmarks of modernity. Two of these men—Maritain and Berdyaev—came from non-religious environments, where the prejudices and dogmas of modernity were the "received ideas" of the culture. A third—Paul Tillich—coming from a religious environment, had to achieve a certain "distancing" before he could establish his spiritual autonomy; and in another sense, the same is true of the fourth, Martin Buber. For each of these men the "frontier" on which he has stood has been not merely the frontier of his religious communion but also the frontier of the religious life, the frontier of human existence. Each of these men has felt in his own existence the metaphysical disquiet that is disturbing the complacency of the late-modern world, and each has experienced in his own thinking the metaphysical hunger that cannot be stilled with the dry husks of nineteenth-century platitudes. Each theologizes in this radical spirit, and therefore each has become, in his own way, a pioneer of the "new thinking" that Franz Rosenzweig, a generation ago, saw as the emerging consciousness of the age. In this, more than in anything else, lies the enduring meaning and significance of their thought.

WILL HERBERG

JACQUES MARITAIN

※ ※ ※ ※

JACQUES MARITAIN

Jacques Maritain, the most widely known and most influential of contemporary Catholic philosophers, was born in Paris on November 18, 1882, into a cultured middle-class family. His father was a lawyer; his mother a daughter of Jules Favre, who became President of the Republic. Since the mother was Protestant, the children were baptized as Protestants, but the Maritain home was religiously indifferent. Jacques entered the Lycée Henri IV without any particular religious convictions, and then went on to the Sorbonne to study philosophy and natural science in very much the same temper of mind. Yet already he was deeply dissatisfied with the prevailing intellectual atmosphere, that curious mixture of rationalism, positivism, and scientism that formed the substance of French modernist "free thought." At the Sorbonne he met a fellow-student, Raissa Oumansoff, of a Russian Jewish family, who shared his perplexities. Looking back years later, Maritain described himself and Raissa at this time as "carrying in themselves that distress which is the only serious product of modern culture, and a sort of active despair, lightened only (they did not know why) by the inner assurance that the truth for which they hungered, and without which it was almost impossible for them to accept life, would one day be shown to them . . ."[1] Upon the suggestion of Charles Péguy, a friend of the family, they went to hear Henri Bergson's lectures at the Collège de France, and there found, at least for the time being, "the spiritual perspectives of life" and the "intellectual certainty" for which they were hungering. In November 1904, Jacques and Raissa were married. Just six months later, in June 1905, came the great and decisive "accident" of their lives, which shattered and remade their entire existence.

Through a chance reference in a newspaper article, Jacques Maritain heard of Léon Bloy, and came to read his book, *La Femme Pauvre*. The Maritains wrote to him appreciatively and received from Bloy an invitation to visit him. This they did on June 25, and came face to face with "this Christian of the second century astray in the Third Republic." The impact was immense, and within a year, in June 1906, Jacques, Raissa, and the latter's sister Vera, entered the Church and were baptized.

A new life began for the Maritains. At first they believed that their Catholicism meant an end to philosophy, and Maritain turned to biology. With some financial aid obtained through a fellowship, the Maritains left for Germany in August 1906, and settled at Heidelberg, where Maritain studied under Hans Driesch, the neo-vitalist. In 1908 they returned to France, but Maritain was not eager to teach, and so accepted hack work from publishers until he could find his bearings. Under the influence of Humbert Clérissac, the Dominican who became his spiritual adviser, Maritain began the study of Thomas Aquinas, and discovered that he "was already a Thomist without knowing it."[2] His voca-

[1] These are the words of Léon Bloy; see his "Letters of Léon Bloy to His Godchildren," *Pilgrim of the Absolute* (Pantheon, 1947), p. 21.

[2] Jacques Maritain, *La Philosophie Bergsonienne* (2nd ed., 1948), preface.

tion as philosopher and teacher of philosophy became clear
to him, and for this he now set to work to prepare himself.
In 1910 he published an article on "Reason and Modern
Science"; in 1911 a critique of Bergson's thinking ("The
Evolutionism of M. Bergson"); and the next year he accepted a position as instructor in philosophy at the Collège
Stanislas, where he made a minor sensation by his forth-
right Thomism, then still regarded as something of an in-
novation in conservative Catholic circles. In 1914 he was
called to the chair of philosophy at the Institut Catholique
in Paris, and he settled down to a life of teaching logic,
metaphysics, and the other disciplines that fell within the
scope of his philosophic concern. The first of his significant
works were published in this period.

But the whole course of his thought was now unexpectedly diverted in a direction quite remote from his earlier
interests. Hitherto the Maritains had shown only a very
slight regard for social and political questions. Under the
influence of their environment, however, and more particularly under the influence of Father Clérissac, Maritain had
become loosely associated with the Action Française, the
monarchist, proto-fascist organization directed by Charles
Maurras, and occasionally he contributed to its journal, La
Revue Universelle. In 1926 the Action Française was condemned by Pius XI, and was repudiated as an organization
speaking for or on behalf of French Catholicism. Even before the papal condemnation Maritain had begun to have
his doubts, and he set about to clarify his thinking in a field
that had not hitherto engrossed his interest. Primauté du
Spirituel (translated into English under the title of The
Things That Are Not Caesar's) appeared in 1927 as a
statement of his basic position. He still continued his more
strictly philosophical work, publishing The Degrees of
Knowledge in 1932 and A Preface to Metaphysics: Seven
Lectures on Being in 1934; but more and more his concern
shifted to ethical, political, and social questions. Freedom

in the Modern World appeared in 1933, and the definitive work, *True Humanism,* three years later.

The collapse of France in World War II found Maritain in the United States, engaged in a university lecture tour. (He had visited and lectured in South America four years before.) Maritain was deeply afflicted by the plight of his country and immediately identified himself with the resistance movement. During these years he taught at Columbia, Princeton, and the Pontifical Institute of Medieval Studies in Toronto.

As soon as the war was over he returned to France and was appointed Ambassador to the Vatican by General De Gaulle, head of the provisional government. From 1945 to 1948 he served in this diplomatic post, though he did not abandon his philosophical work or lose contact with the intellectual currents of his time. In 1948 he published *Existence and the Existent,* in which he presented Thomism as the "only authentic existentialism." In *The Person and the Common Good,* published a year earlier, Maritain had developed a distinctively personalistic interpretation of the Thomist tradition.

The same year, he returned to the United States to teach at Princeton and, with some interruptions, the Maritains have remained in this country ever since.

Jacques Maritain is widely recognized as the greatest living Catholic philosopher, and he has had a deep impact on the thinking of our time far beyond Catholic circles. His thinking has at all points—even on the most abstract metaphysical questions, let alone the more "practical" problems with which he has been preoccupied since the 1930s— aroused sharp controversy even among his fellow Catholics. Nor has he been reluctant to challenge the favorite dogmas of the contemporary secular culture, particularly, to use his own phrase, the "pseudo-metaphysics of scientism." What is so characteristic of him as a thinker is not so much the rigor and consistency of his Thomism, as his unquenchable thirst for the truth and his extraordinary capacity to discover ever new facets of it within the framework of the "perennial philosophy" he espouses.

SELECTED BIBLIOGRAPHY

WORKS BY MARITAIN

(Only books available in English are listed.)

Three Reformers: Luther, Descartes, Rousseau. Scribner's, 1929.

Art and Scholasticism. Scribner's, 1930.

The Things That Are Not Caesar's. Scribner's, 1930.

Freedom in the Modern World. Scribner's, 1936.

The Degrees of Knowledge. Scribner's, 1938.

True Humanism. Scribner's, 1938.

A Christian Looks At the Jewish Question. Longmans, Green, 1939.

A Preface to Metaphysics. Sheed and Ward, 1939.

Science and Wisdom. Scribner's, 1940.

Scholasticism and Politics. Macmillan, 1940.

Ransoming the Time. Scribner's, 1941.

St. Thomas and the Problem of Evil. Marquette University Press, 1942.

Art and Poetry. Philosophical Library, 1943.

The Rights of Man and Natural Law. Scribner's, 1943.

Education at the Crossroads. Yale, 1943.

Christianity and Democracy. Scribner's, 1944.

The Person and the Common Good. Scribner's, 1947.

Existence and the Existent. Pantheon, 1948.

Man and the State. University of Chicago Press, 1951.

The Philosophy of Nature. Philosophical Library, 1951.

The Range of Reason. Scribner's, 1952.

Creative Intuition in Art and Poetry. Pantheon, 1953; Meridian, 1953.

Approaches to God. Harper, 1954.

"Natural Law and Moral Law," in Ruth Nanda Anshen, ed., *Moral Principles of Action.* Harper, 1952.

Bergsonian Philosophy and Thomism. Philosophical Library, 1955.

On the Philosophy of History. Scribner's, 1957.

Reflections on America. Scribner's, 1958.

WORKS ABOUT MARITAIN

Allen, Edgar L., *Christian Humanism: A Guide to the Thought of Jacques Maritain.* Philosophical Library, 1951.

Evans, Joseph W. and Leo R. Ward, eds., *The Social and Political Philosophy of Jacques Maritain* (selections). Scribner's, 1955.

Fecher, Charles A., *The Philosophy of Jacques Maritain.* Newman Press, 1953.

Horton, Walter Marshall, *Contemporary Continental Theology,* pp. 41–65. Harper, 1938.

Maritain, Raissa, *We Have Been Friends Together.* Longmans, Green, 1942.

Maritain, Raissa, *Adventures in Grace.* Longmans, Green, 1945.

Phelan, Gerald B., *Jacques Maritain.* Sheed and Ward, 1937.

The Thomist, Vol. I (January 1943). Issue dedicated to essays on Jacques Maritain. Sheed and Ward, 1943.

The Desire to See God

18. It is as First Cause of things that all the proofs of the existence of God make us know God. Whether they be philosophical or prephilosophical, the approaches to God of which our nature is capable lead us to God, known in and through His effects or in the mirror of the things which proceed from Him.

But how could the intellect, knowing God in His effects, fail to aspire to know Him in Himself? It is natural and normal that, knowing a reality—and the most important of all—from without and by means of signs, we should desire to know it in itself and to grasp it without any intermediary. Such a desire follows from the very nature of that quest of being which essentially characterizes the intellect. There is in the human intellect a natural desire to see in His essence that very God whom it knows through the things which He has created.

But this desire to know the *First Cause through its essence* is a desire which does not know what it asks, like the sons of Zebedee when they asked to sit on the right and on the left of the Son of Man. *Ye know not what ye ask,* Jesus

(From Jacques Maritain, *Approaches to God* [Harper, 1954], Chap. V, pp. 109–14.)

replied to them. For to know the First Cause in its essence, or without the intermediary of any other thing, is to know the First Cause otherwise than as First Cause; it is to know it by ceasing to attain it by the very means by which we attain it, by ceasing to exercise the very act which bears us up to it. The natural desire to know the First Cause in its essence envelops within itself the indication of the impossibility in which nature is placed to satisfy it.

To know God in His essence is evidently something which transcends the powers of every created or creatable nature, for it is to possess God intuitively, in a vision in which there is no mediation of any idea, but in which the divine essence itself replaces every idea born in our mind, so that it immediately forms and determines our intellect. This is to know God divinely, as He Himself knows Himself and as He knows us, in His own uncreated light.

Nothing is more human than for man to desire naturally things impossible to his nature. It is, indeed, the property of a nature which is not closed up in matter like the nature of physical things, but which is intellectual or infinitized by the spirit. It is the property of a *metaphysical* nature. Such desires reach for the infinite, because the intellect thirsts for being and being is infinite. They are natural, but one may also call them transnatural. It is thus that we desire to see God; it is thus that we desire to be free without being able to sin; it is thus that we desire beatitude.[1]

To say that our intellect naturally desires to see God is to say that it naturally desires a knowledge of which nature itself is incapable. This desire is transnatural, it moves toward an end which is beyond the end for which the nature of man is constituted. According as it reaches thus for an end which transcends every end proportioned to nature, the

[1] On the transnatural desire for beatitude, or of absolutely and definitively saturating happiness, as distinct from the strictly natural desire for happiness or felicity in general, see our *Neuf Leçons sur les Notions Premières de la Philosophie Morale* (Paris, Téqui, 1950), pp. 97–98.

desire to see God is an "inefficacious" desire—a desire which
it is not in the power of nature to satisfy, and it is a "conditional" desire—a desire whose satisfaction is not due to
nature.

Yet, according as it emanates from nature, it is a natural
and necessary desire. It is not a simple velleity, a superadded desire, a desire of supererogation. It is born in the
very depths of the thirst of our intellect for being; it is a
nostalgia so profoundly human that all the wisdom and all
the folly of man's behavior has in it its most secret reason.

And because this desire which asks for what is impossible
to nature is a desire of nature in its profoundest depths, St.
Thomas Aquinas asserts that it cannot issue in an absolute
impossibility.[2] It is in no wise necessary that it *be* satisfied,
since it asks for what is impossible for nature. But it is necessary that by some means (which is not nature) it *be able*
to be satisfied, since it necessarily emanates from nature. In
other words it is necessary that an order superior to nature
be possible in which man is capable of that of which nature
is incapable but which it necessarily desires. It is necessary
that there be in man an "obediential potency" which, answering to the divine omnipotence, renders him apt to receive a life which surpasses infinitely the capacities of his
nature. It is necessary that we be able to know God in His
essence through a gift which transcends all the possibilities
of our natural forces. It is necessary that this knowledge,
impossible to nature alone, to which nature inevitably aspires, be possible through a gratuitous gift.[3]

[2] Cf. *Summa Theologica,* I, 12, 1; and our work *Les Degrés
du savoir,* p. 562, note 1.

[3] Thus the argumentation of St. Thomas in the question 12,
a.1, of the *Prima Pars,* establishes rationally the *possibility,* I do
not say of *the supernatural order* such as the faith presents it to
us and as it implies the specifically Christian notion of grace, but
of *an order superior to nature,* the notion of which remains still
indeterminate, except in this, that through the divine generosity
man can therein be rendered capable of knowing God in His
essence.

Shall we go beyond philosophy in order to get our answer?[4] Through the night of faith it is given us to attain in His inner life—on the testimony of His Word—the very God who will be intuitively grasped when faith gives way to vision. And in the intellect elevated to the life of faith, the natural desire to see God supernaturally becomes a desire which knows what it asks for—a knowledge of God through His essence, *such as He gives Himself, in His own uncreated light*—and which from now on has *in germ* the wherewithal to attain what it asks for.

Thus the natural desire to see that First Cause whose existence is shown to us through the natural approaches to God is, in human reason, the mark of the possibility—through a gift which transcends the whole order of nature, and in which God communicates what belongs only to Himself—of a knowledge of God superior to reason, which is not due to reason, but to which reason aspires.

[4] Cf. *Neuf Leçons sur les Notions Premières de la Philosophie Morale,* pp. 102–108.

The Existent

THE SUBJECT (SUPPOSITUM)

16. I have spoken of the existential (practical-existential) character of the judgment of conscience whose truth is measured by the rightly orientated voluntary dynamism of the subject. It is time now to furnish a few indications concerning this very notion of subject and the place it occupies in the over-all vision of Thomist philosophy. Precisely because of the existentialism (existentialist intellectualism) of this philosophy, the notion of subject plays a capital part in it; we may even say that *subjects* occupy all the room there is in the Thomist universe, in the sense that, for Thomism, only subjects exist, with the accidents which inhere in them, the action which emanates from them, and the relations which they bear to one another. Only individual subjects exercise the act of existing.

What we call *subject* St. Thomas called *suppositum*. Essence is *that which* a thing is; suppositum is *that which* has an essence, *that which* exercises existence and action —*actiones sunt suppositorum*—*that which* subsists. Here we meet the metaphysical notion which has given students so many headaches and baffles everyone who has not grasped

(From Jacques Maritain, *Existence and the Existent* [Pantheon, 1948], Chap. III, pp. 62–84.)

the true—the existential—foundation of Thomist metaphysics, the notion of *subsistence*.

We are bound to speak of this notion of subsistence with great respect, not only because of the transcendent applications made of it in theology, but because, in the philosophical order itself, it bears witness to the supreme tension of an articulated thought bent on seizing intellectually something which seems to escape from the world of notions or ideas of the intellect, namely, the typical reality of the subject. The existential subject has this in common with the act of existing, that both transcend the concept or the idea considered as the terminus of the first operation of mind or simple apprehension. I have tried to show in an earlier section how the intellect (because it envelops itself) grasps in an idea which is the first of its ideas, that very thing, the act of existing, which is the intelligible (or rather the super-intelligible) proper to the judgment, and not to simple apprehension. Now we are no longer dealing with the act of existing but with that which exercises that act. Just as there is nothing more commonplace in language than the word being (and this is the greatest mystery of philosophy) so there is nothing more commonplace than the 'subject' to which in all our propositions we attribute a predicate. And when we undertake a metaphysical analysis of the reality of this subject, this individual thing which maintains itself in existence, this supremely concrete reality, and undertake to do justice to its irreducible originality, we are forced to appeal to that which is most abstract and most elaborate in our lexicon of notions. How can we be astonished that minds which are fond of facility should regard as so many vain scholastic refinements and Chinese puzzles the elucidations in which Cajetan and John of St. Thomas show us that subsistence is distinct both from essence and from existence, and describe it as a substantial mode? I concede that the style of their dissertations seems to carry us very far from experience into the third heaven of abstraction. And yet, in reality their aim was to form an *objective notion* of the *subject* itself or the suppositum, to reach objectively, within the ontological analysis of the structure of reality, the property which makes the subject to be subject and not object, and to transcend, or rather exceed in depth, the whole universe of objects.

When they explain that an essence or a nature, considered strictly, cannot exist outside the mind as an object of thought, and that nevertheless individual natures do exist, and that, consequently, in order to exist, a given nature or essence must be other than it has to be in order to be an object of thought, that is to say, it must bear in itself a supreme achievement which adds nothing to it in the line of its essence (and consequently does not enrich our understanding by any new note which qualifies it), but which *terminates* it in that line of essence (closes or situates it, constitutes it as an *in-itself* or an inwardness face to face with existence) in order that it may take possession of this act of existing for which it is created and which transcends it;[1] when they explain in this fashion *that by which,* on the

[1] Cf. J. Maritain, *Les Degrés du savoir*, Annexe IV, pp. 845–853, specially pp. 846–848. (The appendixes which were published in the French original have been omitted from the English translation.—Translator's Note.) 'In all other cases where we have to deal with the potency—act couple, for example in the case of a faculty in relation to its operation, there exists between the potency and the act, which are in the same line, a proportion such that, all the conditions being given, the act received in the potency can be received only in it, and is strictly adapted to it alone, because in itself it limits that act to itself, to the exclusion of every other potency. It is *its* act, *its* actuation, *its* determination.

'In the special case of which we are now speaking, it is a whole order which is potency in respect of another order. Essence and existence belong to two different orders, and essence is in potency with respect to existence.

'It cannot properly be said here that the act is received in a potency because the words "to be received in a potency" relate to an act which itself is posited in existence as a determination of that potency's own reserves of determinability.

'Consequently, it should rather be said here, that it is the act

plane of reality, the *quod* which exists and acts is other than the *quid* which we conceive, they attest the existential character of metaphysics, they shatter the Platonic world of pure objects, they justify the passage into the world of

---

which, if it does not receive, at least holds essence up and sustains it by causing it formally to be. In other terms, if I may be allowed to put it so, there is a sort of transcendence of the act of existing by reason of which (not being the achievement of a potency *in the order proper* to that potency—for, existence is not the achievement of essence in the order of essence; it does not form part of the order of essence), the potency which the act achieves, considered with respect to its quidditative constituents, *has not in itself anything by which to make* ITS OWN the act in question.

'Considering any substantial nature exclusively in its quidditative constituents, it is made to exist *per se;* it is made to possess existence in itself, not in another thing. But if we consider the act of existing, it becomes clear that since, according to a universal principle, it is potency which limits act, there is nothing in this act taken in itself which limits existence to this particular potency rather than to another one; and if we view essence itself exclusively in its quidditative constituents, there is, as we have just seen, nothing in it either which limits or appropriates this act of existing to itself alone, to the exclusion of any other essence. It summons existence, but existence is not one of *its* determinations. Existence is not a quidditative determination; existence does not form part of the line of essence; it is not a determination of essence. By a unique paradox, it actuates essence and it is not an actuation of the reserves of potency within essence.

'Consequently nothing stands, metaphysically, in the way of its being joined with another substantial essence in the act of existing; under this aspect it is *unterminated.* Nevertheless, it cannot exist (and act) except it be terminated. Existence must be *its own.* Briefly, every (substantial) finite essence (really distinct from existence) requires to be terminated on the side of existence, face to face with existence, in such fashion that it *cannot* be joined to another substantial essence in order to receive existence. When it is thus terminated, it will limit existence to itself and to its own finitude. It will be terminated in this fashion by a substantial mode which is precisely *subsistence,* and which is not a quidditative constituent of essence any more than the point which terminates a line is itself an extent, a segment of the line. On the one hand this subsistence is not one of the quidditative constituents of essence, and on the other hand it is not yet existence. Its proper office is to terminate

subjects or supposita, they rescue for the metaphysical intellect the value and reality of subjects.

17. God does not create essences to which He can be imagined as giving a last rub of the sandpaper of subsistence before sending them forth into existence! God creates existent subjects or supposita which subsist in the individual nature that constitutes them and which receive from the creative influx their nature as well as their subsistence, their existence, and their activity. Each of them possesses an essence and pours itself out in action. Each is, for us, in its individual existing reality, an inexhaustible well of knowability. We shall never know everything there is to know about the tiniest blade of grass or the least ripple in a stream. In the world of existence there are only subjects or supposita, and that which emanates from them into being. This is why ours is a world of nature and adventure, filled with events, contingency, chance, and where the course of events is flexible and mutable whereas the laws of essence are necessary. We know those subjects, we shall never get through knowing them. We do not know them as subjects, we know them by objectising them, by achieving objective insights of them and making them our objects; for the object is nothing other than something of the subject transferred into the state of immaterial existence of intellection in act. We know subjects not as subjects, but as objects, and therefore only in such-and-such of the intelligible aspects, or rather *inspects,* and perspectives in which they are rendered present to the mind and which we shall never get through discovering in them.

As we pass progressively to higher degrees in the scale

---

substantial essence, to bring it to pass that the essence be rendered incommunicable—by which is to be understood *not to be able to communicate with another substantial essence in the existence that actuates it;* to cause it to be divided off from every other, not only as regards *that which* it is (as individual substance), but divided off from every other *in order to exist.'*

of beings we deal with subjects of existence or supposita
more and more rich in inner complexity, whose individuality is more and more concentrated and integrated, whose
action manifests a more and more perfect spontaneity, from
the merely transitive activity of inanimate bodies to the oc-
cultly immanent activity of vegetable life, the definitely immanent activity of sentient life, and the perfectly immanent
activity of the life of the intellect.[2] At this last degree the
threshold of free choice is crossed, and therewith the threshold of independence properly so-called (however imperfect
it be) and of personality. With man, liberty of spontaneity
becomes liberty of autonomy, the *suppositum* becomes *persona*, that is, a whole which subsists and exists in virtue of
the very subsistence and existence of its spiritual soul, and
acts by setting itself its own ends; a universe in itself; a
microcosm which, though its existence at the heart of
the material universe is ceaselessly threatened, nevertheless
possesses a higher ontological density than that whole universe. Only the person is free; only the person possesses,
in the full sense of these words, inwardness and subjectivity
—because it contains itself and moves about within itself.
The person, St. Thomas says, is that which is noblest and
highest in all nature.

SUBJECTIVITY AS SUBJECTIVITY

18. By sense or experience, science or philosophy, each
of us, as I said a moment ago, knows the environing world
of subjects, supposita, and persons in their rôle as objects.
The paradox of consciousness and personality is that each
of us is situated precisely *at the centre* of this world. Each
is at the centre of infinity. And this privileged subject, the
thinking self, is to itself not object but subject; in the midst
of all the subjects which it knows only as objects, it alone

---

[2] Cf. J. Maritain, *De Bergson à Thomas d'Aquin*, Chap. VI
('Spontaneity and Independence').

is subject as subject. We are thus confronted by subjectivity as subjectivity.

I know myself as subject by consciousness and reflexivity, but my substance is obscure to me. St. Thomas explains that in spontaneous reflection, which is a prerogative of the life of the intellect, each of us knows (by a kind of knowledge that is not scientific but experimental and incommunicable) that his soul exists, knows the singular existence of this subjectivity that perceives, suffers, loves, thinks. When a man is awake to the intuition of being he is awake at the same time to the intuition of subjectivity; he grasps, in a flash that will never be dimmed, the fact that *he is a self*, as Jean-Paul said. The force of such a perception may be so great as to sweep him along to that heroic asceticism of the void and of annihilation in which he will achieve ecstasy in the substantial existence of the *self* and the 'presence of immensity' of the divine Self at one and the same time—which in my view characterises the natural mysticism of India.[3]

But the intuition of subjectivity is an existential intuition which surrenders no essence to us. We know *that which* we are by our phenomena, our operations, our flow of consciousness. The more we grow accustomed to the inner life, the better we decipher the astonishing and fluid multiplicity which is thus delivered to us; the more, also, we feel that it leaves us ignorant of the essence of our self. Subjectivity *as subjectivity* is inconceptualisable; is an unknowable abyss. It is unknowable by the mode of notion, concept, or representation, or by any mode of any science whatsoever—introspection, psychology, or philosophy. How could it be otherwise, seeing that every reality known through a concept, a notion, or a representation is known as object and not as subject? Subjectivity as such escapes by defini-

---

[3] Cf. J. Maritain, *Quatre essais sur l'Esprit dans sa condition charnelle*, Chap. III ('Natural Mystical Experience and the Vacuum').

tion from that which we know about ourselves by means of notions.

19. Yet it is known in a way, or rather in certain ways, which I should like briefly to enumerate. At the very beginning and above all, subjectivity is known or rather felt in virtue of a formless and diffuse knowledge which, in relation to reflective consciousness, we may call unconscious or pre-conscious knowledge. This is knowledge of the 'concomitant' or spontaneous consciousness, which, without giving rise to a distinct act of thought, envelops in fact, *in actu exercito*, our inner world in so far as it is integrated into the vital activity of our spiritual faculties.[4] Even for the most superficial persons, it is true that from the moment when they say *I*, the whole unfolding of their states of consciousness and their operations, their musings, memories, and acts, is subsumed by a virtual and ineffable knowledge, a vital and existential knowledge of the totality immanent in each of its parts, and immersed, without their troubling to become aware of it, in the diffuse glow, the unique freshness, the maternal connivance as it were, which emanates from subjectivity. Subjectivity is not known, it is felt as a propitious and enveloping night.

There is, secondly, a knowledge of subjectivity as such, imperfect and fragmentary of course, but in this instance formed and actually given to the mind, and which is thrown into relief by what St. Thomas calls knowledge by mode of inclination, sympathy, or connaturality, not by mode of knowledge. It appears before us under three specifically distinct forms: (1) practical knowledge, which judges both moral matters and the subject itself, by the inner inclinations of the subject. I mentioned this some pages back in connection with moral conscience and prudence; (2) poetic knowledge, in which subjectivity and the things of this

[4] Cf. J. Maritain, *De Bergson à Thomas d'Aquin*, pp. 160–161.

world are known together in creative intuition-emotion and
are revealed and expressed together, not in a word or concept but in a created work;[5] (3) mystical knowledge,
which is not directed towards the subject but towards
things divine, and does not of itself issue in any expression,
but in which God is known by union and by connaturality
of love, and in which this very love that becomes the formal
means of knowledge of the divine Self, simultaneously renders the human self transparent in its spiritual depths. Let
the mystic reflect an instant upon himself, and a St. Theresa
or a St. John of the Cross will show us to what extent the
divine light gives him a lucid and inexhaustible knowledge
of his own subjectivity.

But in none of these instances is the knowledge of subjectivity as subjectivity, however real it be, a knowledge by
mode of knowledge, which is to say, by mode of conceptual
objectisation.

20. In none of these instances is it philosophical knowledge. It would be a contradiction in terms to seek to make
a philosophy of that sort of knowledge, since every philosophy—like it or not—proceeds by concepts. This is the
first point to which the consideration of subjectivity as subjectivity draws our attention; and it is a point of capital
importance. Subjectivity marks the frontier which separates
the world of philosophy from the world of religion. This
is what Kierkegaard felt so deeply in his polemic against
Hegel. Philosophy runs against an insurmountable barrier
in attempting to deal with subjectivity, because while philosophy of course knows subjects, it knows them only as
objects. Philosophy is registered whole and entire in the relation of intelligence to object; whereas religion enters into
the relation of subject to subject. For this reason, every
philosophical religion, or every philosophy which, like

[5] Cf. Jacques and Raïssa Maritain, *Situation de la poésie*,
Paris, 1947.

Hegel's, claims to assume and integrate religion into itself, is in the last analysis a mystification.

When philosophy, taking its start in the being of things, attains to God as the cause of being, it has then, thanks to ana-noetic knowledge,[6] rendered the divine Self an object of philosophical knowledge expressed in concepts. These concepts do not circumscribe the supreme reality presented by them. On the contrary, that divine reality infinitely overflows the banks of conceptual knowledge. But philosophy knows thereby, or ought to know, that the reality thus objectised 'through a glass, darkly,' is the reality of a transcendent Self inscrutable in its being and its goodness, in its liberty and its glory. And all the other intelligent *selves* who know it, from the instant that they do know it, owe to it, as their first duty, obedience and adoration. St. Paul blamed pagan wisdom for not recognising that glory of God of which it was in fact aware. But in fact, to recognise that glory is already to adore it. It is something to know that God is a transcendent and sovereign Self; but it is something else again to enter oneself and with all one's baggage—one's own existence and flesh and blood—into the vital relationship in which created subjectivity is brought face to face with this transcendent subjectivity and, trembling and loving, looks to it for salvation. This is the business of religion.

Religion is essentially that which no philosophy can be: a relation of person to person with all the risk, the mystery, the dread, the confidence, the delight, and the torment that lie in such a relationship. And this very relationship of subject to subject[7] demands that into the knowledge of un-

[6] Cf. *Les Degrés du savoir*, pp. 432–447, Eng. trans., pp. 268–278.

[7] Is it necessary to explain that when we employ the word *subject* in speaking of God, we do not do so in the sense in which this word signifies receptivity as regards forms or accidents (for in this sense God is obviously not a 'subject': cf. *Sum. theol.*, I, q. 3, a. 6 and 7), but in the sense in which, as

created subjectivity which the created subjectivity possesses there shall be transferred something of that which the latter is as *subjectivity,* i.e., as that uncreated subjectivity is in the mystery of its personal life. Whence all religion comports an element of revelation. Therefore in the true faith it is the First Truth in Person which makes known to man the mystery of the divine subjectivity: *unigenitus filius, qui est in sinu patris, ipse enarravit.*[8] This knowledge is still 'through a glass, darkly,' and therein the divine subjectivity is still objectised in order to be grasped by us. But this time it is in the glass of the super-analogy of faith,[9] in concepts which God Himself has chosen as His means of speaking to us about Himself—until at the last every glass falls away and then we know truly as we are known. Then shall we truly know the divine subjectivity as subjectivity in the vision in which the divine essence itself actuates our intellect and transports us in ecstasy within itself. While awaiting this state, the connaturality of love gives us, in apophatic contemplation, a dim sort of substitute and obscure foretaste of such a union.

21. Generally speaking, to *situate* the privileged subject which knows itself as subject in respect of all other subjects, which it knows as objects; to situate the self, that thinking reed in the crowd of thinking reeds, sets a singular problem. Each of us is able to say with Mr. Somerset Maugham: 'To myself I am the most important person in the world; though I do not forget that, not even taking into consideration so grand a conception as the Absolute, but from the standpoint of common sense, I am of no con-

---

the moderns employ it, the word signifies subsistence and Self. In this circumstance the word *subject* is like the word *hypostasis* which has a similar etymology and which is predicated formally-eminently of God (cf. *Sum. theol.,* I, q. 29, a. 3).

[8] John I, 18.

[9] Cf. *Les Degrés du savoir,* pp. 478–484, Eng. trans., pp. 297–301.

sequence whatever. It would have made small difference to the universe if I had never existed.'[10] This is a simple remark; but its implications are very wide.

Being the only subject which is a subject for me in the midst of a world of subjects which my senses and my intelligence can know only as objects, I am at the centre of the world, as we observed a moment ago. With regard to my subjectivity in act, I *am* the centre of the world ('the most important person in the world'). My destiny is the most important of all destinies. Worthless as I know myself to be, I am more interesting than all the saints. There is me, and there are all the others. Whatever happens to the others is a mere incident in the picture; but what happens to me, what I myself have to do, is of absolute importance.

And yet, as regards the world itself, from the most obvious 'standpoint of common sense,' I know perfectly well that 'I am of no consequence whatever' and that 'it would have made small difference to the universe if I had never existed.' I know that I am one of the herd, not better than the rest, worth no more than the rest. I shall have been a tiny crest of foam, here one moment, gone in the twinkling of an eye, on the ocean of nature and humanity.

These two images—of myself and of my situation in respect of other subjects—can positively not be superposed. These two perspectives cannot be made to coincide. I oscillate rather miserably between them. If I abandon myself to the perspective of subjectivity, I absorb everything into myself, and, sacrificing everything to my uniqueness, I am riveted to the absolute of selfishness and pride. If I abandon myself to the perspective of objectivity, I am absorbed into everything, and, dissolving into the world, I am false to my uniqueness and resign my destiny. It is only from above that the antinomy can be resolved. If God exists, then not I, but He is the centre; and this time not in relation to a certain particular perspective, like that in

[10] W. Somerset Maugham, *The Summing Up*, 1938, § 5.

which each created subjectivity is the centre of the universe it knows, but speaking absolutely, and as transcendent subjectivity to which all subjectivities are referred. At such time I can know both that I am without importance and that my destiny is of the highest importance. I can know this without falling into pride, know it without being false to my uniqueness. Because, loving the divine Subject more than myself, it is for Him that I love myself, it is to do as He wishes that I wish above all else to accomplish my destiny; and because, unimportant as I am in the world, I am important to Him; not only I, but all the other subjectivities whose lovableness is revealed in Him and for Him and which are henceforward, together with me, a *we*, called to rejoice in His life.

22. I am known to other men. They know me as object, not as subject. They are unaware of my subjectivity as such; unaware not merely of its inexhaustible depth, but also of that presence of the whole in each of its operations, that existential complexity of inner circumstances, data of nature, free choice, attractions, weaknesses, virtues perhaps, loves and pains; that atmosphere of immanent vitality which alone lends meaning to each of my acts. To be known as object, to be known to others, to see oneself in the eyes of one's neighbour (here M. Sartre is right) is to be severed from oneself and wounded in one's identity. It is to be always unjustly known—whether the *he* whom they see condemns the *I*, or whether, as occurs more rarely, the 'he' does honour to the 'I.' A tribunal is a masquerade where the accused stands accoutered in a travesty of himself, and *it* delivers his acts to be weighed in the balance. The more the judges stray from the crude outward criteria with which formerly they contented themselves, and strive to take account of degrees of inner responsibility, the more they reveal that the truth of him whom they judge remains un-

knowable to human justice. Interrogated by such a tribunal, Jesus owed it to Himself to remain silent.

I am known to God. He knows all of me, me as subject. I am present to Him in my subjectivity itself; He has no need to objectise me in order to know me. Then, and in this unique instance, man is known not as object but as subject in all the depth and all the recesses of subjectivity. Only God knows me in this wise; to Him alone am I uncovered. I am not uncovered to myself. The more I know of my subjectivity, the more it remains obscure to me. If I were not known to God, no one would know me. No one would know me in my truth, in my own existence. No one would know me—*me*—as subject.

What this comes to is that no one would render justice to my being.[11] There could be no justice for me anywhere. My existence would be immersed in the injustice of the knowledge of me possessed by all the others and by the world itself; and in my own ignorance of myself. But if there is no justice possible with regard to my being, then there is no possible hope for me. If man is not known to God, and if he has the profound experience of his personal existence and his subjectivity, then he has also the experience of his desperate solitude; and the longing for death—more than this, the aspiration to total annihilation, is the sole spring that can gush forth within him.

Finally, to know that I am known as subject in all the dimensions of my being is not only to know that my truth is known, and that in this knowledge justice is done me; it

[11] ' "You're tying yourself up more and more," said the Head Waiter. "If we're to believe you, we've got to keep forgetting what you said before." . . .
' "It's impossible to defend oneself where there is no good will," Karl told himself, and he made no further answer. . . . He knew that all he could say would appear quite different to the others, and that whether a good or a bad construction was to be put on his actions depended alone on the spirit in which he was judged.' Franz Kafka, *Amerika*, New York, 1946, p. 174 (English translation by Edwin Muir).

is also to know that I am *understood.* Even though God condemn me, I know that He understands me. The idea that we are known to Him who scrutinises the loins and the heart dissolves us at first in fear and trembling because of the evil that is within us. But on deeper reflection, how can we keep from thinking that God Who knows us and knows all those poor beings who jostle us and whom we know as objects, whose wretchedness we mostly perceive—how can we keep from thinking that God Who knows all these in their subjectivity, in the nakedness of their wounds and their secret evil, must know also the secret beauty of that nature which He has bestowed upon them, the slightest sparks of good and liberty they give forth, all the travail and the impulses of good-will that they drag from the womb to the grave, the recesses of goodness of which they themselves have no notion? The exhaustive knowledge possessed by God is a loving knowledge. To know that we are known to God is not merely to experience justice, it is also to experience mercy.

23. In any case, what I should like to say is that our acts are tolerable to ourselves only because our consciousness of them is immersed in the obscure experience of subjectivity. Our acts are hatched in it as in a nest where everything, even the worst rendings and the worst shames, connives with us to emanate from us in the unique freshness of the present instant that we are living. They bathe in that maternal atmosphere emanating from subjectivity, of which I spoke earlier. There is nothing which crushes us so much as our own acts when, forgotten and then one day evoked by some relic of past time, they pass to the state of objects, separated from the living waters of subjectivity. Even if they were not specifically evil, we are no longer sure that they were good and that some unknown illusion or hidden impurity had not tainted them—those strangers

who fling themselves upon us like the dead come forth from within to bring doubt and death to us.

It must be one of the natural features of the state of damnation that the subject, not seeing himself in God, and therefore not seeing his whole life in the eternal instant to which everything is present, all his good and evil acts come back upon him in the sterile endlessly questioning light of the memory of the dead, like enemy objects wholly detached from the actual existence in which subjectivity is definitively set, in the solitude of its ill-will which renders its own past a separate thing for it.

But when the subject reaches his end and sees himself in God and in divine eternity, all the moments of his past life are known to him in the actuality and the presentness of the instant in which they were lived, and all his acts (even the evil, now not only forgiven but leaving no spot nor shadow) are known as emanating presently out of the freshness of subjectivity, now itself become trans-luminous. And in the virtue of the vision in which his intelligence possesses the *Ipsum esse subsistens* he knows not only himself and all his life in a sovereignly existential manner, but also the other creatures whom in God he knows at last as subjects in the unveiled depth of their being.

THE STRUCTURE OF THE SUBJECT

24. To objectise is to universalise. The intelligibles in which a subject objectises itself for our mind are universal natures. It is in relation to the individuality itself of the subject (which the intelligence is not capable of grasping directly); in relation to its subjectivity as subjectivity, as something unique and singular, incommunicable and unconceptualisable, and in relation also to the subject's own experience of its own subjectivity, that objectisation is false to the subject and that, known as object, it is unjustly known, as we have already observed. On the other hand,

in relation to its essential structures, the subject is in no wise betrayed when it is made object. The objectisation which universalises it and discerns in it intelligible natures, makes it known by a knowledge destined doubtless to continue to deepen, but not one that is in any sense unjust. Such a knowledge does no violence to the truth of the subject, but renders that truth present to the mind.

The subject, or suppositum, or person has an essence, an essential structure. It is a substance equipped with properties and which is acted upon and acts by the instrumentality of its potencies. The person is a substance whose substantial form is a spiritual soul; a substance which lives a life that is not merely biological and instinctive, but is also a life of intellect and will. It is a very simple-minded error to believe that subjectivity possesses no intelligible structure, on the ground that it is an inexhaustible depth; and to conceive of it as without any nature whatsoever for the purpose of making of it an absurd abyss of pure and formless liberty.

These observations allow us to understand why many contemporary philosophers, while they talk of nothing but person and subjectivity, nevertheless radically misunderstand those words. They remain lightheartedly ignorant of the metaphysical problem of that *subsistence* concerning which something was said in a preceding section. They do not see that personality, metaphysically considered, being the subsistence of the spiritual soul communicated to the human composite, and enabling the latter to possess its existence, to perfect itself and to give itself freely, bears witness in us to the generosity or expansivity of being which, in an incarnate spirit, proceeds from the spirit and which constitutes, in the secret springs of our ontological structure, a source of dynamic unity and unification from within.[12]

Because analysis wearies them, they are ignorant of what

[12] Cf. J. Maritain, *La Personne et le Bien Commun*, Paris, 1947, p. 34 (Eng. trans., N.Y., 1947, p. 31).

the proper life of the intelligence consists in, and in what the proper life of the will consists. They do not see that, because his *spirit* makes man cross the threshold of independence properly so-called, and of self-inwardness, the subjectivity of the person demands as its most intimate privilege communications proper to love and intelligence. They do not see that, even before the exercise of free choice, and in order to make free choice possible, the most deeply rooted need of the person is to communicate with *the other* by the union of the intelligence, and with *others* by the affective union. Their subjectivity is not a *self*, because it is wholly phenomenal.

25. I have already cited St. Thomas's aphorism, that the whole root of liberty is established in the reason. What reveals subjectivity to itself is not an irrational break (however profound and gratuitous it may be) in an irrational flow of moral and psychological phenomena, of dreams, automatisms, urges, and images surging upwards from the unconscious. Neither is it the anguish of forced choice. It is self-mastery for the purpose of self-giving. When a man has the obscure intuition of subjectivity, the reality, whose sudden invasion of his consciousness he experiences, is that of a secret totality, which contains both itself and its upsurge, and which superabounds in knowledge and in love. Only by love does it attain to its supreme level of existence —existence as self-giving.

'This is what I mean: Self-knowledge as a mere psychological analysis of phenomena more or less superficial, a wandering through images and memories, is but an egotistic awareness, however valuable it may be. But when it becomes ontological, then knowledge of the Self is transfigured, implying intuition of Being and the discovery of the actual abyss of subjectivity. At the same time, it is the discovery of the basic generosity of existence. Subjectivity, this essentially dynamic, living and open centre, both receives and gives. It receives through the intellect, by superexisting in knowledge. It gives through the will, by superexisting in love; that is, by having within itself other beings as inner attractions directed towards them and giving oneself to them, and by spiritually existing in the manner of a gift. And "it is better to give than to receive." The spiritual existence of love is the supreme revelation of existence for the Self. The Self, being not only a material individual but also a spiritual personality, possesses itself and holds itself in hand in so far as it is spiritual and in so far as it is free. And to what purpose does it possess itself and dispose of itself, if not for what *is better,* in actual existence and absolutely speaking, or to give of itself? Thus it is that when a man has been really awakened to the sense of being or existence, and grasps intuitively the obscure, living depth of the Self and subjectivity, he discovers by the same token the basic generosity of existence and realises, by virtue of the inner dynamism of this intuition, that love is not a passing pleasure or emotion, but the very meaning of his being alive.'[13]

By love, finally, is shattered the impossibility of knowing another except as object. I have emphasised this impossibility above at length and noted that it directly concerns the senses and the intellect. To say that union in love makes the being we love another *ourself* for us is to say that it makes that being another subjectivity for us, another subjectivity that is ours. To the degree that we truly love (which is to say, not for ourselves but for the beloved; and when—which is not always the case—the intellect within us becomes passive as regards love, and, allowing its concepts to slumber, thereby renders love a formal means of knowledge), to this degree we acquire an obscure knowledge of the being we love, similar to that which we possess of ourselves; we know that being in his very subjectivity (at least

[13] Cf. J. Maritain, 'A New Approach to God,' in *Our Emergent Civilization,* ed. by Ruth Nanda Anshen, Harper & Bros., N.Y., 1947, pp. 285–286. By permission of the publishers.

in a certain measure) by this experience of union. Then he himself is, in a certain degree, cured of his solitude; he can, though still disquieted, rest for a moment in the nest of the knowledge that we possess of him as subject.

The People and the State

I. NATION, BODY POLITIC, AND STATE

There is no more thankless task than trying rationally to distinguish and to circumscribe—in other words, trying to raise to a scientific or philosophical level—common notions that have arisen from the contingent practical needs of human history and are laden with social, cultural, and historical connotations as ambiguous as they are fertile, and which nevertheless envelop a core of intelligible meaning. Such concepts are nomadic, not fixed; they are shifting and fluid. Now they are used synonymously, now in opposition to one another. Everybody is the more at ease in using them as he does not know exactly what they mean. But as soon as one tries to define them and separate them from one another, hosts of problems and difficulties arise. One runs the risk of being switched onto a wrong track while attempting to bring out the truth, and to make analytical and systematic what has been conveyed to him by confused experience and concrete life.

The preceding remarks apply strikingly to the notions of *Nation, Body Politic* (or Political Society), and *State.* Yet nothing is more necessary, for a sound political philosophy,

(From Jacques Maritain, *Man and the State* [University of Chicago Press, 1951], Chap. I, pp. 1–27.)

than to try to *sort out* these three notions, and clearly circumscribe the genuine meaning of each.

Often, when we speak in the current, more or less vague
manner, these three concepts are used, and can be legiti-
mately used, as synonymous with one another. But when it
comes to their genuine sociological meaning and to political
theory, they must be sharply distinguished. The confusion
between, or the systematic identification of, *Nation* and
Political Society—or *Political Society* and *State*—or *Nation*
and *State,* has been a woe to modern history. A correct re-
statement of the three concepts in question is badly needed.
The austerity of my analysis may perhaps be excused,
therefore, on account of the importance of the principles in
political philosophy it may make us aware of.

II. COMMUNITY AND SOCIETY

A preliminary distinction must be made—namely between *community* and *society.* Of course these two terms
may licitly be used synonymously, and I myself have done
so many times. But it is also licit—and proper—to assign
them to two kinds of social groups which are actually different in nature. This distinction, though it has been misused in the most grievous manner by the theorists of the
superiority of "life" over reason, is in itself an established
sociological fact. Both community and society are ethico-
social and truly human, not mere biological realities. But a
community is more of a work of nature and more nearly
related to the biological; a society is more of a work of reason, and more nearly related to the intellectual and spiritual
properties of man. Their inner social essences and their characteristics, as well as their spheres of realization, do not
coincide.[1]

[1] The concept of community, as it is used here, is a generic
concept, covering the three specific forms of sociability that
Professor Georges Gurvitch distinguishes under the names of

In order to understand this distinction, we must remember that social life as such brings men together by reason of a certain common *object*. In social relations there is always an object, either material or spiritual, around which the relations among human persons are interwoven. In a *community*, as J. T. Delos[2] has rightly pointed out, the object is a *fact* which precedes the determinations of human intelligence and will, and which acts independently of them to create a common unconscious psyche, common feelings and psychological structures, and common mores. But in a *society* the object is a *task* to be done or an *end* to be aimed at, which depends on the determinations of

---

"masses," "community," and "communion" (cf. Georges Gurvitch, *Essais de sociologie* [Paris: Recueil Sirey, 1938]; "Masses, Community, Communion," *Philosophical Review*, August, 1941). We agree with Professor Gurvitch on the distinction between Political Society and State (*Essais de sociologie*, p. 60) and the fact that the Political Society as well as the State are "functional," not "suprafunctional," forms of organized sociability. We dissent from him on three main points: (1) His theory deals only with communities (in the generic sense of the word), so as to miss the basic distinction between community (especially the Nation) and society (especially the Political Society), with the essential rational characteristic of the latter, and thus makes of the Political Society a mere "superstructure" of the Nation. (2) He insists that the Nation is *supra-functional* (*ibid.*, p. 58), whereas we deny the existence of any *supra-functional* social group (that is, implying "an infinite ensemble of ends and values" [*ibid.*, p. 59]). The infinity in question is merely potential, therefore cannot be a specific determination of any social group whatever. Every social group is determined by an object (which is a *fact*, not an *end*, in the case of the Nation as of any community in general). The Nation is acephalous, it is not supra-functional: it is rather *infra-functional*. (3) Professor Gurvitch, like many modern authors, defines the State by the "monopoly of unconditional constraint" (cf. Georges Gurvitch, *Sociology of Law* [New York: Philosophical Library, 1942], pp. 238 ff.). The criterion of unconditional constraint is a merely empirical note, deriving from more essential characteristics, and does not make clear the nature of the State. The true criterion is the maintenance of law and public order, as relating to the common good of the Political Society.

2 Cf. J. T. Delos, *La Nation* (Montréal: L'Arbre, 1944).

human intelligence and will and is preceded by the activity
—either decision, or, at least, consent—of the reason of individuals; thus, in the case of society the objective and
rational element in social life explicitly emerges and takes
the leading role. A business firm, a labor union, a scientific
association are *societies* as much as is the body politic.
Regional, ethnic, linguistic groups, social classes are *communities*. The tribe, the clan are communities that pave the
way for, and foreshadow the advent of, the political society.
The *community* is a product of instinct and heredity in
given circumstances and historical frameworks; the *society*
a product of reason and moral strength (what the Ancients
called "virtue").

In the *community*, social relations proceed from given
historical situations and environments: the collective patterns of feeling—or the collective unconscious psyche—have
the upper hand over personal consciousness, and man appears as a product of the social group. In *society*, personal
consciousness retains priority, the social group is shaped by
men, and social relations proceed from a given initiative,
a given idea, and the voluntary determination of human
persons.

Even in *natural* societies, such as the family society and
political society—that is, in societies which are both necessarily required and spontaneously rough-hewn by nature
—*society* finally springs up from human freedom. Even in
communities—regional communities, for instance, or voca-
tional communities—that grow around some particular society, like an industrial or commercial establishment, *community* springs up from nature; I mean, from the reaction
and adjustment of human nature to a given historical environment, or to the factual impact of the industrial or
commercial society in question upon the natural condition-
ing of human existence. In the *community*, social pressure
derives from coercion imposing patterns of conduct on man
and comes into play in a deterministic mode. In *society*, so-

cial pressure derives from law or rational regulations, or from an idea of the common aim; it calls forth personal conscience and liberty, which must obey the law freely.

A society always gives rise to communities and community feelings within or around itself. Never can a community develop into a society, though it can be the natural soil from which some societal organization springs up through reason.

III. THE NATION

Now the *Nation* is a community, not a society. The Nation is one of the most important, perhaps the most complex and complete community engendered by civilized life. Modern times have been faced with a conflicting tension between the Nation and another momentous human community, the Class; yet, as a matter of fact, the dynamism of the Nation has appeared to be the stronger—because it is more deeply rooted in nature.

The word nation originates from the Latin *nasci,* that is, from the notion of *birth,* but the nation is not something biological, like the Race. It is something ethico-social: a human community based on the fact of birth and lineage, yet with all the moral connotations of those terms: birth to the life of reason and the activities of civilization, lineage in familial traditions, social and juridical formation, cultural heritage, common conceptions and manners, historical recollections, sufferings, claims, hopes, prejudices, and resentments. An ethnic community, generally speaking, can be defined as a *community of patterns of feeling* rooted in the physical soil of the origin of the group as well as in the moral soil of history; it becomes a *nation* when this factual situation enters the sphere of self-awareness, in other words when the ethnic group *becomes conscious* of the fact that it constitutes a community of patterns of feeling—or rather, has a common unconscious psyche—and possesses its own unity and individuality, its own will to endure in existence. A nation is a community of people who become aware of themselves as history has made them, who treasure their own past, and who love themselves as they know or imagine themselves to be, with a kind of inevitable introversion. This progressive awakening of national consciousness has been a characteristic feature of modern history. Though it is normal and good in itself, it finally became exacerbated and gave rise to the plague of Nationalism, while—and probably because—the concept of Nation and the concept of State were confused and mixed up in an unfortunate and explosive manner.

The Nation has, or had, a soil, a land—this does not mean, as for the State, a territorial area of power and administration, but a cradle of life, work, pain, and dreams. The Nation has a language—though the linguistic groups by no means always coincide with the national ones. The Nation thrives on institutions—the creation of which, however, depends more on the human person and mind, or the family, or particular groups in the society, or the body politic, than on the Nation itself. The Nation has rights, which are but the rights of human persons to participate in the peculiar human values of a national heritage. The Nation has a historic calling, which is not its *own* calling (as if there were primordial and predestined national monads each of which was possessed of a supreme mission), but which is only a historical and contingent particularization of man's calling to the unfolding and manifestation of his own multifarious potentialities.

Yet for all of that the Nation is not a society; it does not cross the threshold of the political realm. It is a community of communities, a self-aware network of common feelings and representations that human nature and instinct have caused to swarm around a number of physical, historical and social data. Like any other community the Nation is

"acephalous"[3]: it has élites and centers of influence—no
head or ruling authority; structures—no rational form or
juridical organization; passions and dreams—no common
good; solidarity among its members, faithfulness, honor—no
civic friendship; manners and mores—no formal norms and
order. It does not appeal to the freedom and responsibility
of personal conscience, it instils in human persons a second
nature. It is a general pattern in private life, it does not
know any principle of public order. Thus it is that in reality
the national group cannot *transform itself* into a political society: a political society can progressively differentiate itself
within a confused social life in which political functions and
community activities were first commingled; the idea of the
body politic can arise in the bosom of a national community; but the national community can only be a propitious
soil and an occasion for that blossoming. In itself the idea
of the body politic belongs to another, superior order. As
soon as the body politic exists, it is something other than a
national community.

The preceding analysis makes us realize how serious have
been for modern history the confusion between Nation and
State, the myth of the National State, and the so-called
principle of nationalities understood in the sense that each
national group must set itself up as a separate State.[4] Such
a confusion has wrenched both Nation and State out of
shape. The trouble began in the democratic theater, during
the XIXth century. It came to full madness in the anti-
democratic reaction of the present century. Let us consider
the result in the most acute cases.

Uprooted from its essential order, and therefore losing its
natural limits in the course of an anti-natural growth, the
Nation has become an earthly divinity whose absolute self-

[3] Cf. M. Hauriou, *Principes de droit constitutionnel* (Paris,
1923), p. 29.
[4] Cf. René Johannet, *Le Principe des nationalités* (2d ed.;
Paris: Nouvelle Librairie Nationale, 1923).

ishness is sacred, and it has used political power to subvert
any steady order among peoples. The State, when it has
been identified with the Nation, or even with the Race, and
when the fever of the instincts of the earth has thus invaded
its own blood—the State has had its will to power exasper-
ated; it has presumed to impose by force of law the so-
called type and genius of the Nation, thus becoming a
cultural, ideological, caesaro-papist, totalitarian State. At
the same time, that totalitarian State has degenerated by
losing the sense of the objective order of justice and law,
and by swerving toward what is peculiar to tribal as well
as to feudal community achievements. For the universal
and objective ties of law and for the specific relationship
between the individual person and the political body, have
been substituted personal ties derived from blood, or from
a particular commitment of man to man or to the clan, the
party, or the chief.

I have just emphasized the distinction between that sociological reality which is a *National Community* and that
other sociological reality which is a *Political Society*. It must
now be added that, as I have previously remarked, the existence of a given society naturally calls forth the birth
of new communities within or around that societal group.
Thus, when a *political society* has been formed, especially
when it has a century-old experience strengthening genuine civic friendship, it naturally gives rise, within itself, to a
national community of a higher degree, either with regard
to the self-awareness of such an already existing community, or with regard to the very formation of a new National
Community in which various nationalities have been
merged. Thus, to the exact contrary of the so-called principle of nationalities, the Nation here depends on the existence of the body politic, not the body politic on the existence of the Nation. The Nation does not become a State.
The State causes the Nation to be. Thus it is that a multi-

national *Federation of States,* as is the United States, is at the same time a multinational *Nation.* A genuine principle of nationalities would be formulated as follows: the body politic should develop both its own moral dynamism and the respect for human freedoms to such a point that the national communities which are contained within it would both have their natural rights fully recognized, and tend spontaneously to merge in a single higher and more complex National Community.

Let us compare from this point of view four significant instances: Germany, the old Austro-Hungarian Empire, France, and the United States. Germany is a complex of nations, and has been unable to bring about a genuine body politic; it has made up for that frustration by an unnatural exaltation of the national feeling and an unnatural Nation-State. The Austro-Hungarian double crown created a State but was unable to produce a Nation. France and the United States enjoyed particularly favorable circumstances, —as well as a sense of freedom and of the basic role of free choice or consent by people in political life; in each case this helped to produce a single Nation centered on the body politic—a Nation which achieved unity, as a result either of century-old trials or of a ceaseless process of self-creation. So for practical purposes we may use the expression the American Nation, the French Nation, to denote the American or French political body. Yet such a practical synonymity must not deceive us and make us forget the fundamental distinction between National Community and Political Society.

IV. THE BODY POLITIC

In contradistinction to the *Nation,* both the *Body Politic* and the *State* pertain to the order of society, even society in its highest or "perfect" form. In our modern age the two terms are used synonymously,[5] and the second tends to supersede the first. Yet if we are to avoid serious misunderstandings, we have to distinguish clearly between the State and the Body Politic. These do not belong to two diverse categories, but they differ from each other as a part differs from the whole. The *Body Politic* or the *Political Society* is the whole. The *State* is a part—the topmost part—of this whole.

Political Society, required by nature and achieved by reason, is the most perfect of temporal societies. It is a concretely and wholly human reality, tending to a concretely and wholly human good—the common good. It is a work of reason, born out of the obscure efforts of reason disengaged from instinct, and implying essentially a rational order; but it is no more Pure Reason than man himself. The body politic has flesh and blood, instincts, passions, reflexes, unconscious psychological structures and dynamism—all of these subjected, if necessary by legal coercion, to the command of an Idea and rational decisions. Justice is a primary condition for the existence of the body politic, but Friendship is its very life-giving form.[6] It tends toward a really human and freely achieved communion. It lives on the devotion of the human persons and their gift of themselves. They are ready to commit their own existence, their pos-

[5] "The State is a particular portion of mankind viewed as an organized unit" (John W. Burgess, *Political Science and Constitutional Law* [Boston: Ginn & Co., 1896], I, 50).

A similar confusion between Body Politic and State is usual among jurists. According to Story and Cooley, "a state is a body politic, or society of men, united together for the purpose of promoting their mutual safety and advantage by the joint efforts of their combined strength" (Thomas M. Cooley, *Constitutional Limitations* [Boston, 1868], p. 1; cf. Joseph Story, *Commentaries on the Constitution of the United States* [Boston, 1851], I, 142). The word "state," Story goes on to say (*ibid.*, p. 143), "means the whole people, united into one body politic; and the state, and the people of the state, are equivalent expressions."

[6] Cf. Gerald B. Phelan, *Justice and Friendship*, in the "Maritain Volume" of the *Thomist* (New York: Sheed & Ward, 1943).

sessions and their honor for its sake. The civic sense is made up of this sense of devotion and mutual love as well as of the sense of justice and law.

The entire man—though not by reason of his entire self and of all that he is and has—is part of the political society; and thus all his community activities, as well as his personal activities, are of consequence to the political whole. As we have pointed out, a national community of a higher human degree spontaneously takes shape by virtue of the very existence of the body politic, and in turn becomes part of the substance of the latter. Nothing matters more, in the order of material causality, to the life and preservation of the body politic than the accumulated energy and historical continuity of that national community it has itself caused to exist. This means chiefly a heritage of accepted and unquestionable structures, fixed customs and deep-rooted common feelings which bring into social life itself something of the determined physical data of nature, and of the vital unconscious strength proper to vegetative organisms. It is, further, common inherited experience and the moral and intellectual instincts which constitute a kind of empirical, practical wisdom, much deeper and denser and much nearer the hidden complex dynamism of human life than any artificial construction of reason.

Not only is the national community, as well as all communities of the nation, thus comprised in the superior unity of the body politic. But the body politic also contains in its superior unity the family units, whose essential rights and freedoms are anterior to itself, and a multiplicity of other particular societies which proceed from the free initiative of citizens and should be as autonomous as possible. Such is the element of pluralism inherent in every truly political society. Family, economic, cultural, educational, religious life matter as much as does political life to the very existence and prosperity of the body politic. Every kind of law, from the spontaneous, unformulated group regulations to customary law and to law in the full sense of the term, contributes to the vital order of political society. Since in political society authority comes from below, through the people, it is normal that the whole dynamism of authority in the body politic should be made up of particular and partial authorities rising in tiers above one another, up to the top authority of the State. Finally, the public welfare and the general order of law are essential parts of the common good of the body politic, but this common good has far larger and richer, more concretely human implications, for it is by nature the good human life of the multitude and is common to both the *whole* and the *parts,* the persons into whom it flows back and who must benefit from it. The common good is not only the collection of public commodities and services which the organization of common life presupposes: a sound fiscal condition, a strong military force; the body of just laws, good customs, and wise institutions which provides the political society with its structure; the heritage of its great historical remembrances, its symbols and its glories, its living traditions and cultural treasures. The common good also includes the sociological integration of all the civic conscience, political virtues and sense of law and freedom, of all the activity, material prosperity and spiritual riches, of unconsciously operating hereditary wisdom, of moral rectitude, justice, friendship, happiness, virtue and heroism in the individual lives of the members of the body politic. To the extent to which all these things are, in a certain measure, *communicable* and revert to each member, helping him to perfect his life and liberty as a person, they all constitute the good human life of the multitude.[7]

[7] Cf. our book, *The Person and the Common Good* (New York: Charles Scribner's Sons, 1947).

V. THE STATE

From this enumeration of the features of the body politic, it should be evident that the body politic differs from the State. The State is only that part of the body politic especially concerned with the maintenance of law, the promotion of the common welfare and public order, and the administration of public affairs. The State is a part which *specializes* in the interests of the *whole*.[8] It is not a man or a body of men; it is a set of institutions combined into a topmost machine: this kind of work of art has been built by man and uses human brains and energies and is nothing without man, but it constitutes a superior embodiment of reason, an impersonal, lasting superstructure, the functioning of which may be said to be rational in the second degree, insofar as the reason's activity in it, bound by law and by a system of universal regulations, is more abstract, more sifted out from the contingencies of experience and individuality, more pitiless also, than in our individual lives.

The State is not the supreme incarnation of the Idea, as Hegel believed; the State is not a kind of collective superman; the State is but an agency entitled to use power and coercion, and made up of experts or specialists in public order and welfare, an instrument in the service of man. Putting man at the service of that instrument is political perversion. The human person as an individual is for the body politic and the body politic is for the human person as a person. But man is by no means for the State. The State is for man.

When we say that the State is the superior part in the body politic, this means that it is superior to the other organs or collective parts of this body, but it does not mean

---

[8] Harold Laski described the State as a public service corporation (*A Grammar of Politics* [London: Allen & Unwin, 1935], p. 69).

that it is superior to the body politic itself. The part as such is inferior to the whole. The State is inferior to the body politic as a whole, and is at the service of the body politic as a whole. Is the State even the *head* of the body politic? Hardly, for in the human being the head is an instrument of such spiritual powers as the intellect and the will, which the whole body has to serve; whereas the functions exercised by the State are for the body politic, and not the body politic for them.

The theory which I have just summarized, and which regards the State as a part or an instrument of the body politic, subordinate to it and endowed with topmost authority not by its own right and for its own sake, but only by virtue and to the extent of the requirements of the common good, can be described as an "instrumentalist" theory, founding the genuinely *political* notion of the State. But we are confronted with quite another notion, the *despotic* notion of the State, based on a "substantialist" or "absolutist" theory. According to this theory the State is a subject of right, i.e., a moral person, and consequently a whole; as a result it is either superimposed on the body politic or made to absorb the body politic entirely, and it enjoys supreme power by virtue of its own natural, inalienable right and for its own final sake.

Of course there is for everything great and powerful an instinctive tendency—and a special temptation—to grow beyond its own limits. Power tends to increase power, the power machine tends ceaselessly to extend itself; the supreme legal and administrative machine tends toward bureaucratic self-sufficiency; it would like to consider itself an end, not a means. Those who specialize in the affairs of the whole have a propensity to take themselves for the whole; the general staffs to take themselves for the whole army, the Church authorities for the whole Church; the State for the whole body politic. By the same token, the State tends to ascribe to itself a peculiar common good—

its own self-preservation and growth—distinct both from the public order and welfare which are its immediate end, and from the common good which is its final end. All these misfortunes are but instances of "natural" excess or abuse.

But there has been something much more specific and serious in the development of the *substantialist* or *absolutist* theory of the State. This development can be understood only in the perspective of modern history and as a sequel to the structures and conceptions peculiar to the Mediaeval Empire, to the absolute monarchy of the French classical age, and the absolute government of the Stuart kings in England. Remarkably enough, the very word *State* only appeared in the course of modern history; the notion of the State was implicitly involved in the ancient concept of city (*polis, civitas*) which meant essentially body politic, and still more in the Roman concept of the Empire: it was never explicitly brought out in Antiquity. According to a historical pattern unfortunately most recurrent, both the normal development of the State—which was in itself a sound and genuine progress—and the development of the spurious—absolutist—juridical and philosophical conception of the State took place at the same time.

An adequate explanation of that historical process would require a long and thorough analysis. Here I merely suggest that in the Middle Ages the authority of the Emperor, and in early modern times the authority of the absolute King, descended from above on the body politic, upon which it was superimposed. For centuries, political authority was the privilege of a superior "social race" which had a right—and believed it to be an innate or immediately God-given and inalienable right—to supreme power over, and leadership as well as moral guidance of, the body politic—made up, it was assumed, of people under age who were able to make requests, remonstrances, or riots, not to govern themselves. So, in the "baroque age," while the reality of the State and the sense of the State progressively took

shape as great juridical achievements, the concept of the
State emerged more or less confusedly as the concept of a
whole—sometimes identified with the person of the king—
which was superimposed on or which enveloped the body
politic and enjoyed power from above by virtue of its own
natural and inalienable right,—that is to say, which possessed sovereignty. For in the genuine sense of this word
—which depends on the historical formation of the concept
of sovereignty, prior to jurists' various definitions—sovereignty implies not only actual possession of and right to
supreme power, but a right which is *natural and inalienable,* to a supreme power which is supreme *separate from*
and *above* its subjects.[9]

At the time of the French Revolution that very concept
of the State considered as a whole unto itself was preserved,
but it shifted from the King to the Nation, mistakenly identified with the body politic; hence Nation, Body Politic and
State were identified.[10] And the very concept of sovereignty
—as a *natural* or *innate* and *inalienable* right to supreme
transcendent power—was preserved, but shifted from the
King to the Nation. At the same time, by virtue of a volun-
tarist theory of law and political society, which had its
acme in eighteenth-century philosophy, the State was
made into a person (a so-called moral person) and a subject
of right,[11] in such a way that the attribute of absolute sov-

[9] See chap. ii.

[10] This confusion between State, Body Politic, and Law was
to become classical. It appeared in a striking manner in the
theory of A. Esmein (see his *Éléments de droit constitutionnel*
[6th ed.; Paris: Recueil Sirey, 1914]), who insisted that "the
State is the juridical personification of the Nation."

[11] The notion of moral or collective personality—in which
"personality" has a *proper analogical* value—applies to the
people as a whole in a genuine manner: because the people as
a whole (a *natural whole*) are an ensemble of real individual
persons and because their unity as a social whole derives from a
common will to live together which originates in these real individual persons.

Accordingly, the notion of moral or collective personality

ereignty, ascribed to the Nation, was inevitably, as a matter of fact, to be claimed and exercised by the State.

Thus it is that in modern times the despotic or absolutist notion of the State was largely accepted among democratic tenets by the theorists of democracy—pending the advent of Hegel, the prophet and theologian of the totalitarian, divinized State. In England, John Austin's theories only tended to tame and civilize somewhat the old Hobbesian Leviathan. This process of acceptance was favored by a symbolical property which genuinely belongs to the State, namely, the fact that, just as we say twenty head of cattle meaning twenty animals, in the same way the topmost part in the body politic naturally *represents* the political whole. Nay more, the notion of the latter is raised to a higher degree of abstraction and symbolization,[12] and the consciousness of

---

applies in a genuine manner to the *body politic,* which is the organic whole, composed of the people. As a result, both the people and the body politic are *subjects* (*or holders*) *of rights:* the people have a right to self-government; there is a mutual relationship of justice between the body politic and its individual members.

But that same notion of moral personality does not apply to the *State* (which is not a whole, but a part or a special agency of the body politic), except in a *merely metaphorical* manner and by virtue of a juridical fiction. The State is not a subject of rights, a *Rechtssubjekt,* as many modern theorists, especially Jellinek, mistakenly put it. (On the opposite side, Léon Duguit clearly realized that the State is not a subject of rights, but he went to the other extreme, and his general theory jeopardized the very notion of right.)

The rights of the people or of the body politic are not and cannot be *transferred* or given over to the State. Furthermore, in so far as the State *represents* the body politic (in the external relations of the latter with the other bodies politic), "the State" is a merely abstract entity which is neither a moral person nor a subject of rights. The rights ascribed to it are no rights of its own; they are the rights of the body politic—which is *ideally* substituted for by that abstract entity, and *really* represented by the men who have been put in charge of public affairs and invested with specific powers.

[12] So it happened that a great theorist like Kelsen could make out of the State a mere juridical abstraction and identify it with

the political society is raised to a more completely individualized idea of itself in the idea of the State. In the absolutist notion of the State, that symbol has been made a reality, has been hypostasized. According to this notion the State is a metaphysical monad, a person; it is a whole unto itself, *the* very political whole in its supreme degree of unity and individuality. So it absorbs in itself the body politic from which it emanates, as well as all the individual or particular wills which, according to Jean-Jacques Rousseau, have engendered the General Will in order mystically to die and resurge in its unity. And it enjoys absolute sovereignty as an essential property and right.

That concept of the State, enforced in human history, has forced democracies into intolerable self-contradictions, in their domestic life and above all in international life. For this concept is no part of the authentic tenets of democracy, it does not belong to the real democratic inspiration and philosophy, it belongs to a spurious ideological heritage which has preyed upon democracy like a parasite. During the reign of individualist or "liberal" democracy the State, made into an absolute, displayed a tendency to substitute itself for the people, and so to leave the people estranged

---

Law and the legal order—a concept which uproots the State from its true sphere (that is, the political sphere) and which is all the more ambiguous as the real State (as topmost part and agency of the body politic) will in actual fact avail itself of that fictitious essence, ascribed to it as juridical *ens rationis,* to claim for itself the saintly attributes and "sovereignty" of the Law.

Be it noted, moreover, that the expression "sovereignty of the law" is a merely metaphorical expression, which relates to the rational nature of the law and its obligatory moral and juristic quality but has nothing to do with the genuine concept of sovereignty.

The concrete function of the State—its principal function—is to ensure the legal order and the enforcement of the law. But the State is not the law. And the so-called "sovereignty" of the State (see chap. ii) is in no way the moral and juridical "sovereignty" (that is, the property of binding consciences and being enforceable by coercion) of the Law (the just law).

from political life to a certain extent; it also was able to launch the wars between nations which disturbed the XIXth Century. Nevertheless, after the Napoleonic era the worst implications of this process of State absolutization were restrained by the democratic philosophy and political practices which then prevailed. It is with the advent of the totalitarian régimes and philosophies that those worst implications were released. The State made into an absolute revealed its true face. Our epoch has had the privilege of contemplating the State totalitarianism of Race with German Nazism, of Nation with Italian Fascism, of Economic Community with Russian Communism.

The point which needs emphasis is this. For democracies today the most urgent endeavor is to develop social justice and improve world economic management, and to defend themselves against totalitarian threats from the outside and totalitarian expansion in the world; but the pursuit of these objectives will inevitably involve the risk of having too many functions of social life controlled by the State from above, and we shall be inevitably bound to accept this risk, as long as our notion of the State has not been restated on true and genuine democratic foundations, and as long as the body politic has not renewed its own structures and consciousness, so that the people become more effectively equipped for the exercise of freedom, and the State may be made an actual instrument for the common good of all. Then only will that very topmost agency, which is made by modern civilization more and more necessary to the human person in his political, social, moral, even intellectual and scientific progress, cease to be at the same time a threat to the freedoms of the human person as well as of intelligence and science. Then only will the highest functions of the State— to ensure the law and facilitate the free development of the body politic—be restored, and the sense of the State be regained by the citizens. Then only will the State achieve its true dignity, which comes not from power and prestige, but from the exercise of justice.

VI. NORMAL GROWTH AND THE SIMULTANEOUS PROCESS OF PERVERSION

At this point I should like not to be misunderstood. I hope that my previous remarks have made it sufficiently clear that I by no means condemn or depreciate the State and its astonishing growth in the course of modern history. That would be as blindly unreal and futile as to condemn or reject the mechanical achievements which have transformed the world, and which could and should become instruments for the liberation of man. From the last period of the XIXth Century on, state intervention has been needed to compensate for the general disregard for justice and human solidarity that prevailed during the early phases of the industrial revolution. State legislation with regard to employment and labor is in itself a requirement of the common good. And without the power of the State—the democratic State—how could a free body politic resist the pressure or the aggression of totalitarian States? The growth of the State, in modern centuries, as a rational or juridical machine and with regard to its inner constitutive system of law and power, its unity, its discipline; the growth of the State, in the present century, as a technical machine and with regard to its law-making, supervising, and organizing functions in social and economic life, are in themselves part of normal progress.

Such progress has been entirely corrupted in totalitarian States. It remains normal progress, though subject to many risks, in democratic States, especially as regards the development of social justice.

We may dislike the State machinery; I do not like it. Yet many things we do not like are necessary, not only in fact, but by right. On the one hand, the primary reason for which men, united in a political society, need the State, is the order of justice. On the other hand, social justice is the crucial need of modern societies. As a result, the primary duty of the modern State is the enforcement of social justice.

As a matter of fact, this primary duty is inevitably performed with abnormal emphasis on the power of the State to the very extent that the latter has to make up for the deficiencies of a society whose basic structures are not sufficiently up to the mark with regard to justice. Those deficiencies are the first cause of the trouble. And thus any theoretical objections or particular claims, even justified in their own particular spheres, will inevitably be considered as but minor things in the face of the vital necessity—not only factual but moral—of meeting the long-neglected wants and rights of the human person in the deepest and largest strata of the human society.

The problem, in my opinion, is to distinguish the normal progress of the State from the false notions, connected with the concept of sovereignty, which prey upon it; and also to change the backward general conditions which, by imposing a too heavy burden upon it, make it liable to become seriously vitiated. For both those backward social conditions and those false absolutist notions give rise to a process of perversion combined with and preying upon normal growth. How to describe this process of perversion? It occurs—that is apparent from all our previous remarks—when the State mistakes itself for a whole, for *the* whole of the political society, and consequently takes upon itself the exercise of the functions and the performance of the tasks which normally pertain to the body politic and its various organs. Then we have what has been labelled "the paternalist State": the `State not only supervising from the political point of view of the common good (which is normal), but directly organizing, controlling, or managing, to the extent which it judges the interests of public welfare to demand, all forms—economic, commercial, industrial, cultural, or dealing with scientific research as well as with relief and security—of the body politic's life.

Let us point out in this connection that what is called "nationalization," and is in reality "statization," can be opportune or necessary in certain cases, but should by nature remain exceptional—limited to those public services so immediately concerned with the very existence, order, or internal peace of the body politic that a risk of bad management is then a lesser evil than the risk of giving the upper hand to private interests. The fact remains that the State has skill and competence in administrative, legal, and political matters, but is inevitably dull and awkward—and, as a result, easily oppressive and injudicious—in all other fields. To become a boss or a manager in business or industry or a patron of art or a leading spirit in the affairs of culture, science, and philosophy is against the nature of such an impersonal topmost agency, abstract so to speak and separated from the moving peculiarities, mutual tensions, risks, and dynamism of concrete social existence.

By virtue of a strange intermingling in human vocabulary, the word *nationalization* conveys a socialistic meaning, whereas the word *socialization,* on the contrary, if it were correctly understood, would have rather personalist and pluralist implications. For, taken in its genuine sense, it refers to that process of social integration through which association in a single enterprise extends not only to the capital invested, but also to labor and management, and all persons and various groups involved are made participants in some form or other of co-ownership and co-management. This process is not an attack on, but an expansion of private ownership. It depends on the search of free initiative for new economic modalities and adjustments, the more successful of which will be one day sanctioned by the law. It rises from the natural growth of the system of free enterprise, when common consciousness becomes aware of the social function of private property and of the necessity of giving organic and institutional forms to that law of the "common use" on which Thomas Aquinas has laid particular stress.[13]

As a result I would say that if our present social structure is to evolve along normal lines, a first step, made necessary by the requirements of public welfare, would consist in having the State start and support—as has been shown possible by the outstanding example of the Tennessee Valley Authority—large scale undertakings planned and managed *not* by the State and not from the center of the country's political administration, but on the spot, by private enterprises co-ordinated with one another and by the various communities of the very people concerned, under the leadership of independent responsible appointees. Thus the State itself would launch a movement of progressive decentralization and "destatization" of social life, tending toward the advent of some new personalist and pluralist[14] régime.

The final step would take place, in such a new régime, when prodding by the State would no longer be necessary, and all organic forms of social and economic activity, even the largest and most comprehensive ones, would start from the bottom, I mean from the free initiative of and mutual

13 Cf. our book, *Freedom in the Modern World* (New York: Charles Scribner's Sons, 1936), Appendix I, "Person and Property."

14 On the notion of pluralism see my books, *Du régime temporel et de la liberté* ("Freedom in the Modern World"), chap. i, and *Humanisme intégral* ("True Humanism"), chap. v. See also Professor R. M. MacIver's observations on the "multigroup society" (*The Web of Government* [New York: Macmillan Co., 1947], pp. 421 ff.).

When I developed this theory of the pluralist principle, forging the expression for my own purposes, I had not read Harold Laski's books; it was only later on that I became aware of the fundamental part played by the concept of pluralism in his political philosophy. Such phenomena of intellectual convergence between quite different, even conflicting, lines of thought (as was also the case, in another connection, with "personalism") are a sign of the inner necessity for the appearance of certain basic ideas at a given moment in history.

tension between the particular groups, working communities, co-operative agencies, unions, associations, federated bodies of producers and consumers, rising in tiers and institutionally recognized. Then a definitely personalist and pluralist pattern of social life would come into effect in which new societal types of private ownership and enterprise would develop. And the State would leave to the multifarious organs of the social body the autonomous initiative and management of all the activities which by nature pertain to them. Its only prerogative in this respect would be its genuine prerogative as topmost umpire and supervisor, regulating these spontaneous and autonomous activities from the superior political point of view of the common good.

So perhaps it will be possible, in a pluralistically organized body politic, to make the State into a topmost agency concerned only with the final supervision of the achievements of institutions born out of freedom, whose free interplay expressed the vitality of a society integrally just in its basic structures.

To sum up, the common good of the body politic demands a network of authority and power in political society, and therefore a special agency endowed with uppermost power, for the sake of justice and law. The State is that uppermost political agency. But the State is neither a whole nor a subject of right, or a person. It is a part of the body politic, and, as such, inferior to the body politic as a whole, subordinate to it, and at the service of its common good. The common good of the political society is the final aim of the State, and comes before the immediate aim of the State, which is the maintenance of the public order. The State has a primary duty concerning justice, which should be exercised only in the manner of an ultimate supervision in a body politic basically just in its inner structures. Finally the body politic must control the State, which however contains the functions of government within its own fabric. At the point of the pyramid of all the particular structures of authority which in a democratic society should take form in the body politic from the bottom up, the State enjoys topmost supervising authority. But this supreme authority is received by the State *from the body politic*, that is, from the people; it is not a natural right to supreme power which the State possesses of itself. As follows from a critical elucidation of the concept of sovereignty—with which the second chapter of this book is concerned—the supreme authority of the State should in no way be called sovereignty.

In the eyes of a sound political philosophy there is no sovereignty, that is, no natural and inalienable right to *transcendent* or *separate* supreme power in political society. Neither the Prince nor the King nor the Emperor were really sovereign, though they bore the sword and the attributes of sovereignty. Nor is the State sovereign; nor are even the people sovereign. God alone is sovereign.

VII. THE PEOPLE

We have discussed the Nation, the Body Politic, the State. Now what about the People?

I just said that the people are not sovereign in the genuine sense of this word. For in its genuine sense the notion of sovereignty relates to a power and independence which are supreme *separately from* and *above* the whole ruled by the sovereign. And obviously the power and independence of the people are not supreme *separately from* and *above the people themselves*. Of the people as well as of the body politic we have to say, not that they are sovereign, but that they have a natural right to *full autonomy,* or to self-government.

The people exercise this right when they establish the Constitution, written or unwritten, of the body politic; or when, in a small political group, they meet together to make a law or a decision; or when they elect their representatives. And this right remains always in them. It is by virtue of it that they control the State and their own administrative officials. It is by virtue of it that they cause to pass into those who are designated to take care of the common good, the right to make laws and to govern, so that, by investing those particular men with authority, within certain fixed limits of duration and power, the very exercise of the right of the people to self-government restricts to the same extent its further *exercise*, but does not make the *possession* of this right itself cease or lessen in any way. The administrative officials, or the Administration, that is, the human persons who are invested with executive power, are (in the strictest sense of the word "governing") the governing organ *in the State*, because the people have made them, *in the body politic*, the deputies for the very whole. All this is fully consistent with our conclusion that the most accurate expression concerning the democratic régime is not "sovereignty of the people." It is Lincoln's saying: "government of the people, by the people, for the people." This means that the people are governed by men whom they themselves have chosen and entrusted with a right to command, for functions of a determined nature and duration, and over whose management they maintain a regular control—first of all by means of their representatives and the assemblies thus constituted.[15]

As concerns furthermore the very notion of the people, I would say that the modern concept of the people has a long history and stems from a singular diversity of meanings which have fused together.[16] But considering only the po-

[15] See infra, pp. 65–66 and 127–39; and, on Lincoln's saying, *Scholasticism and Politics* (New York: Macmillan Co., 1940), pp. 107–8.

[16] Cf. our book, *Raison et raisons* (Paris: Luf, 1947), chap. xi.

litical significance of the word, suffice it to say that the people are the multitude of human persons who, united under just laws, by mutual friendship, and for the common good of their human existence, constitute a political society or a body politic. The notion of body politic means the whole unit composed of the people. The notion of the people means the members organically united who compose the body politic. Thus what I have said concerning either Body Politic and Nation or Body Politic and State holds good for either People and Nation or People and State. Nay more, since the people are human persons who not only form a body politic, but who have each one a spiritual soul and a supratemporal destiny, the concept of the people is the highest and noblest concept among the basic concepts that we are analyzing. The people are the very substance, the living and free substance, of the body politic. The people are above the State, the people are not for the State, the State is for the people.

I should finally like to point out that the people have a special need of the State, precisely because the State is a particular agency specializing in the care of the whole, and thus has normally to defend and protect the people, their rights and the improvement of their lives against the selfishness and particularism of privileged groups or classes. In ancient France the people and the King relied upon each other, somewhat ambiguously, in their struggle against the supremacy of the great feudal lords or the nobility. In modern times it has been the same with the people and the State in regard to the struggle for social justice. Yet, as we have seen, this normal process, if it becomes corrupted by the absolutism of the totalitarian State, which raises itself to the supreme rule of good and evil, leads to the misfortune and enslavement of the people; and it is impaired and jeopardized if the people surrender themselves to a State, which, as good as it may be, has not been freed from the notion of its so-called sovereignty, as well as from the factual deficiencies of the body politic itself. In order both to maintain and make fruitful the movement for social improvement supported by the State, and to bring the State back to its true nature, it is necessary that many functions now exercised by the State should be distributed among the various autonomous organs of a pluralistically structured body politic—either after a period of State capitalism or of State socialism, or, as is to be hoped, in the very process of the present evolution. It is also necessary that the people have the will, and the means, to assert their own control over the State.

Natural Law and Moral Law

In this chapter I should like to try to clarify certain basic concepts—basic for the theory of Natural Law—in the perspective of Thomistic philosophy.

NATURAL LAW (LEX NATURALIS)

Reason is "the measure of human actions." Thus reason —human reason—is a measuring measure (*mensura mensurans*). Yet reason is also a measured measure (*mensura mensurata*), for human reason is not the supreme rule of good and evil. In order to measure human conduct, practical reason has to be measured by something. What is it by which practical reason is measured? Natural Law (*lex naturalis*. In the expression "natural law" it is appropriate to understand "law" in the sense of *lex*, not of *jus*). Let us summarize as briefly as possible the fundamental characteristics of Natural Law.[1]

Two essential components must be recognized in the notion of Natural Law: the *ontological* and the *gnoseological*.

(From Ruth Nanda Anshen, ed., *Moral Principles of Action* [Harper, 1952], Chap. IV, pp. 62–76.)
[1] Cf. my book, *Man and the State* (The University of Chicago Press: 1951).

Considered in its ontological component, Natural Law is the normality of functioning of the human being. Every kind of being existing in nature, a plant, a dog, a horse, has its own "natural law," that is, the proper way in which, by reason of its specific structure and ends, it "should" achieve fullness of being in its growth or in its behavior. Now this very word "should" begins to have a *moral* sense, that is, to imply moral obligation, when we pass the threshold of the world of free agents. Natural Law—strictly speaking, Natural Law for man—is moral law, because man obeys or disobeys it freely. We might compare natural law in general with an algebraic equation according to which a curve develops in space. But with man the curve must conform freely to the equation.

Let us say, then, that in its ontological aspect Natural Law is an ideal order or a *divide* between the suitable and the unsuitable, the proper and the improper, which depends on human nature and its essential ends. In this first consideration (ontological) Natural Law is co-extensive with the whole field of moral regulations which concern man as man—even if they are grounded on the most subtle and refined considerations—with the whole field of ethical philosophy, as universally valid.

But the second essential component of the notion of Natural Law, the gnoseological component, causes the extent of this notion to be greatly restricted. For Natural Law is natural not only insofar as it is the normality of functioning of human nature, but also insofar as it is *naturally known:* that is to say, known *through inclination,* by way of congeniality or connaturality, not through conceptual knowledge and by way of reasoning. Here we have a crucial point, which in my opinion has been too often disregarded. It deals with the manner in which Natural Law is made manifest to practical reason. Natural Law is made manifest to practical reason in certain judgments, but these very judgments do not proceed from any conceptual, discursive, rational exercise of reason. They proceed from *connaturality or congeniality* through which what is consonant with the essential inclinations of human nature is grasped by the intellect as good; what is dissonant, as bad. And they therefore remain always more or less immersed in the vital and experiential, conceptually inexpressible dynamism of inclinations and tendencies. The motive power on which they depend is not reason, demonstration, *logos,* but nature and nature's root inclinations. Thus it is that Natural Law is, in the fullest sense of this word, *unwritten* law. And, by the same token, it appears that Natural Law, considered not in its ontological component alone but also in its gnoseological component, only embraces those requirements of the human being's normality of functioning which are *known through inclination*—in other words, the principles "immediately" known (that is, without conceptual or rational medium) of human morality.

At this point two observations of the utmost importance should be made, which, to my regret, I cannot discuss here as fully as I should like. First, the inclinations to which I have just referred are not the animal instincts, qua animal, but the inclinations—ontological, animal and rational—of the human being *insofar as they are human,* or insofar as they are vitally rooted in the non-conceptual life of the mind, that is, in reason as "form" or entelechy of our psychological energies (a function of reason which is performed in a pre-conscious manner). Let us say, then, inclinations of nature as refracted through the crystal of reason in its unconscious or pre-conscious life. For what is consonant with reason spontaneously pleases the rational animal.

Second, these natural inclinations rooted in reason presuppose a primary, self-evident principle: "the good is to be done, the evil to be avoided," of which all men are aware. But as to further determinations, they are dependent upon historical progress which is characteristic of mankind. For man is an animal of culture, an historical animal. As a result, the essential inclinations of which we are speaking either developed or were released in the course of an historical progress which was constantly thwarted, moreover, by any kind of accidental process of regression or perversion. Thus it is that man's knowledge of the content of Natural Law was progressively formed and molded by the inclinations of human nature, starting with the most basic ones. The very history of human conscience distinguishes genuine human inclinations from spurious or perverted ones. The truly authentic inclinations were those which, in the long history of human conscience, led reason to an awareness of the regulations which, recognized more or less indeterminately from the time of the oldest social communities, have remained permanent in the human race, while assuming forms more definite and more clearly determined. At this point nothing appears more valuable to moral philosophy, especially to the theory of Natural Law, than the data of anthropology. An attentive examination of such data shows that what I venture to call the fundamental *dynamic schemes* of Natural Law are susceptible only of indeterminate expression (for example: "no family group exists without some kind of fixed pattern"), but that they are the object of a considerably more universal knowledge —at all times and in all places—than would appear upon superficial inspection.

We can understand, moreover, why there is a large measure of variability in the particular rules, customs, standards of life through which, among all of the earth's people, mankind has conveyed its knowledge of the most fundamental and deep-seated principles of Natural Law. This spontaneous knowledge does not bear upon conceptually discovered and rationally deduced moral regulations but upon regulations known through inclination, and in its ultimate source, upon general frameworks, which are tendential in nature, dynamic schemes of moral regulations still in a primitive state. Within such tendential frameworks or dynamic schemes the content may be considerably varied and more or less deficient, not to mention those warped, perverted or devious inclinations which may be intermingled with authentic and fundamental inclinations.

ETERNAL LAW

These explanations, although summary, provide a sufficiently clear idea of what Natural Law is. It is necessary, however, to proceed further, for the concept of Natural Law is given its definitive meaning only when that of Eternal Law has been established.

This concept of Eternal Law is not solely theological. It is a philosophical truth as well, one which the philosopher with his means alone can reach and establish. God exists. He is the first cause of being, activating all beings. It is by His intellect and will that He acts: whence the notion of Providence. The entire community of the universe is governed by the divine reason. Hence there is in God, as in One who governs the entirety of created beings, this very reality which is the judgment and command of the practical intellect applied to the governing of a unified community: in other words, this very reality which we call *law*. Eternal Law is one with the eternal wisdom of God and the divine essence itself. Saint Thomas defines this Eternal Law as "nothing other than the exemplar of divine wisdom insofar as this wisdom directs all the actions and movements of things."[2]

It is evidently to this Eternal Law that we must have recourse if we are in search of the first foundation of Natural Law. Because every law is a work of reason, at the source of Natural Law there must be reason: not human reason but Subsistent Reason, the intellect which is one with the First Truth itself. "Law is a measure and a rule," says Saint

[2] *Sum. Theol.*, I–II, 93, 1.

Thomas, "and hence is found in him who rules, and also in that which is measured and ruled, for a thing is ruled and measured insofar as it participates in the measure and rule existing in the one who rules. Now, since all things are ruled and measured by the Eternal Law, we must conclude that they participate in this Law insofar as they derive from it the inclinations through which they tend naturally toward their proper operations and ends. Now among all creatures, the rational creature is subject to divine providence in a particular and more excellent way, inasmuch as it has a share in providential government, by being provident both for itself and others. Thus the rational creature by its very rationality participates in the eternal reason, and because of this participation has a natural inclination to the actions and ends proper to it." (What is meant here are those inclinations "rooted in reason" of which we were just speaking.) "It is this participation in the Eternal Law enjoyed by the rational creature which is called the Natural Law."[3]

What emerges from this doctrine—and this is a fundamental point—is that the Natural Law is known by human reason, but that human reason, in its rational exercise, has no part in its establishment. The divine reason alone is the author of Natural Law. It alone causes that Law to exist, and it alone causes it to be known, insofar as it is the cause of human nature and of its essential inclinations. Let us not say merely (as was generally held in the sixteenth and seventeenth centuries) that God guarantees the exercise and value of our reason as though it were our reason which instituted Natural Law, or at least deciphered it in nature and made it known by its own effort and authority. Let us say rather that here the divine reason is *the only reason* to be considered. The law, in effect, is essentially an ordinance of reason (*ordinatio rationis*), so that without an ordering reason there is no law. The notion of law is essentially

[3] *Sum. Theol.*, I–II, 91, 2.

bound up with that of an ordering reason. Indeed, in the case of Natural Law, human reason has no share in the initiative and authority establishing the Law, either in making it exist or in making it known. How then does it know Natural Law? It knows it through inclination, by connaturality —through the inclinations of nature, which is the work of God, and not by its own rational effort. It knows the Law; it in no way makes it. According as human reason knows Natural Law through inclination, it is in a very precise sense "natural reason," *ratio naturalis,* and the light of this natural reason is "nothing other than a certain impression of the divine light upon us."[4] The author of Natural Law is exclusively the divine reason.

The fact that the divine reason is the only reason which is author of the Law enables us to understand better the meaning of Saint Thomas' expression: Natural Law is a participation in the Eternal Law. It is the divine reason which is involved. If human reason had a hand in it, the Law would, to that extent, have no more than the value of human authority.

The formal medium by which we advance in our knowledge of the regulations of Natural Law is not the conceptual work of reason, but rather those inclinations to which the practical intellect conforms in judging what is good and what is bad. Through the channel of natural inclinations the divine reason imprints its light upon human reason. This is why the notion of knowledge through inclination is basic to the understanding of Natural Law, for it brushes aside any intervention of human reason as a creative factor in Natural Law.

It is evident, then, how strongly and decisively Natural Law obliges *by virtue* of Eternal Law. It is from the divine reason that it possesses its rational character, and consequently, it is from the divine reason that it possesses its genuine nature as law and its obligatory character.

[4] Saint Thomas Aquinas, *loc. cit.*

We can understand at this point in what the error in the conceptions of a thinker like Grotius consisted. While maintaining that Natural Law presupposed in fact God's existence, he wrote the celebrated sentence in which he said that even if, on an absurd supposition, God did not exist, Natural Law would continue to exercise its dominion and its authority over us. The fact is that he was concentrating solely upon the order of nature—as deciphered by human reason —and did not perceive the relationship between the order of nature and the eternal reason.

Two things are to be considered here. Suppose, absurdly, that God does not exist and that nothing is changed in things: then, by hypothesis, nature would continue to exist, and consequently the normality of functioning of human nature; the exigencies of the ideal order based upon the essence of man would likewise continue to exist. But a second question presents itself: is this order rational, is it wise, does it oblige me in conscience? Indeed, the only foundation for its rationality is the Eternal Law, the divine reason, and it is precisely this which Grotius did not perceive. Thus began the process (prepared by scholastic doctors who came after Saint Thomas and who neglected the essential importance of the component: knowledge through inclination) of a rationalistic deformation of the concept of Natural Law. At that moment a separation took place, a schism, between Eternal Reason and the order of nature. God became merely the guarantor of that order, and Natural Law ceased to be a participation in Eternal Law. It became the order of a nature which was sufficient to herself, an order for which the conceptual and discursive reason provided knowledge. But why should I be obliged in conscience by a purely factual order? In reality, if God does not exist, the Natural Law lacks obligatory power. If the Natural Law does not commit the divine reason, it is not a law, and if it is not a law, it does not oblige.

I would like to remark further, concerning the concept

of Eternal Law, that this concept enables us to realize the essentially analogical character of the notion of law. The word "law" in the expression "natural law" admits of the danger of a misunderstanding because the most obvious and the most immediate notion that we have of law is that of written law or positive law: consequently, if we overlook the analogical character of the notion of law, we run the risk of conceiving Natural Law and every species of law after the pattern of the type of law best known to us, written law.

But the very notion of Eternal Law brings this analogical character to light in an undeniable manner. For the definition of law: "A certain ordinance of reason for the common good, promulgated by him who has the care of the community,"[5] has its first realization—in itself, *secundum se*, and not with regard to us and our manner of knowing —in the Eternal Law. But God is not a legislator like the others. The community that He heads is the entire created universe. The Eternal Law is not written upon paper, it is promulgated in the divine intellect and is known in itself solely by God and by those who see Him in His essence. However, Saint Thomas writes that every rational creature knows a certain reflection of it insofar as this creature knows truth. "For all knowledge of truth is a sort of reflection of and participation in the Eternal Law, which is the unchangeable truth."[6] The Eternal Law is as infinitely distant from written or human law as the divine essence is from created being. Between the two there is only an analogical community. Likewise, the notion of law is only analogically common to the concepts of Natural Law and positive law, and so also to the concepts of Natural Law and Eternal Law. This analogicity of the notion of law will be even more readily grasped if we discuss the concept of "right" (*jus*)

[5] *Sum. Theol.*, I–II, 90, 4.
[6] *Ibid.*, I–II, 93, 2.

and compare it with that of "law" (*lex*).[7] What is the relation between law and right?

NATURAL RIGHT

When it is a question of positive law (written law), the relation between law and right is very simple—it is a relation of identity. Positive right and positive law are the same thing; they are synonyms, because the notion of right, or of juridical order, signifies a code of laws suited to a certain type of common life which men are not only obliged to obey in conscience, but can be constrained to obey by the coercive power of society. We are confronted, therefore, with the notion of *debitum legale*, of what is legally due or legally just, the neglect of which is punishable by the external sanctions established by law. Given this meaning of the word "right," it is clear that positive right and positive law are the same thing: positive right and positive law emanate from social authority and are sanctioned by the constraints of society. We have here the order of legality or the juridical order which supposes the moral order, but which adds something to it, namely, this possibility of constraint by society.

But let us consider now the domain of Natural Law, which is that of morality, and not of legality. As we have already remarked, although the notion of Natural Law in itself (*secundum se*) is prior to that of positive law, nevertheless, *as far as we ourselves* and our manner of knowing are concerned (*quoad nos*), it is from the idea of the positive law, which is first known, that we proceed to the idea of the Natural Law. Consequently, since we say positive law and positive right with equivalent meaning, it seems

[7] In current language, these two concepts are expressed in English by the same word, "law." Hence a supplementary difficulty arises. For the sake of clarity, we may be permitted to use the word "right" to signify *jus* (*droit, Recht*), and the word "law" to signify solely *lex* (*loi, Gesetz*).

natural to say *right* and *law* equivalently when the question is one of Natural Law. Hence the use of the expression "natural right" (*Naturrecht, droit naturel*) in the habitual language of philosophers and jurists.

The application of the notion of right in such a domain, however, involves us in serious difficulties. Natural Law—which is not written, which concerns man as man, and a community which is neither the body politic nor the civilized community but simply the community of the human species, and which obliges us in conscience—Natural Law is promulgated in our reason as knowing (insofar as it knows through inclination), and not as legislating; and it concerns the moral, not the juridical order. What we have here is nothing other than the notion of *debitum morale,* of that which is morally due by virtue of right reason, or by virtue of Natural Law, but not by virtue of a juridical constraint. How, then, under these conditions, can we speak of natural *right?* Is there not a simple contradiction in terms here, and would it not be preferable to rid oneself of such an expression? This is a temptation for the philosopher, for it would be the most convenient thing to do. Nevertheless, I do not believe that we must yield to it. In considering things more closely, we see that, in spite of everything, we do have a solid basis for speaking of natural right, and not only in the sense that this or that precept of Natural Law may become an object of a prescription of the positive law. For in a considerably more profound and universal sense it is necessary to say that each man bears within himself the *judiciary authority* of humanity. (It is not a question here of the civilized community, as in the case of the law of nations, but of the human species.) This is true in an analogical but nonetheless real sense. Each member of the human species bears within him in a certain manner the judiciary authority of humanity, and consequently, the right of imposing constraint which derives from this authority.

How can we justify philosophically the right of legitimate defense? How can we say that a man has the right of killing another man when he is attacked by the latter, or that I have the right of putting to death a man who before my eyes throws himself upon a child to assassinate it? Is this simply a biological reflex? If so, there could be no question of a right. No, we are faced with a properly *judiciary* act. That is why this act is moral, by virtue of a judiciary authority which transcends me and which goes back to the Author of nature and of humanity. Without possessing the function of a judge in society—and outside of the order of constituted tribunals to which punishment normally belongs—but simply as a member of the human species, I exercise in such a case a judiciary authority which is virtually inherent in the species and which may be actualized, in any man whatsoever, under such exceptional circumstances. And this is not only the case in the examples I have just given. Each time that we give a counsel, or guide another man, or try to dispose circumstances so as to help him avoid an error in his moral life, we exercise in a certain measure and to a certain degree an authority which is derived in us from the Author of human reason. Each time that States, in the absence of an international judiciary power, have recourse to sanctions such as war or just reprisals against the aggression of another State, or against the barbarous procedures it employs, it is the judiciary authority virtually inherent in the human species which is being exercised. These acts of political power would have neither meaning nor moral justification if it were merely a question of defensive reflexes; they have human meaning and moral value only if the States in question decide upon such acts in the name of the judiciary authority of which they are the organs so long as there does not yet exist a supranational political society capable of putting the judgments of its tribunals into effect.

By reason of the fundamental notion which I have just expressed, we can say, in an analogical but real sense, that there is a natural juridical order contained within the Natural Law and the natural order of morality, but in a simply virtual manner. And in this sense the expression *natural right* is valid, but, once again, in an altogether analogical sense.

We have, then, the notion of a virtual juridical order which always remains virtual, and which never unfolds as a juridical order expressed in positive law and in the judiciary authority of human society, for we cannot conceive of a tribunal which would be charged with enforcing the Natural Law. As soon as a precept of Natural Law is expressed in written law, it becomes a precept of written law and by this token it is part of positive right, of the juridical positive order. But the *natural right* itself, insofar as it is natural *right*, remains *virtual*, enveloped in the Natural Law, and it is actualized in exceptional cases, for example, as we have seen, when a man or a State finds it necessary to exercise the judiciary authority of which the human species as such is depositary and which is derived from its Author, from the Divine Reason and Subsistent Justice.

Thus, natural right does not require, as a fulfillment which it should receive, formulation in positive law and in the juridical order in the full and formal sense of the word. It remains enveloped in the Natural Law.

JUS GENTIUM

With the *jus gentium* (the law of nations),[8] on the contrary, we enter a domain in which the notion of right (*jus*) no longer takes on merely a virtual but a formal and actual

---

[8] We use the expression "law of nations" as equivalent to *jus gentium* (*le droit des gens*), because the term is so well established in the language of political science and political philosophy, although the term "right of nations" would perhaps correspond better to our use of "positive right" and "natural right." (It is true that the *law* of nations is distinguished in this section from natural and positive *law*.)

meaning as well. For the philosopher or jurist, there is no notion more fraught with difficulties than that of the law of nations. The different theories which have been advanced since the sixteenth century have succeeded in obscuring the concept rather than clarifying it. It is difficult to define the law of nations, because it is intermediary between the Natural Law and the positive law—although Saint Thomas does connect it rather with the positive law. Our thought on the subject would profit greatly if, as a result of the systematic elucidation to which we now proceed, we were able to determine clearly and exactly in what the law of nations consists.

Let us say, then, that in its most profound meaning, as we are able to disengage it from the thought of Saint Thomas, the law of nations (I would prefer to say the common law of civilization) differs from the Natural Law in the manner in which it is *known,* or in relation to the second essential component, the gnoseological component of the Natural Law. It is necessary to insist on the manner in which the law in question is known. The law of nations is known, not through inclination, but through the conceptual exercise of reason. This is the specific difference distinguishing the law of nations from the Natural Law. The Natural Law is known through inclination, the law of nations is known through the conceptual exercise of the human reason (considered not in such and such an individual, but in common civilized humanity). In this sense, it pertains to the positive law, and for this reason Saint Thomas relates it to positive law: since wherever human reason intervenes as author, we are in the general domain of the positive law. In this case, the human reason does not intervene as the author of the *existence of the law* (which is the case with positive law in the strict sense), but it does intervene as the author of the *knowledge of the law.* In consequence, with the law of nations, we have already a juridical order, no longer virtual as in the case of natural right but formal, although not necessarily written into a code. As to the manner in which the regulations of the law in question are known, it must be said that they are known through the rational, logical, conceptual exercise of the common reason, starting from more profound and more primary principles which are the principles of Natural Law.

Now it is necessary to make a distinction concerning the *content* of the law of nations. In the first place, the law of nations may include regulations pertaining also to the Natural Law (since the principle of distinction is not the content of the law, but the manner in which the knowledge of the law takes place). Hence, certain regulations which are based upon human nature, and which are connected necessarily with the first principle: "Do good and avoid evil," may be known on the one hand through inclination (in which sense they belong to Natural Law), and on the other hand through the conceptual exercise of reason (in which sense they belong to the law of nations).

Take this example: "We must obey the laws of the social group." This prescription may be a rational conclusion, established through the logical exercise of reason, for the common sense of humanity can deduce it from a more primitive principle: "Men should live in society," in which case we are in the presence of a precept of the law of nations. Now this same regulation: "Obey the laws of the group," is also a norm known not by way of conceptual demonstration, but through inclination, by conformity with the radical tendency which urges men to dwell in society, in which case it is a principle of the Natural Law. Hence the same thing may belong to the Natural Law if it is known through inclination and if the divine reason is the only operative principle causing it to be known as well as to exist, and to the law of nations if it is known by human reason which, intervening between the Divine Reason, the cause of nature, and the knowledge of the precept, acts on its own account and thus introduces an element of positive law.

In the second place, and this is the most general and most interesting case, the content of the law of nations may concern things which, although universally obligatory since they are deduced from a principle of the Natural Law, and although necessarily connected with the first principle: "Do good and avoid evil," go beyond the Natural Law because they are not previously known through inclination but are known *only* as the result of the conceptual exercise of reason, a deduction made not by jurists or philosophers, but by the common reason of humanity. Take this example: "Do not condemn anyone without a hearing." I do not think that this rule is first known through inclination; it is known only as a conclusion logically deduced from what is due in justice to an accused man. In such a case we have a precept of the law of nations which is not a precept of the Natural Law. Similarly, the precept: "Treat prisoners of war humanely," is known only through a logical operation accomplished by the human reason starting from a first principle of the Natural Law.

The law of nations or the common law of civilization has to do with duties which are necessarily bound up with the first principle: "Do good and avoid evil," but in cases like those I have just mentioned, this necessity is seen and established by human reason. And precisely because the regulations dealing with social life are *par excellence* the work of human reason, we have been gradually led to regard the law of nations as pertaining more to the social domain and especially to the international domain. But it is absurd to reduce the law of nations to the laws of international morality. According to what we have seen, every norm of conduct which is universally valid, but which is known to common consciousness because necessarily deduced by human reason, is a part of *jus gentium* or the common law of civilization.

The law of nations belongs at once to the moral order and to the juridical order; it presupposes a *debitum morale,* a moral obligation appealing to conscience, before the legal obligation, *debitum legale.* At the same time the law of nations is a formal juridical order, although not necessarily a written one. Hence it differs at once from natural right because it is not merely virtually contained in the order of natural morality, and from positive right because it is not necessarily promulgated by social authority and applied by judiciary authority. It may be formulated juridically; in fact, it seeks to be, but is not necessarily so formulated. Before it is at some future time formulated in the code of a supranational world society whose tribunals would be required to enforce it, the law of nations is first of all formulated in the common conscience by human reason in its legislative role, making the law known through its own conceptual means. In a word, it is based upon the natural order of morality, but it emanates necessarily from this order as the first formal juridical order.

POSITIVE RIGHT

We come finally to positive law. The positive law in force in any particular social group, whether it be a question of customary right or written right, has to do with the rights and duties which are bound up in a *contingent,* not a necessary, manner with the first principle of the practical intellect: "Do good and avoid evil." And it has as its author not the divine reason but the human reason.[9] By virtue of determined rules of conduct, established by the reason and will of men when they institute the laws or engender the customs of a particular social group, certain things will be

[9] We are speaking here of human positive law and passing over what concerns the divine positive law (which has God for its Author, but whose regulations are contingent with regard to what is required by the nature of the human being).

good and permissible and certain things bad and not permissible, but it is the human reason which establishes this. Human reason intervenes here as a creative factor not only in that which concerns the knowledge of the law—as in the case of the law of nations—but in that which concerns the very existence of the law. It has the astounding power of laying it down that certain things will henceforth be good and others bad. Thus, for example, a police ordinance has decreed that it will henceforth be good for motorists to stop at the red light and to go when the light is green. There is no kind of natural structure which requires this; it depends uniquely upon the human reason. But once this regulation has been promulgated, it is evil not to stop at the red light. There is thus a moral good and a moral evil which depend upon the human reason because it takes into consideration the particular exigencies of the common good in these given circumstances, in conformity, however, with principles of the Natural Law, as for example: "Do not harm your fellow men." But the Natural Law itself does not prescribe the rules in question, it leaves them to the ultimate determination and initiative of the human reason. The Natural Law itself requires that what it leaves undetermined be ultimately determined by human reason.

Hence, the positive law obliges men in conscience—in other words the *debitum legale* that it institutes is also a *debitum morale*—because it obliges by virtue of the Natural Law. By the same token we see that an unjust law is not a law. This follows as a consequence from what I have just said, that is, from the fact that the positive law obliges by virtue of the Natural Law which is a participation in the Eternal Law. It is inconceivable that an unjust law should oblige by virtue of the Natural Law, by virtue of regulations which go back to the Eternal Law and which are in us a participation in that Law. It is essential to a philosophy such as that of Saint Thomas to regard an unjust law as not obligatory. It is the counterpart of this truth that the just law binds in conscience because it binds by virtue of the Natural Law. If we forget the one, we forget the other.

NICOLAS BERDYAEV

❇ ❇ ❇ ❇

NICOLAS BERDYAEV

Nicolas (Nikolai Aleksandrovitch) Berdyaev, who, despite all his heterodoxies, may be taken as a brilliant exponent of an important strain in Eastern Orthodox spirituality, was born in Kiev in 1874. His father, an "enlightened liberal" of the time, was a man of culture and social standing; his mother, half French, possessed certain Roman Catholic sympathies. The home, however, probably under the father's influence, was almost entirely devoid of religion.

The boy early acquired a dislike for the "gentlefolk society" from which he sprang and in which he was brought up. Early, too, he showed a strong inclination to follow his own bent in everything he undertook. "It was from freedom," he was later to testify, "that I made my start upon my journey."[1] Nikolai was destined to follow the military traditions of his forbears, and he was sent to the cadet school in Kiev, but he intensely disliked the military environment. He turned to philosophy instead, and he soon entered the University of Kiev, supposedly to study natural science, but actually to devote himself to his own intellectual interests. At the university he was caught up in

[1] Nicolas Berdyaev, *Slavery and Freedom* (Scribner's, 1944), p. 11.

the radical stirrings of the time, and in 1898 was arrested
and exiled to Vologda. The brief term of exile was for
Berdyaev a crucial period of intellectual and spiritual clarification, perhaps even reorientation. He was greatly attracted by Marxist thought, then beginning to make its
way in Russia, and by the literary and cultural revival associated with the names of Merezhkovsky, Rozanov, Blok,
and Ivanov. Even before his exile he had published an essay on F. A. Lange in the German social-democratic journal, *Neue Zeit*, and by the time he returned from exile he
was a convinced socialist, though of a very unorthodox kind.
His first book, *Subjectivism and Individualism in Social
Philosophy*, published in 1900, marked out the lines of his
thinking, which might be described as an attempt to make
a synthesis out of Marxism, idealistic philosophy, and the
"God-seeking" spirituality that was already permeating a
significant section of the Russian intellectuals. This direction of his thinking was deepened by his marriage, in 1904,
to Lydia Yudifovna, who although coming from a wealthy
and "freethinking" family, was herself deeply religious and
strongly radical in her sympathies. Not long after the marriage she became a Roman Catholic.

In St. Petersburg, where they settled, the Berdyaevs met
Sergei Bulgakov, another religio-idealist fellow traveler of
Marxism. For the next two years, Berdyaev and Bulgakov
edited a review, *The New Way*, and its successor, *Problems of Life*, both devoted to religion and radical politics.
Berdyaev also took active part in the discussions of the
Religious-Philosophical Society in Petersburg, and later
(after a visit to Paris) in Moscow. In 1907 he returned to
the Russian Orthodox Church.

But this return was not a return to a safe harbor after
the storms of life. On the contrary, it meant the intensifi-
cation of the struggle against what Berdyaev felt were reac-
tionary tendencies within the Church. At the same time,
Berdyaev continued his attacks on the materialism and de-

terminism of the left intelligentsia. In his contribution to the symposium, *Landmarks,* edited by M. Gershenson and published at this time, Berdyaev formulated his mature position, and aroused the wrath of left and right alike. In 1914 proceedings against him were initiated with the Holy Synod, the governing body of the Russian Church, and he was again threatened with exile. But the war diverted attention, and in 1917 the case was dropped.

Berdyaev hailed the revolution in 1917, the moderate revolution in February (under which he was made a member of the Council of the Republic), and the Bolshevik revolution in October. As a result of his own social radicalism and his strong belief in the messianic vocation of the Russian people, he found himself in essential agreement with the economic outlook and political orientation of the Bolsheviks, though differing sharply from them in philosophy and spiritual outlook. In 1918 he established the Free Academy of Spiritual Culture in Moscow, where he continued holding lectures to crowded audiences on religious and cultural subjects. In 1920 he was elected to a professorship in Moscow University, but the very next year, with a shift of Soviet policy, he was arrested and exiled. The rest of his life he spent abroad.

The Berdyaevs first went to Berlin, where the refugee philosopher took part in the work of the Y.M.C.A. and founded a religious-philosophical academy. In 1924, however, they removed to Paris. In Paris, Berdyaev continued in the work of the Y.M.C.A. and the Student Christian Movement. Because of his support, though qualified, of the Soviet revolution—he long continued to insist that communism "answered more truly to Christianity than capitalism"[2] —he was thoroughly out of sympathy with Russian emigré Church sentiment, and was in constant conflict with his fellow countrymen in exile. In 1926, through the help of John

[2] Oliver Fielding Clarke, *Introduction to Berdyaev* (Bles, 1950), pp. 64–65.

R. Mott of the International Y.M.C.A., Berdyaev founded a Russian religio-philosophical journal, *The Way*, and continued editing it until 1939. But most of his apparently limitless energies he devoted to lecturing in France and many other countries, and to participating in innumerable conferences. He also organized private discussions with Roman Catholics and Protestants, which proved of considerable influence in their time. Yet throughout, Berdyaev felt very much alone. "There was no direction in which I could bring the whole of me completely to bear," he later testified, "and I felt rather lonely. The motif of loneliness has always been basic with me. But owing to the activity and combativeness of my character, I took part from time to time in a good deal that was going on; and this was torture to me, for it led to disillusion."[3]

Yet it was at this time, a very difficult time, that he did his best work both in developing the religio-philosophical gnosis (*Freedom and the Spirit*) that came to form his spiritual outlook, and the social philosophy that he named "personalist socialism" (*Slavery and Freedom*).

This creative period was brought to an end by the outbreak of war. When the Germans entered Paris, Berdyaev and his wife left the city for the southwest but they soon returned. Though under surveillance, they were not disturbed; Berdyaev's public activities, however, were reduced to a minimum. The end of the war brought a resumption of work. His wife died in 1945, after more than forty years of life together. Berdyaev himself followed three years later, on March 24, 1948, in his seventy-fifth year.

Berdyaev's thinking was greatly affected, as he himself repeatedly indicated, by the German romantic-idealist tradition. In one way or another the influence of Kant, Schelling, and Nietzsche is to be detected, and, going further back, the influence of the German mystics, such as Meister Eckhart and Jakob Boehme, to whom the romantic philoso-

[3] Nicolas Berdyaev, *Slavery and Freedom*, p. 16.

phers themselves owed so much. But over and above everything else, Berdyaev was a Russian and an Orthodox Russian. The doctrine he taught, insofar as he taught any doctrine, was not the official doctrine of the Russian Orthodox Church, but his quasi-gnostic mystical-eschatological speculations can only be understood in the context of the Orthodox tradition. But again, like that other thorough Russian, Fyodor Dostoevsky, with whom he felt himself so much akin, his appeal has been a universal appeal and has found a powerful response wherever the existential concerns of the spiritual life have been taken seriously.

SELECTED BIBLIOGRAPHY

WORKS BY BERDYAEV

(Only books available in English are listed.)

The Russian Revolution. Sheed and Ward, 1931.
Dostoevsky. Sheed and Ward, 1934.
Freedom and the Spirit. Scribner's, 1935.
The Meaning of History. Scribner's, 1936.
The Destiny of Man. Scribner's, 1937.
Solitude and Society. Scribner's, 1937.
The Origin of Russian Communism. Scribner's, 1937.
Spirit and Reality. Scribner's, 1939.
Slavery and Freedom. Scribner's, 1944.
The Russian Idea. Macmillan, 1948.
The Divine and the Human. London: Bles, 1949.
Towards a New Epoch. London: Bles, 1949.
Dream and Reality. Macmillan, 1951.
The Beginning and the End. Harper, 1952.
The Realm of Spirit and the Realm of Caesar. London: Gollancz, 1952.
Truth and Revelation. Harper, 1954.
The Meaning of the Creative Act. Harper, 1955.

WORKS ABOUT BERDYAEV

Allen, Edgar L., *Freedom in God: A Guide to the Thought of Nicolas Berdyaev*. Philosophical Library, 1951.

Clarke, Oliver Fielding, *Introduction to Berdyaev*. London: Bles, 1950.

Horton, Walter Marshall, *Contemporary Continental Theology*, pp. 1–40. Harper, 1938.

Lampert, Evgeny, "Nicolas Berdyaev," in Donald Atwater, ed., *Modern Christian Revolutionaries*. Devin-Adair, 1947.

Seaver, George, *Nicolas Berdyaev: Introduction to His Thought*. London: Clarke, 1950.

Spinka, Matthew, *Nicolas Berdyaev: Captive of Freedom*. Westminster, 1950.

Tillich, Paul, "Nicolas Berdyaev," *Religion in Life*. Summer, 1938.

Religion of the Spirit

A DEVOUT MEDITATION

The greatest error of which historical Christianity is guilty
is due to the circumscribing and deadening notion that revelation is finished and that there is nothing more to be expected, that the structure of the Church has been completely built and that the roof has been put on it. Religious
controversy is essentially concerned with the problem of the
possibility of a new revelation and of a new spiritual era.
All other questions are of secondary importance. The new
revelation is certainly not to be thought of as a new religion
distinct from Christianity, but as the fulfilment and crowning of the Christian revelation, and the achievement of its
true œcumenicity. There is as yet no œcumenicity. The
revelation of the Spirit cannot be just simply waited for;
it depends also upon the creative activity of man; it cannot be understood simply as a new revelation of God to
man; it is also a revelation of man to God. This means that
it will be a divine-human revelation. The separation and
opposition of the divine and the human will be overcome
in the Spirit, although the distinction between them will be
preserved. This is the crowning point in the mystical dia-

(From Nicolas Berdyaev, *The Divine and the Human* [Lon-
don: Bles, 1949], Chap. XIII, pp. 183–94.)

lectic of the divine and the human. It is also the end of objectivization, of the projection of revelation into the external, and of naïve realism in the conception of revelation.

In the relation between man and God an infinite spiritual experience is possible. It may be thought that the religion of the Spirit—and it is that precisely of which we are speaking—is a new form of immanentism. But the old controversies about immanentism and transcendentism must be regarded as completely out of date. The very way in which the matter was put was entirely wrong, it was abstract and not dialectic. Just as one cannot break the bond between the divine and the human, and affirm one of these principles in the abstract, so we must not make a break between the transcendent and the immanent, and affirm either of them in the abstract. Real life is in the inter-relation between the one and the other. The transcendent becomes immanent and without its immanence it is abstract and lifeless. It is merely objectivization at its limit. And equally the immanent must not be thought of without the transcendent. Life in the immanent postulates a process of transcendence. Pure immanentism which denies the transcendent is continuance in a circle which has no outlet. When the human is looked upon as the divine, and the identity of the two is affirmed, authentic life comes to an end and its dramatic character exists no longer. When the transcendent is thought of exclusively as immanent and there is no transcendent mystery and remoteness, the immanent is deprived of life and content. On these grounds what was known as immanentism in controversies of an earlier day, which are now out of date, ought to be decisively rejected.

The Holy Spirit is the principle of union between God and the creature,[1] and it is in Him that the mystery of creation, a mystery which is anthropological and cosmological must be revealed. The religion of the Spirit, which is also

[1] The Catholic writer Henstenberg writes in an interesting way on this subject, *Das Bund zwischen Gott und Schöpfung.*

the religion of the Trinity, will not be in the least like E. von Hartmann's monistic religion of the spirit, in which there is nothing Christian whatever.[2] The coming of a new era of the Spirit into which the highest attainments of spirituality will enter, presupposes a change in human consciousness and that it is given a new orientation. It is a revolutionary change in consciousness, which has been hitherto conceived in a static way. Myths, legends, dogmas will appear in a different light according to the degrees of consciousness, according to the extent to which its immobility and induration have been overcome. The religion of the Spirit will be the religion of man when he has come of age; it will constitute his emergence from childhood and youth.

Certain traits of this eternal religion, which is new only in external appearance, of this Christian and Trinitarian religion, this religion freed from slavery to the world of objects, can be guessed. In the religion of the Spirit, the religion of freedom, everything will appear in a new light. There will be no authority and no retribution; the nightmare of a legalistic conception of Christianity and of an everlasting hell, will finally disappear. It will have as its basis not judgment at a tribunal and retribution, but creative development and transfiguration, assimilation to God. A new anthropology will be revealed and the religious meaning of human creativeness will be recognized. It will be understood that freedom is its primary basis. The idea of God will be purified from servile sociomorphism. The idea of God as sufficient unto Himself and as a potentate who wields power, still includes relics of an idolatry which is not yet overcome. It is only the conception of God as suffering, and yearning for the Other, and as sacrificed, which subdues atheism and the fight against God. There is a paradox in the knowledge of God which must be courageously faced and put into words, thus: the affirmation of God by my whole being means that God exists; human

[2] E. von Hartmann, *Die Religion des Geistes.*

freedom creates God, and this means that God is; my creating of God is a divine-human act of creation.

All this leads to a revaluation of the idea of Providence, a matter with which atheism is more closely connected than with anything else. The religion of the Spirit is the expectation that a new community of mankind will be revealed, a sense of communion of spirit which is really human, one which radiates kindness and love. The religion of the Spirit is also the expectation of the revelation of a new relation between man and the cosmos, and an expectation of the transfiguration of the cosmos. The process of the disintegration of the cosmos which is due to a merely scientific and technical relation to it, is coming to an end. Its final phase will be the disintegration of the atom. All this finds support in the subject of eschatology, in an active view of eschatology. But in no degree whatever does it mean an optimistic conception of history. Of this I have already spoken. The revelation of light in no sense means the denial of darkness. On the contrary, before the coming of the era of the Spirit, man will have to pass through a thickening of the darkness, through a period of dark night. We are living in tragic times as we witness the process by which as a result of discoveries in the realm of physics, nature is deprived of its soul and devastated, and the cosmos, so to speak, made to disappear. Marx and historical materialism have deprived history of its soul and devastated it. Freud and psycho-analysis have done the same thing to the human soul itself. The end of the war and the revolution are revealing terrible cruelty; humanity is dim and fading out; the Creator is, as it were, withdrawing from His creation; He is present in it only *incognito* (a favourite expression of Kierkegaard). But all this can be understood as a dialectic moment in the revelation of the Spirit and the new spiritual life. One must die in order to come to life again. The crucifixion of man and of the world is taking place, but the last word will belong to Resurrection.

We are not yet entering into the era of the Spirit; we are entering into the dark era. There have been forerunners of the new revelation of the Spirit throughout the whole extent of the history of Christianity, and such there are also now. There are always spiritually-minded people who live before their time. The Eastern doctors of the Church were of great importance in their contribution to the interpretation of Christianity as the religion of the Spirit, especially Origen and St Gregory of Nyssa, the latter more than any other. His doctrine of man was the most exalted in the history of Christian thought, and his spirituality anticipates the whole history of Christian mysticism.[3] Further, the religious movement in Italy at the end of the twelfth and the beginning of the thirteenth centuries, which was a quest for the Christianity of the Holy Spirit, is of enormous importance.[4] Its central figures were St Francis of Assisi whose character most nearly approached to the pattern of the person of Christ, and Joachim of Floris who had prophetic premonitions, although sometimes they were naïvely expressed. In popular religious movements there was already something new. The apocalyptic frame of mind made its appearance in Europe after the French Revolution and the Napoleonic Wars, although it found very confused expression.[5] The German mystical movement which began in the fourteenth century and is represented by Eckhardt, Tauler and others, was of still greater importance for this change in consciousness. But Jacob Boehme and later Angelus Silesius were of greater significance than all.

German idealistic metaphysics of the beginning of the nineteenth century also constituted a most outstanding event in the history of the European spirit, in the dialectic of the divine and the human; and in spite of the mistaken

[3] See Jean Daniélou, *Platonisme et théologie mystique. Essai sur la doctrine spirituelle de St Grégoire de Nysse.*
[4] See E. Gebhart, *L'Italie mystique.*
[5] See Viatte, *Les sources occultes du Romantisme,* Vol. II.

nature of the monistic tendency in them they did prepare
the way which led to the possibility of a new consciousness. German mysticism as a whole, however, inclines to
be hostile to eschatological thought. It was in Russia that
eschatological aspiration, with its expectation of a new
epoch of the Spirit, and belief in the possibility of a crowning revelation, was most forcibly expressed. If we compare
one of the greatest of Russian saints, Saint Seraphim of
Sarov, with one of the most recent of Roman Catholic
saints, Jean Baptiste Vianney, the Curé d'Ars, we are struck
by the fact that in St Seraphim all his aspiration is directed
exclusively towards the resurrection, towards the transfiguration of the whole creation in the Holy Spirit, that is to
say, towards the future. In the Curé d'Ars everything is
directed exclusively to the Cross, that is to say, to the past.
The apocalyptic and eschatological trend is to be found
also in popular religious movements in Russia and in the
quest for truth by the Russian intelligentsia, as well as
in the supreme moments of Russian religious thought.
Here I ought again to mention names to which I have already many times referred, especially Dostoyevsky, Vladimir Solovëv and N. Fedorov, and even a man who stood
apart from Orthodox thought, that seeker after truth, that
seeker after God—Leo Tolstoy. The religious and philosophical movements which belong to the beginning of the
twentieth century were coloured in the same way.

But quite one of the most notable of the forerunners of
the religion of the Spirit was Cieszkowski, the philosopher
of Polish messianism.[6] In him the conception of a religion
of the Spirit as the crowning and complete revelation is expressed more clearly than in Solovëv. His thought passes
outside the framework of historical Christianity, but it preserves a link with the Roman Catholic Church. The link
with the Church is of great importance in this respect, that

[6] See the book already referred to, Cieszkowski, *Notre Père,*
in 4 volumes.

it saved the movement towards a new revelation of the
Spirit from assuming a sectarian character. And this link
becomes a possibility in the Orthodox Church in particular,
for there are greater potentialities in Orthodoxy than in Roman Catholicism. In the Roman Catholic sphere Léon Bloy
stands out as the great man of Apocalypse. There was a
strong prophetic element in him. But in that stupendous
writer, as indeed in many others, the prophetic premonitions were mingled with survivals of the old ideas of a sac-
rosanct monarchy, with the cult of Napoleon and the like.
People like Kierkegaard have been of vast significance, but
their influence acted indirectly. Charles Péguy may also be
considered as a forerunner of the era of the Spirit.[7]

But we must recognize as forerunners of the era of the
Spirit not only those who deliberately regard themselves as
Christians, we must include also those who do not call
themselves Christians and even those who are anti-Christian
in their thought. The fact is that even the fight against God
may be a way of serving God, it may be more truly religious
than coldness and indifference. New ground is made ready
by the tragic experience of man and the creative activity of
man. Such forerunners of the era of the Holy Spirit cannot
be called devout in the traditional sense. Nietzsche has
enormous importance; his appearance was a highly significant moment in the dialectic of the divine and the human,
without the consummation of which no new religious era
can follow. Moreover, there is an important element of
messianic consciousness in socialism too, for all that it is associated nowadays with atheism. Among the great writers
of the end of the nineteenth century, Ibsen is to be noted
as being of prophetic mentality; he used to speak of the
Third Kingdom, the Kingdom of the Spirit. It is impossible
to decide on rational grounds the position of the line which
separates the Holy Spirit from Spirit, and that which is re-

[7] In this connection there are rich materials in Romain Rol-
land, *Péguy.*

ferred simply to Spirit may have a relation to the Holy Spirit, whose operation in the world is universal. God may not be where one would like to see Him, and He may be where one refuses to see Him. The presence of God in the world is mysterious, and not susceptible to precise definition. It is equally impossible to state precisely the boundaries of the Church. These limits are rigidly fixed only for the purpose of exercising power. Politics are the most fatal force in human life, it is they which have perverted the life of religion and stained the history of the Church with blood. The era of the Spirit will not tolerate the sway of politics over the life of the Spirit.

There was a very long period of human history in which consciousness was stabilized, and appeared to be immobile and unchangeable.[8] And corresponding to this stable consciousness was a certain condition of the world, which was regarded as the one reality. Belief, which is the unveiling of things invisible, was directed to a different world than the world which corresponds to the structure of average and normal human consciousness. The traditional spiritual philosophy of the schools, very abstract in character, recognized the spiritual nature of the human soul. But it opened up no new horizons upon other worlds than this, it has not stressed the possibilities of spiritual experience. Everything has gone on moving within established limits, within the order of the objectivization of Spirit, within the sphere of the antithesis of subject and object. But the objectivization of Spirit, its alienation from itself, its projection into the external, is the chief hindrance to a new out-pouring of the Holy Spirit in the world. The acknowledgment of objective Spirit which is indeed the objectivization of Spirit, is the greatest obstacle which the new spirituality, and the advent of the era of Spirit have to encounter.

Indian religious and philosophical thought has believed

[8] See my book, *Creativity and Objectivization*. An essay in eschatological metaphysics.

in the possibility of changing consciousness; in its view consciousness is dynamic. But any conception of the dynamism of history has been entirely lacking. In Christian Europe on the other hand there has been immense awareness of the dynamism of history, but the dynamic conception of consciousness has been lacking. Consciousness has taken a static form in the thought of Christian Europe, and with this has been connected the idea of the unchanging nature of man. The Indian conception of the dynamism of consciousness cannot satisfy us because of the monism of Indian thought and its failure to recognize the rôle of the human principle. It is in Christianity that this rôle is revealed.[9] The new era of the Spirit, the new consummating revelation will have as its counterpart a corresponding change in the structure of human consciousness. And this change in the structure of consciousness may be prepared for by spiritual effort. Objectivizations have corresponded with degrees of revelation. In the process of revelation, that which ought to be revealed from within and out of the depth, has appeared instead as something revealed from without and from above. Objectivization always means disruption and dichotomy; what Hegel calls the unhappy consciousness. The new revelation of the Holy Spirit brings alienation and objectivization to an end, not in thought only but in life itself, in vital spiritual experience; it is a movement in depth. Consciousness passes into super-consciousness and a world is revealed which lies beyond the sphere in which subject and object fall apart. This will mean a loosening movement of the indurated, petrified phenomenal world, and greater translucency in the noumenal core of the world.

Œcumenical religion is the religion of Spirit purified from enslaving elements; it is the religion of the Holy Spirit in whom is the fullness of revelation and all power of eman-

[9] See the recently published book, O. Leombre, *L'Absolu selon le Vedanta. Les Notions de Brahman et de l'Atman dans les systèmes de Cankara et Romanoaja.*

cipation. And that is the eternal Gospel. Man is a mixture; there is in him a combination of creature and creator, he is compact of matter, absurdity and chaos, and yet he is the possessor of creative power to realize things that are new. Creativeness in the world is, as it were, the eighth day of creation. Really new life is created, not by the fact of man's setting before himself external aims in the realization of which he acquiesces in, and is even compelled to make use of, criminal means, but by this above all, that he radiates from within, from his own self, a gracious transfiguring creative energy. The new life, the new era of Spirit presupposes a total change in man and not merely a change in this or that separate part of him. It is a moral, intellectual and aesthetic change, and at the same time a social change. And above all it is a manifest renewal of soul. There will be no special religious and ecclesiastical side of life but the whole of life will have become religious. It is only spiritually that man is an independent being. Biologically and socially he depends upon nature and society. That is why any social movement alone, unless a spiritual movement goes with it, is powerless, and may turn out to be merely the resumption of the old, though it wears new clothing.

Apocalypse depicts in symbolical form the destructive course of evil. But we must not interpret apocalypse as fate, as though the terrible results of the world process were inevitable. This would amount to a complete denial of freedom. It is only the path of evil which is fated. The path of good is constructed upon the freedom of man, who shares in the creation of the world. In the revelation of the Spirit, the apocalyptic end must appear in another light. The apocalypse of historical Christianity depicts the final destinies of mankind as a complete separation and breach between God and mankind, as being what Hegel called the 'unhappy consciousness'. The apocalypse of the religion of the Spirit depicts the final destinies of mankind as a divine-human creative act, as a work achieved by the collaboration of God and man. The positive end, the end which decides things, must depend upon man as well, not only upon God. Fate can be overcome by freedom.

The historical process divides into two, and its results may be appraised in two ways; but if there were nothing positive in its end the creation of the world would have been a failure. In the Book of the Revelation there is a prophecy of the thousand years' reign and the positive result of the world process is symbolized by this. But the historical Church has been much afraid of millenarianism and hushes it up. This symbolism must again reveal its meaning in a new way in the final revelation of the Spirit. The idea of the thousand years' reign has been left in historical Christianity in a lifeless and abstract state. It has been given life and made concrete in social movements which to all appearance lie outside Christianity. If the negative results of the universal historical process ought to be consumed in fire, its positive results must be thought of concretely, as a revived community life in all its fullness, as community inspired and maintained by freedom. If human life were to become the incarnate expression of a completely organized, mechanized and rationalized life of masses and not of peoples, if it were to become divided up into categories and at the same time completely totalitarian, that is to say if the last traces of freedom were to disappear, then spirit and spirituality also would disappear, for spirit is freedom. Free community can only be the result of a movement which is both spiritual and social, and in which the spiritual and the social cease to be separate and opposed.

The Incarnation and the earthly life of Jesus were an interpenetration of the two natures; the hand of God was laid upon the Chosen One. Only in the Resurrection was Jesus finally raised to infinite height. That which happened individually in the God-Man ought to happen in God-

manhood, and that will be the third revelation of the Spirit.
It is impossible to reconcile oneself to the idea that the
creative vital impulse, the moments of luminous joy, of
creative love and liberation, which have been experienced
in ecstasy, will all disappear for ever, come to nothing and
leave no trace. At the end of revelation there is infinity,
not the sinister infinity which knows no end, but the good
infinity which is eternity. There will be darkness and suffering in the future such as there have not yet been. But
there will also be unprecedented light, there will be the appearance of a new man, of a new society, a new cosmos.
There will be the crowning point of the mystical dialectic
of the threefold being of God.

Pneumocentrism is already to be seen in the Gospel.
Everything happens in the Spirit and through the Spirit.
From a certain moment onwards this pneumocentrism will
begin to increase. The Spirit has been stifled in historical
Christianity and history has taken a line which is opposed
to Christianity. This was the passage through the severance
and rupture of the divine-human link. In the end it has
been a death before the resurrection to a new life. A deadly
anguish has gripped mankind, but the time will be short-
ened and the end of time will come. The Church which
is beginning to convey the impression of powerlessness, of
having lost the gift of the Spirit, will appear in its eternal
nature, as inspired by the prophetic spirit. This is the
Church as St John conceived it, the Church to which Orthodoxy makes the nearest approach. A Russian apocalyptic said that in Orthodoxy a great eschatological pa-
tience was to be found but in the deeps of it there was also
great eschatological expectation. Into the Church of the
Holy Spirit there will enter also everything creatively positive which has in appearance been outside the Church, and
even been opposed to it. The eschatological problem is the
final problem in the dialectic of the divine and the human.

Personality

Personality is not a biological or a psychological category, but an ethical and spiritual. Personality cannot be identified with the soul. Personality has an elemental-unconscious foundation. Man in his sub-conscious is submerged in the blustering ocean of elemental life and is but partially rationalized. It is necessary to distinguish in man, the profound and the superficial ego. Too often, to other people, to society and civilization man presents his superficial ego, which is capable of various sorts of external communication, but is not capable of communion. Tolstoy understood this admirably. He always depicts the double life of man, the outwardly conditional, unreal life, replete with falsehood, which he brings into relation with society, the state and civilization, and his inner real life in which man confronts primary reality, and the deeps of life. When Prince Andrew is gazing at the starry heavens, that is more real life than when he is engaged in conversation in a Petersburg drawing-room. The superficial ego in man which is much socialized, rationalized and civilized, is not the personality in man. It may be even a distortion of the form

(From Nicolas Berdyaev, *Slavery and Freedom* [Scribner's, 1944], Part I, Chap. I, pp. 25–29, 35–37, 42–47.)

of man and a thing which conceals his personality. The
personality of man may be crushed, man may assume
many disguises, and his form may not be capable of being
grasped. Man often plays a part in life, and he may play
a part which is not his. Dichotomy of personality is especially striking in primitive man and in the psychologically
unstable and unsound. In semi-normal civilized man it as-
sumes another character, the duality acquires the normative
character of adaptation to the conditions of civilization, and
gives rise to the necessity of falsehood as a means of self-
defence. Social training and the civilizing of barbarous man
may be a beneficial process, but it does not mean the formation of personality. The completely socialized and civilized man may be entirely impersonal; he may be a slave
and not notice that he is.

Personality is not a part of society, as it is not part of
a race. The problem of man, that is to say, the problem
of personality, is more primary than the problem of society.
All the sociological doctrines about man are erroneous, they
know only the superficial, objectified stratum in man. Looking at things from the sociological point of view it is only
externally that personality is seen as a subordinate part of
society; and a very small part at that, compared with the
massiveness of society. But only an existential philosophy,
and not a sociological philosophy, any more than a biological philosophy can construct the true doctrine of man as
personality.

Personality is a subject, and not an object among other
objects, and it has its roots in the inward scheme of existence, that is in the spiritual world, the world of freedom.
Society on the other hand is an object. From the existential
point of view society is a part of personality, it is its social
side, just as the cosmos is a part of personality, its cosmic
side. Personality is not an object among other objects and
not a thing among other things. It is a subject among subjects and the turning of it into an object or a thing means

death. The object is always evil, only the subject can be
good. It might be said that society and nature provide the
material for the formation of personality. But personality
is emancipation from dependence upon nature, from dependence upon society and the state. It opposes all determination from without, it is determination from within. And
even within, the determination is self-determination, not
even God can do it. The relation between personality and
God is not a causal relation, it lies outside the realm of determination, it is within the realm of freedom, God is not
an object to personality. He is a subject with whom existential relations exist. Personality is the absolute existential
centre. Personality determines itself from within, outside
the whole object world, and only determination from within
and arising out of freedom, is personality. Everything defined from without, everything determined, everything that
is based upon the power of the object world is not personal,
it is the impersonal in man. Everything determined in the
human ego is past and has become impersonal.

But personality is the coming into being of the future, it
consists of creative acts. Objectivization is impersonality,
the ejection of man into the world of determinism. The existence of personality presupposes freedom. The mystery of
freedom is the mystery of personality. And this freedom is
not freedom of the will in the elementary sense, freedom
of choice, which presupposes rationalization. The worth of
man is the personality within him. Human worth consists
solely in personality. Human worth is liberation from slavery, liberation also from the servile understanding of religious life and of the relation between man and God. God
is the guarantee of the freedom of personality from the enslaving power of nature and society, of the Kingdom of
Caesar and of the object world. This takes place in the
realm of the spirit and not in the realm of the object world.
And no categories of the object world can be transferred

to these inward existential relations. Nothing in the object world is an authentic existential centre.

Personality as an existential centre, presupposes capacity to feel suffering and joy. Nothing in the object world, nation or state or society, or social institution, or church, possesses this capacity. They speak of the sufferings of the masses of the people in an allegorical sense. No communities in the object world can be recognized as personality. Collective realities are real values, but not real personalities, their existentiality refers to the realities of personalities. One can allow the existence of collective souls, but not of collective personalities. The conception of collective or 'symphonic' personality is a disputable conception. To this we shall return again later on.

It is true that we hypostatize everything we love, and everything we pity, inanimate things and abstract ideas. But this is a mythopœic process, without which there is no intensity of life, but it does not mean a real bestowal of personality. Personality is not only capable of experiencing suffering, but in a certain sense personality is suffering. The struggle to achieve personality and its consolidation are a painful process. The self-realization of personality presupposes resistance, it demands a conflict with the enslaving power of the world, a refusal to conform to the world. Refusal of personality, acquiescence in dissolution in the surrounding world can lessen the suffering, and man easily goes that way. Acquiescence in slavery diminishes suffering, refusal increases it. Pain in the human world is the birth of personality, its fight for its own nature. Already in the animal world individuality suffers. Freedom gives rise to suffering. One can lessen it if one refuses freedom. The worth of man, that is to say personality, and again that is to say freedom, presupposes acquiescence in pain, and the capacity to bear pain. The degradation of my people or my faith causes pain in me, but not in the people and not in the religious community, which do not possess an existential centre, and consequently are devoid of capacity to feel pain. Capacity to experience pain is inherent in every living creature, above all in man, but it is in animals also, and perhaps in another way in plants as well, but not in collective realities nor in ideal values. This question is of first importance, it is by it that the ethics of personalism are defined. Man, human personality is the supreme value, not the community, not collective realities which belong to the object world, such as society, nation, state, civilization, church. That is the personalist scale of values. We shall repeat it over and over again.

Personality is connected with memory and certitude; it is linked with the whole of a man's fate, and with his whole life history. And, therefore, the existence of personality is difficult and painful. In Christianity there has always been a twofold attitude to man. On the one hand Christianity has, as it were, degraded man by regarding him as a sinful and fallen being who is called to humility and obedience. And it is this they can never forgive Christianity. But on the other hand Christianity extraordinarily exalts man in that it regards him as made in the image and likeness of God, recognizes a spiritual principle in him, which raises him above the natural and social world, it recognizes in him a spiritual freedom which is independent of the Kingdom of Caesar, and it believes that God Himself became man and by this exalted man to heaven. And only on this Christian basis can a doctrine of personality be constructed and the personalist transvaluation of values be worked out. Personalist philosophy must recognize that spirit does not generalize but individualizes, that it creates, not a world of ideal values, suprahuman and common, but a world of personalities with their qualitative content, that it forms personalities. The triumph of the spiritual principle means, not the subordination of man to the universe, but the revelation of the universe in personality. If one imagined oneself endowed with the highest universal qualities of mind, genius, beauty, goodness, holiness, but with the removal of the existential centre, with the transference of the centre of gravity of the ego to the universal qualitative principles, that would be just as if the ego had endowed another being with those qualities, just as if the ego had seen another as such. The unity of the subject and its life history disappears, memory does not preserve personality. Herein lies the falsity of the idealist philosophy of values and of ideal existence.

Man is a being who surmounts and transcends himself. The realization of personality in man is this continuous transcending of self. Man desires to go out from the closed circle of subjectivity and this movement always takes place in two different and even opposite directions. Emergence from subjectivity proceeds by way of objectivization. This is the way which leads out into society with its forms of universal obligation, it is the way of science with its laws of universal obligation. On this path there takes place the alienation of human nature, its ejection into the object world: personality does not find itself. The other path is emergence from subjectivity through the process of transcendence. This is a passing over into the trans-subjective and not to the objective. This path lies in the deeps of existence, on this path there take place the existential meeting with God, with other people, with the interior existence of the world. It is the path not of objective communication but of existential communion. Personality reaches full realization of itself only on this path.

. . . .

In order to understand what personality is, it is very important to establish the difference between personality and the individual. The French Thomists very justly insist upon this distinction, though they take their stand upon different philosophical ground from mine. The individual is a category of naturalism, biology, and sociology. The individual is indivisible in relation to some whole; he is an atom. He not only can be a member of a species or community, as well as of the cosmos as a whole, but he is invariably thought of as part of a whole, and outside that whole he cannot be called an individual.

The individual is characterized alike, on the one hand as a subordinate part of the whole and on the other as a part which is self-affirming as an ego. Therefore, individualism, which is derived from the word individual, certainly does not signify independence in relation to the whole, that is to the cosmic, biological and social process. It signifies only the isolation of the subordinate part in its feeble revolt against the whole. The individual is closely linked with the material world, he is brought to birth by the generic process. The individual is born of a father and a mother, he has a biological origin, which is determined by family heredity and also by social heredity. There is no individual without the family and no family without the individual. The individual is found entirely within categories which distinguish what belongs to the species from what is of the individual.

The individual carries on a struggle for existence in the family, the biological and the social processes. Man certainly is an individual, but he is not only an individual. The individual is bound up with the material world, and is nourished by it; but he is not universal, as such, he has not a universal content. Man is a microcosm, and a universe; but not in virtue of his being an individual. Man is also personality, the idea of man and his vocation in the world are bound up with his personality. And here everything is changed. Personality is not a naturalistic but a spiritual category. Personality is not the indivisible or the atom in relation to any whole whatever, cosmic, family, or social. Personality is the freedom and independence of man in relation to nature, to society and to the state; but not only is it not egoistic self-affirmation, it is the very opposite. Personalism does not mean, as individualism does, an egocentric isolation. Personality in man is his independence in relation to the material world, which is the material for the work of the spirit. And at the same time personality is a universe, it is filled with universal content. Personality is not born of the family and cosmic process, not born of a father and mother, it emanates from God, it makes its appearance from another world. It bears witness to the fact that man is the point of intersection of two worlds, that in him there takes place the conflict between spirit and nature, freedom and necessity, independence and dependence.

Espinas says that the real individual is a cell. But personality most certainly is not a cell and does not enter into any organism as a part into a whole. It is the primary whole and unity, it is characterized by its relation to an other and to others, to the world, to society, to people, as a relation of creativeness, freedom and love, and not of determination. Personality lies outside the co-relation of individually-particular and that which is common to the species, outside the co-relation of parts and whole, of organs and organism. Personality is not the living individual. Personality in man is not determined by heredity, biological and social; it is freedom in man, it is the possibility of victory over the world of determination. Everything that is personal in man is set in opposition to any kind of automatism, that automatism which plays such a part in human life, automatism both psychical and social. There are not two separate men, but one and the same man is both an individual and a personality. That is not two different beings, but two kinds of qualitativeness, two different forces in man. Péguy says that the individual is every man's own bourgeois which he is called upon to conquer. Man, as an individual, endures the experience of isolation, egocentrically engulfed in himself, and called upon to wage a tormenting struggle for life, as he defends himself against the dangers that lie in wait for him. He finds his way out of difficulties through conformism, through adaptation. Man as a person, the same man, gains the mastery of the egocentric self-confinement, discloses a universe in himself, but insists upon his independence and dignity in relation to the surrounding world.

But it must always be remembered that our language often gets confused. We constantly make use of words which do not bear the meaning which we assign to them. That which is individual, individuality, denotes the unique within its kind, the original, distinguished from any other and from the rest. In this sense the individual is inherent in every person.

Personality has a higher degree of individuality than the individual. The individual also often denotes the irrational, in opposition to that which is common, to the universally binding, to the rational and normative. In this sense personality is irrational; and the individual much more subject to binding law, since it is more determined.

It is interesting, in the history of the discovery of the meaning of personality, to notice that among the romantics individuality is distinguished from personality in our sense of the word. Among the romantics themselves individuality was clearly presented, but personality was often very weakly expressed. The character of individuality is rather vital than spiritual and does not as yet indicate the victory of spirit and freedom. We see a reflection of a profound disintegration, of a dissociation of personality in the contemporary novel, for instance in Proust and among us, Andrei Byely. Inward unity and integrality are inherent in personality; whereas the individual may be torn to pieces by the forces of the world. A person cannot be completely a citizen of the world and of the state, he is a citizen of the Kingdom of God. For this reason personality is a revolutionary element in a profound sense of the word. This is bound up with the fact that man is a being who belongs not to one world, but to two. Personalism is a dualistic not a monistic philosophy.

. . . .

Personalism transfers the centre of gravity of personality from the value of objective communities—society, nation, state, to the value of personality. But it understands personality in a sense which is profoundly antithetic to egoism. Egoism destroys personality. Egocentric self-containment and concentration upon the self, and the inability to issue forth from the self is original sin, which prevents the realization of the full life of personality and hinders its strength from becoming effective. A hysterical woman is a clear example of egoism in her craze for herself and her odd way of referring everything to herself. But she is in the highest degree antithetic to personality; personality is destroyed in her, although it may be the case that she is a distinct individuality. Personality presupposes a going out from self to an other and to others, it lacks air and is suffocated when left shut up in itself. Personalism cannot but have some sort of community in view.

At the same time this going out of the personality from itself to an other does not by any means denote exteriorization and objectivization. Personality is I and Thou, another I. But the Thou to whom the I goes out and with whom it enters into communion is not an object, it is another I, it is personality. With an object, indeed, no communion is possible, no state of community can be shared with it, there can be only mutual obligation. The personal needs an other, but that other is not external and alien: the relation of the personal to it is by no means exteriorization. Personality is to be found in a series of external relations with other people and in acts of communion with them. External relations mean objectivization, whereas communion is existential. External relations, being in the world of objectivization, are to be classed as determination and therefore do not liberate man from slavery. Communion on the other hand, being in the existential world, and having no cognizance of objects, belongs to the realm of freedom, and means liberation from slavery. Egoism denotes a double slavery of man—slavery to himself, his own hardened selfhood, and slavery to the world, which is transformed exclusively into an object which exercises constraint from without. The egocentric man is a slave, his attitude to everything which is non-I is a servile attitude. He is aware of non-I only, he has no knowledge of another I, he does not know a Thou, he knows nothing of the freedom of going out from the I. The egocentric man usually defines his relation to the world and to people in a way that is not personalistic, he very readily adopts the point of view of the objective scale of values. There is something lacking in the humanity of the egocentric man. He loves abstractions which nourish his egoism. He does not love living concrete people.

Any ideology you please, even the Christian, can be turned to the service of egoism. Personalist ethics signify just that going out from the 'common' which Kierkegaard and Shestov consider a break with ethics, which they identify with standards of universal obligation. The personalistic transvaluation of values regards as immoral everything which is defined exclusively by its relation to the 'common' —to society, the nation, the state, an abstract idea, abstract goodness, moral and logical law—and not to concrete man and his existence. Those who are no longer under the law of the 'common', it is they who are the really moral people; while those who are subject to the law of the 'common' and determined by the social routine of daily life, they are the immoral people. Such people as Kierkegaard, are the victims of the old antipersonalistic ethics and antipersonalist religion, the religion of the social routine. But the tragedy which such people have lived through has an immense im-

portance in the transvaluation of values which is now in
progress.

In order to understand personality it is most important
always to remember that personality is defined above all
not by its relation to society and the cosmos, not by its relation to the world which is enslaved by objectivization, but
by its relation to God, and from this hidden and cherished
inward relation it draws strength for its free relation to the
world and to man. The egocentric individual imagines that
he is free in his relation to the world, which for him is non-I.
But in actual fact he is slavishly determined by the world
of the non-I, which shuts him up in himself. Egoism is an
aspect of determination by the world: the egocentric will
is external suggestion, for the world is in an egocentric condition. Of the egoism of the I and the egoism of the non-I,
the latter is always the more powerful. Human personality
is a universe only on condition that it has no egocentric relation to the world. The universality of personality which
absorbs into itself the object world which crushes everything, is not an egocentric affirmation of self, but a throw-
ing open in love.

Humanism is a dialectic moment in the revelation of human personality. The error of humanism certainly did not
lie in the fact that it laid too great an emphasis upon man,
that it was responsible for a forward movement along the
path towards divine humanity, as is frequently asserted in
Russian religious thought, but in the fact that it did not
give sufficient emphasis to man, that it did not carry its
affirmation of man through to the end, that it could not
guarantee the independence of man from the world and included within itself a danger of enslaving man to society
and nature. The image of human personality is not only a
human image, it is also the image of God. In that fact lie
hidden all the enigmas and mysteries of man. It is the mystery of divine-humanity, which is a paradox that cannot
be expressed in rational terms. Personality is only human

personality when it is divine-human personality. The freedom and independence of human personality from the world of objects is its divine-humanity. This means that personality is not formulated by the world of objects but by subjectivity, in which is hidden the power of the image of God. Human personality is theandric existence. Theologians will reply in alarm that Jesus Christ alone was God-man, and that man is a created being and cannot be God-man. But this way of arguing remains within the confines of theological rationalism. Granted man is not God-man in the sense in which Christ is God-man, the Unique One; yet there is a divine element in man. There are, so to speak, two natures in him. There is within him the intersection of two worlds. He bears within himself the image which is both the image of man and the image of God and is the image of man in so far as the image of God is actualized.

This truth about man lies beyond the dogmatic formulas and is not completely covered by them. It is a truth of existential spiritual experience which can be expressed only in symbols, not in intellectual concepts. That man bears within himself the image of God and in virtue of that becomes man, is a symbol. One cannot work out an intellectual concept about it. Divine-humanity is a contradiction for the line of thought which inclines towards monism or dualism. Humanistic philosophy never rose to such a height as to understand the paradoxical truth about divine-humanity. Theological philosophy, however, has endeavoured to rationalize this truth. All theological doctrines of grace have been but the formulations of the truth about the divine-humanity of man, and about the inward action of the divine upon the human. But it is absolutely impossible to understand this mystery of divine-humanity in the light of the philosophy of identity, monism, immanentism. The expression of this mystery presupposes a dualistic moment, an experience of the process of transcendence, of falling into an abyss and of escaping from that abyss. The divine is that which transcends man, and the divine is mysteriously united with the human in the divine-human image. It is for this reason only that the appearance in the world of personality which is not a slave to the world is possible. Personality is humane and it surpasses the human, which is dependent upon the world. Man is a manifold being; he bears within him the image of the world, but he is not only the image of the world, he is also the image of God. Within him conflict between the world and God takes place. He is a being both dependent and free. The image of God is a symbolic expression and if it is turned into a concept it meets with insuperable difficulties. Man is a symbol, for in him is a sign of something different, and he is a sign of something different. With this alone the possibility of liberating man from slavery is connected. This is the religious foundation of the doctrine of personality—not the theological foundation but the religious, that is to say, the spiritually empirical, the existential. The truth about God-humanity is not a dogmatic formula, not a theological doctrine, but an empirical truth, the expression of spiritual experience.

This same truth of the twofold nature of man, twofold and at the same time integral, has its reflection in the relation of human personality to society and to history. But here it is turned upside down, as it were. Personality is independent of the determination of society, it has its own world, it is an exception, it is unique and unrepeatable. And at the same time personality is social, in it there are traces of the collective unconscious. It is man's way out from isolation. It belongs to history, it realizes itself in society and in history. Personality is communal; it presupposes communion with others, and community with others. The profound contradiction and difficulty of human life is due to this communality. Slavery is on the watch to waylay man on the path of his self realization and man must constantly return to his divine image.

Man is subjected to forcible socialization during the very

time that his human personality must be in free communion, in free community, in communality which is based upon freedom and love. And the greatest danger to which a man is exposed on the paths of objectivization is the danger of mechanization, the danger of automatism. Everything mechanical, everything automatic in man is not personal, it is impersonal, it is antithetic to the image of personality. The image of God, and the image of mechanism and the automaton clash against each other, the choice is either God-man or automatic humanity, machine-humanity. Man's difficulty is rooted in the fact that there is no correlation and identity between the inward and the outward, no direct and adequate expression of the one in the other. This is indeed the problem of objectivization. When he objectivizes himself in the external man enslaves himself to the world of objects; and at the same time, man cannot but express himself in the external, cannot dispense with his body, cannot but enter actively into society and history.

Even the religious life of humanity is subject to this objectivization. In a certain sense it may be said that religion in general is social; that it is a social link. But this social character of religion distorts the spirit, subordinates the infinite to the finite, makes the relative absolute, and leads away from the sources of revelation, from living spiritual experience. In the interior world, personality discovers its image through the image of God, through the penetration of the human by the divine. In the exterior world the actualization of truth denotes the subordination of the world, of society, and of history to the image of personality, it signifies permeation by personality. And that is personalism. Inwardly personality is given strength and is liberated through divine-humanity. Outwardly the whole world, all society and all history are transfigured and liberated through humanity, through the supremacy of personality. Communality passes from within outward, and this movement is not objectivization, it does not subordinate personality to objectivity. Personality must be God-human, whereas society must be human. The objectivization of God-humanity in society and in the course of history is a source of falsehood and slavery. It has established a false objective hierarchism which contradicts the dignity and freedom of human personality. With it there is connected the setting up of false ideas of sacredness. We shall see this in all forms of human slavery.

·   ·   ·   ·   ·   ·   ·   ·

Master, Slave and Free Man

It is well to repeat constantly that man is a being who is full of contradictions and that he is in a state of conflict with himself. Man seeks freedom. There is within him an immense drive towards freedom, and yet not only does he easily fall into slavery, but he even loves slavery. Man is a king and a slave. In the *Phänomenologie des Geistes*, Hegel gives expression to some remarkable thoughts on the subject of master and slave, about *Herrschaft* and *Knechtschaft*. He is not there discussing the social categories of master and slave, but something deeper. It is the problem of the structure of consciousness. There are three conditions of man, three structures of consciousness, and they may be distinguished under the names of 'master', 'slave' and 'free man'. Master and slave are correlatives. Neither of them can exist without the other. The free man, however, exists in himself; he has his own quality within him, without correlation to anything placed in antithesis to him. The master is an existing consciousness for himself, but that consciousness is derived through some other, it is through the slave that he exists for himself. If the consciousness of a

(From Nicolas Berdyaev, *Slavery and Freedom* [Scribner's, 1944], Part I, Chap. II, pp. 59–72.)

master is consciousness of the existence of some other for him, then the consciousness of the slave is the existence of himself for the other. The consciousness of the free man, on the other hand, is consciousness of the existence of each one for himself, but with a free outgoing from himself to the other and to all. The boundary of a state of slavery is the absence of awareness of it.

The world of slavery is the world of spirit which is alienated from itself. Exteriorization is the source of slavery, whereas freedom is interiorization. Slavery always indicates alienation, the ejection of human nature into the external. Feuerbach and later on Marx recognized this source of the slavery of man; but they connected it with a materialistic philosophy, which is the legitimatization of the slavery of man. Alienation, exteriorization, the ejection of the spiritual nature of man into the external denote the slavery of man. The economic slavery of man undoubtedly signifies the alienation of human nature and the turning of a man into a thing. Marx was right in this. But for the liberation of man his spiritual nature must be restored to him; he must be aware of himself as a free and spiritual being. If on the other hand man remains a material and economic being and his spiritual nature is regarded as an illusion of consciousness, as the effect of a deceptive ideology, then man remains a slave and he is a slave by nature. In the objectivized world man can be only relatively not absolutely free, and his freedom presupposes conflict and resistance to necessity, which he ought to overcome. But freedom presupposes a spiritual principle in man which offers resistance to enslaving necessity. The freedom which is the result of necessity will not be real freedom, it is only an element in the dialectic of necessity. Hegel in actual fact knew nothing of real freedom.

Consciousness which exteriorizes and alienates is always slavish consciousness. God the Master, man the slave; the church the master, man the slave; the state the master, man

the slave; society the master, man the slave; the family the
master, man the slave; Nature the master, man the slave;
object the master, man-subject the slave. The source of
slavery is always objectivization, that is to say exteriorization, alienation. It is slavery in everything; in the acquisi-
tion of knowledge, in morals, in religion, in art, in political
and social life. Putting an end to slavery is putting an end
to objectivization; and putting an end to slavery does not
mean that mastership will make its appearance, for mastership is the reverse side of slavery. Man must become not a
master but a free man. Plato truly said that the tyrant is
himself a slave. The enslaving of another is also the enslaving of oneself. Mastership and enslavement were originally
connected with magic which has no knowledge of freedom.
Primitive magic was the will to power. The master is nothing but the figure of a slave who leads the world into delu-
sion. Prometheus was a free man and a liberator; whereas a
dictator is a slave and an enslaver; the will to power is always a servile will. Christ was a free man, the freest of the
sons of men. He was free from the world; He was bound
only by love. Christ spoke as one having authority but He
did not have the will to authority, and He was not a master.
Caesar, the hero of imperialism, is a slave; he is the slave
of the world, the slave of the will to power, the slave of the
human masses, without whom he cannot realize his will to
power. The master knows only the height to which his
slaves raise him. Caesar knows only the height to which the
masses raise him. But the slaves, and the masses, also over-
throw all masters and all Caesars. Freedom is freedom not
only from the masters but from the slaves also. The master
is determined from without; the master is not a personality,
just as the slave is not a personality. Only the free man is a
personality and he is that even if the whole world should
wish to enslave him.

The fall of man finds expression most of all in the fact
that he is a tyrant. He is a tyrant, if not on a great scale,

then on a small, if not in the state, if not in the pages of
world history, then in his family, in his shop, in his office,
in the bureaucratic establishment in which he occupies the
very smallest position. Man has an unconquerable inclination to play a part and in that part to assign a special importance to himself, to play the tyrant over those around
him. Man is a tyrant not only in hatred but also in love. A
man in love becomes a dreadful tyrant. Jealousy is a manifestation of tyranny in a passive form. A jealous person is
an enslaver who lives in a world of fiction and hallucination.

Man is a tyrant over himself also and perhaps most of
all over himself. He tyrannizes over himself as a dichoto-
mous creature which has lost its entirety. He tyrannizes over
himself by a false consciousness of guilt. A true consciousness of guilt would set man free. He tyrannizes over himself
by false beliefs, superstitions, myths. He tyrannizes over
himself by every sort of fear that is possible. He tyrannizes
over himself by envy, by self-love, by *ressentiment*. An un-
healthy self-love is a most dreadful form of tyranny. Man
tyrannizes over himself by the consciousness of his weakness
and insignificance and by the thirst for power and great-
ness. By his enslaving will man enslaves not only another
but himself. There exists an age-long tendency to despot-
ism, a thirst for power and mastership. The primary evil is
the power of man over man, the lowering of the dignity of
man, violence and domination. The exploitation of man by
man, which Marx considers the primary evil, is a derivative
evil; it is a phenomenon which becomes possible when man
lords it over man. But a man gets into the position of master over some other man because in accordance with the
structure of his consciousness he has become a slave to the
will to mastership. The same power by which he enslaves
another, enslaves himself also. A free man does not desire to
lord it over anyone.

The 'unhappy consciousness', according to Hegel, is the
consciousness of a being who is aware of another being who

is opposed to him, and so of one who is aware of his own insignificance. When the essential being of a man is felt by another to be opposed to him, then he may suffer the vexation of a slavish consciousness of dependence. But in such a case he often wins back his losses, and compensates himself by the enslavement of others. The most terrible of all is the slave who has become a master. As a master, however, the least terrible is the aristocrat who is conscious of his nobility of origin and dignity, and is free from *ressentiment*. The dictator, a man of the will to power, never becomes such an aristocrat. The psychology of the dictator, who is essentially a *parvenu,* is a perversion of man. He is the slave of his own enslavements. He is, in the most profound sense, the antithesis of Prometheus the liberator. The leader of the crowd is in the same state of servitude as the crowd; he has no existence outside the crowd, outside slavery, over which he plays the master. He is entirely ejected into the external.

The will to power, to dominance, to mastership, is possession; it is not free will nor is it the will to freedom. The man who is possessed by the will to power is in the grip of fate and becomes a man of destiny. The Caesar-dictator, the hero of the imperialistic will, places himself at the disposal of fate. He cannot stop, he cannot set limits to himself; he goes on ever further and further towards perdition. He is a man whose fate has been decided. The will to power is insatiable. It does not witness to an abundance of strength which bestows itself upon men. The imperialistic will creates a fantastic ephemeral kingdom and gives rise to catastrophe and war. The imperialistic will is a demoniacal perversion of the true vocation of man. It contains a perversion of the universalism to which man is called. This universalism tries to realize itself through a false objectivization, through casting out human existence into the external, through the exteriorization which makes man a slave. Man is called to be lord of the earth and the world. Kingship is

inherent in the idea of man. Man is called to expansion and
to take possession of extended spaces; he is attracted to
great adventure. But the Fall of man gives a false, an enslaving, direction to this universal will.

It was the lonely and unhappy Nietzsche who was the
philosopher of the will to power. And how monstrously they
have made use of Nietzsche, how they have vulgarized
him. How they have made his thought the instrument of
purposes which Nietzsche himself would have repudiated.
Nietzsche addressed himself to the few; he was an aristo-
cratic thinker; he despised the human masses, without
whom the imperialistic will cannot be realized. He called
the state the most cold-blooded of monsters and said that
man only begins where the state ends. How in this case is
empire to be organized, for empire is always the organization of the masses, of the average man? Nietzsche was a
weak man who lacked strength of any sort—the very weakest of the men of this world. Nor did he possess the will to
power; what he had was the idea of the will to power. He
called upon men to be harsh, but it is doubtful whether he
understood by harshness the violence of states and revolutions, and the harshness of the imperialistic will. The figure
of Caesar Borgia was to him only a symbol of the inward
tragedy of the spirit which he himself experienced. But the
exaltation of the imperialistic will, the will to power, and to
enslavement, in any case denotes a break with the ethics of
the Gospel. And this break is taking place in the world.
There was still nothing of it in the old humanism, nor did
it exist in the French Revolution. The enslaving gesture of
violence would like to be a gesture of strength, but it is in
its very essence always a gesture of weakness. Caesar is the
very weakest of men. Every man who inflicts punishment
is a man who has wiped out the strength of the spirit, who
has lost all consciousness of it. We come now to the very
complex problem of violence.

That will to power, the imperialistic will, is opposed to the dignity and freedom of man is absolutely clear. And indeed imperialistic philosophy has never said that it defends the freedom and dignity of man. It exalts the exercise of violence upon man, and makes it the mark of man's highest attainment. But the actual problem of force, and one's attitude towards it, are very complex and difficult. When men revolt against violence, they commonly have in view forms of violence which are crude and leap to the eyes. They beat men, put them in prison, kill them. But human life is full of unnoticed, more refined forms of violence. Psychological violence plays a still greater rôle in life than physical. Man is deprived of his freedom and is made a slave not only as the result of physical violence. The suggestion which reaches a man from his social environment and which he undergoes from childhood, may make a slave of him. A system of upbringing may completely deprive a man of his freedom and incapacitate him for freedom of judgment.

The weight and solidity of history use force on a man. It is possible to use force on a man by way of threat, by way of some mental contagion which has been turned into collective action. Enslavement is murder. Man always brings to bear upon man either a flow of life or a flow of death. And hate is always a stream of death brought to bear upon another, and doing violence to him. Hate always desires to take away freedom. But the astonishing thing is that love also can become deadly and send out the stream of death. Love enslaves no less than hate. Human life is permeated by underground streams, and man chances unseeingly upon an atmosphere which does violence to him and enslaves him. There is a psychological force of the individual person, and there is a psychological force of the community, of society. Crystallized, hardened public opinion becomes violence upon man. Man can be a slave to public opinion, a slave to custom, to morals, to judgments and opinions which are imposed by society. It is difficult to overestimate the violence which is perpetrated by the press in our time. The average man of our day holds the opinions and forms the judgments of the newspaper which he reads every morning: it exercises psychological compulsion upon him. And in view of the falsehood and venality of the press, the effects are very terrible as seen in the enslavement of man and his deprivation of freedom of conscience and judgment. And all the while how comparatively little this form of violence is noticed. It is noticed only in countries which live under dictatorship, where the falsification of men's opinions and judgments is an activity of the state.

There is a still more deep-seated form of violence, and that is the strong hand of the power of money. This is the hidden dictatorship in capitalist society. They do not use violence upon a man directly, in a noticeable fashion. The life of a man depends upon money, the most impersonal, the most unqualitative power in the world, and the most readily convertible into everything else alike. It is not directly, by way of physical violence, that a man is deprived of his freedom of conscience, freedom of thought, and freedom of judgment, but he is placed in a position of dependence materially, he finds himself under the threat of death by starvation and in this way he is deprived of his freedom. Money confers independence; the absence of it places a man in a position of dependence.

But even the man who possesses money finds himself in a state of servitude and is exposed to an unnoticed form of violence. In the Kingdom of Mammon, man is compelled to sell his labour and his labour is not free. Man has not known real freedom in labour. The labour of the artisan has been more free, relatively speaking, and so has intellectual labour, which by the way, has also been exposed to unnoticed violence. But the mass of human beings has served its time in toil which is servile, in forced labour, in the new slave labour of the capitalist world, and in bond-service after the pattern of the communist society. Man remains ever more and more a slave.

It is a very interesting fact that psychologically the easiest thing of all to accept as freedom is the absence of movement, the habitual condition. In movement there is already a certain exercise of force upon the surrounding world, upon material environment and upon other people. Movement is change, and it does not ask for the acquiescence of the world in this altered position, which is an effect of that change caused by the movement. Such an acceptance of rest as the absence of force, and of movement, change, as force, has conservative results in social life. Habitual, time-hardened slavery may not appear to be a form of violence, while a movement which is directed to the abolition of slavery may appear to be violence. The social reformation of society is accepted as violence by those to whom a certain habitual social order has presented itself as freedom, even though it may be terribly unjust and wrong. All reforms in the position of the working classes call forth from the side of the bourgeois classes, shouts about the violation of freedom and the use of force. Such are the paradoxes of freedom in social life. Slavery lies in wait for man on all sides. The fight for freedom presupposes resistance and without resistance its pathos is enfeebled. Freedom which has been established by an habitual way of living, passes over into an unnoticed enslavement of men; this is freedom which has become objectivized, whereas all the while freedom is the realm of the subject. Man is a slave because freedom is difficult, whereas slavery is easy.

In the servile world of objects, they regard violence as strength, as strength made manifest. The exaltation of violence always means the worship of power. But violence is not only not identical with power, it should never be connected with power. Power, in its most profound sense means the taking possession of that to which it is directed; not domination, in which externality is always maintained, but a persuasive, inwardly subjugating union. Christ speaks with power. A tyrant never speaks with power. The man who exerts force is absolutely powerless over those upon whom he exerts it. They resort to force as a result of impotence, in consequence of the fact that they have no power whatever against those upon whom they exert violence.

The master has no power at all over his slave. He can put him on the rack, but this torture only means that he is confronted by an insuperable obstacle. And had the master had power, he would have ceased to be a master. The limit of powerlessness in relation to another man finds its expression in the murdering of him. Limitless power would be revealed if it were possible to raise a man from the dead. Power is the transfiguration, the enlightenment, the resuscitation of another. Violence, torture, and murder, on the other hand, are weakness. In the objectivized, assimilated, depersonalized, exteriorized world, that is not called power which is power in the existential sense of the word. This is expressed in the clash between power and value. The higher values in the world appear to be weaker than the lower, the higher values are crucified, the lower triumph. The policeman and the sergeant major, the banker and the lawyer, are stronger than the poet and the philosopher, the prophet and the saint. In the objectivized world, matter is stronger than God. The Son of God was crucified. Socrates was poisoned. The prophets were stoned. The initiators and creators of new thought and a new way of living have always been persecuted, and oppressed and often put to death. The average man of the social routine of daily life has triumphed. Only the master and the slave have triumphed, they could not endure free men. The higher value, that of human personality, they were unwilling to acknowledge, while the lower value, the state, with its violence and falsehood, with its espionage and cold-blooded murder, they regarded as the higher value, and servilely bow down before it.

In the objectivized world they love only the finite, they cannot bear the infinite. And this sway of the finite always shows itself as the slavery of man, whereas the hidden infinite would be liberation. They associated power with the bad means which were considered necessary for ends which were regarded as good. But the whole of life has been filled with these methods, and the purposes have never been attained, and man becomes a slave of the means which supposedly give him power. Man has sought power in false ways, in the ways of impotence, which are shown in acts of violence. Man has consummated acts of will which enslave, and he has not consummated acts of will which liberate. In the so-called great actors of history, the heroes of imperialistic will, it is murder that has always played an enormous part, and this has always been evidence of the metaphysical weakness of those 'strong' men, of a pathological will to power and might, and domination, accompanied by a mania for persecution. Spiritual weakness, powerlessness over the inner life of man, absence of strength which resuscitates to a new life, have led to this, that the tortures of hell have been readily admitted in the life to come, and executions, tortures, and cruel punishments in this life. Truth is crucified in the world, but real power is in truth— the truth of God.

The philosophical source from which the slavery of man derives is monism. The practical expression of monism is tyrannical. Personalism is most profoundly opposed to monism. Monism is the domination of the 'common', of the abstract universal, and the denial of personality and freedom. Personality and freedom are linked with pluralism or, more correctly, externally they take the form of pluralism, while inwardly they may signify concrete universalism. Conscience cannot have its centre in any sort of universal unity; it is not liable to alienation; it remains in the depth of personality. Conscience in the depth of personality does not by any means indicate the confinement of personality within itself; it does not denote egoism. On the contrary it presupposes an opening out inwardly, not in the external, and an inward fulfilling by the concrete universal content. But this concretely universal content of personality never means that it deposits its conscience and its consciousness with society, with the state, with the nation, or a class, or a party, or with the church as a social institution. There is only one acceptable, non-servile meaning of the word *sobornost*, and that is the interpretation of it as the interior concrete universalism of personality, and not the alienation of conscience in any kind of exterior collective body whatever. The free man is simply the man who does not allow the alienation, the ejection into the external of his conscience and his judgment. He who permits this is a slave. The master also permits it, but he is only another form of slave.

Terminologically it is inexact to speak of the autonomy of personality, or of the autonomy of consciousness, or of conscience. In Kant it means subjection to the personal moral-intellectual law. In that case it is not man who is autonomous, but the moral-intellectual law. It is the autonomy of man, as personality, that must be called freedom. Men pitted either reason or nature against the authoritarian and hierarchical order in European history. Reason or nature rebelled against authority, but the freedom of man was not attained in this way. Man remains subjected to impersonal reason, to a sovereign society or simply to natural necessity. To the authoritarian consciousness or to the authoritarian order of life must be opposed, not reason, and not nature, and not a sovereign society, but spirit, that is to say, freedom, the spiritual principle in man, which organizes his personality and is independent of objectivized nature and the objectivized logical world. This presupposes a change of direction in the conflict against the slavery of man, that is to say it presupposes the personalistic transvaluation of values in the defence of which this book is written. The inward existential universalism of personality must be opposed to the outward objectivized universalism which is ever more and more creating new forms of slavery. Everything which is not personal, everything alienated into the sphere of the 'common', is the seduction and slavery of man. The free man is a self-governing being not a governed being; nor is it the self-government of a society and a people, but the self-government of a man who has become a personality. The self-government of a society, and of a people is still the government of slaves.

The change of direction in the fight for the freedom of man, for the manifestation of the free man, is above all a change in the structure of consciousness, a change in the scale of values. This process goes deep and its effects can but slowly become apparent. It is a profound interior revolution which is brought about in existential, not in historical, time. This change in the structure of consciousness is also a change in the interpretation of the relation between immanence and transcendence. The immanent continuity which precipitates man into the continuous evolutionary process is the negation of personality, which presupposes interruption and transcension. Man is subordinated to the universal unity in relation to which God is fully immanent. But God is also completely transcendent in relation to this universal unity and to the process which takes place in it. And this transcendence of God, the freedom of God from world necessity, and from all objectivity, is the source of the freedom of man, it constitutes the very possibility of the existence of personality. But transcendence also can be understood in a servile way and may mean the degradation of man. Transcendence can be interpreted as objectivization and exteriorization, and relation to it not as an inward act of transcension in freedom, but as the relation of slave to master. The way of liberation lies on the other side of traditional immanence and transcendence. The process of transcension in freedom never means subjection to an alien will, which indeed is slavery, but subjection to the Truth which is at the same time also the Way and the Life.

Truth is always connected with freedom and is bestowed upon freedom only. Slavery is always the denial of truth, and the dread of truth. Love for the truth is triumph over enslaving fear. Primitive man who still lives on in contemporary man is under the sway of fear; he is a slave of the past, of what is customary, of the spirit of his ancestors. Myths can enslave. The free man does not live under the sway of myths. He is emancipated from that sway. But people of our contemporary civilization, at the highest point of civilization, are still under the power of myths, and, in particular, under the power of the myth of universal realities, of the realm of the 'common' to which man ought to be subjected. But universal common realities do not exist, they are phantoms and illusions created by objectivization. Universal values exist, for example, truths, but always in a concrete and individual form. Hypostatization of universal values is a false direction for consciousness to take. It is the old metaphysic and it cannot be justified. Outside personality no sort of universality exists. The universe is to be found in the personality of man, in the personality of God. The personification of principles is objectivization and in that process personality disappears.

Slavery is passivity. The victory over slavery is creative activity. Only in existential time is creative activity disclosed. Historical activity is objectivization, the projection of what has been accomplished in the core of personality. And historical time would make man its slave. The free man ought not to bend the knee either before history or before race or before revolution or before any objective unity which makes pretentions to universal significance. The master also bows the knee before history, before common unities, before false universals, as the slave does. Master and slave have a great deal more in common than they think. The free man cannot even desire to be a master. It would

indicate the loss of freedom. In order to prepare the structure of consciousness which overcomes slavery and domination it is necessary to construct an apophatic sociology
on the analogy of apophatic theology. Kataphatic sociology
is to be found in the categories of slavery and domination.
It has no issue in freedom. The usual sociological concepts
are not applicable to thinking about society which is free
from the categories of domination and slavery. Such thinking presupposes renunciation and a negative attitude in relation to everything upon which society in the kingdom of
Caesar rests, that is to say in the objectivized world where
man also becomes an object. A society of free men, a society
of personalities, is not either a monarchy or a theocracy or
an aristocracy or a democracy, nor is it authoritarian society
nor a liberal society, nor a bourgeois society nor a socialist
society: it is not fascism nor communism, nor even anarchism as far as objectivization exists in anarchism. This is pure
apophatics as the knowledge of God is pure apophatics, free
from concepts, free from all rationalization. For all this
means that change in the structure of consciousness in
which objectivization disappears, in which there is no antithesis between subject and object, no master, no slave. It
is infinity, it is subjectivity filled with a universal content;
it is the realm of pure existentiality. It would be a complete
mistake to refer apophatic sociology to the other heavenly
transcendent world, to the life 'beyond the grave' and to
find peace and quiet in the thought that in this earthly immanent world, in the life before death, everything should
be left in the old way. We shall see that this is an absolutely
false understanding of eschatology, one which makes it an
interpretation of the end without any existential significance. In actual fact, change in the structure of consciousness, the putting an end to objectivization, the establishment of a society of free men, which are thinkable only for
apophatic sociology, ought to take place already on this
side of the grave.

Man lives not only in the cosmic time of the natural kaleidoscope of life and in the disrupted historical time which rushes towards the future; he lives also in existential time; he exists also outside the objectivity which he makes for himself. In the last part of this book we shall see that the 'end of the world' which in philosophical language denotes the end of objectivity, presupposes creative activity on the part of man and is accomplished not only 'on the other side' but also 'on this side'. This paradox of human destiny and the destiny of the world must be thought of paradoxically; one cannot think of it in rational categories. Master and slave, generally speaking, cannot think about this. Only free men can think of it. Master and slave will make superhuman efforts to prevent the end of objectivity, the 'end of the world', the coming of the Kingdom of God, the kingdom of freedom and free men. They will establish ever new forms of domination and slavery; they will fashion new disguises for new forms of objectivization in which the creative acts of man will meet with great failures; they will prolong the crimes of history. But free men should prepare their kingdom not only 'there' but also 'here' and above all prepare themselves, make themselves free, make themselves personalities. The free have a responsiblity which lies upon them. Slaves cannot prepare a new kingdom, one to which in fact the very word 'kingdom' is not to be applied; the revolt of slaves always establishes new forms of slavery. Only free men can so grow as to achieve this. The master has one lot with the slave, and we must trace in what a number of varied and refined forms slavery lies in wait for man and seduces him.

The End of Things and
the New Aeon

The whole movement of thought in this book leads to the problem of the end, not as one out of a number of problems but as the all-embracing and principal problem. 'Thesis: The world has a beginning in time and it is confined within the limits of space.' 'Antithesis: The world has neither beginning in time nor bounds in space but is infinite, as in space, so also in time.'[1] This is one of the antinomies of pure reason in the transcendental dialectic of Kant's genius. What interests me here is simply the antinomy as it is associated with time, and it must be extended to include the apocalyptic problem of an end in time. The antinomies of Kant cannot be resolved, cannot be *aufgehoben*, to use Hegel's expression. Reason finds itself in the power of transcendental appearance (*Schein*). Kant is absolutely right in saying that the antinomies cannot be overcome within the limits of the phenomenal world. In the problem with which we are now concerned it is alike impossible to think that the world will exist endlessly in time, and to

(From Nicolas Berdyaev, *The Divine and the Human* [London: Bles, 1949], Chap. XIV, pp. 195–202.)
[1] Kant, *Kritik der reinen Vernunft. Antinomie der reinen Vernunft. Erster Wiederstreit der transcendentalen Ideen.*

think that it will come to an end in time. For Kant there is no development which has its source in antitheses. Hegel's dialectic is quite different in character. With him the antinomies find their solution in dialectic development. Thesis and antithesis overcome each other and are removed in a synthesis.

Contradictions do give rise to development. The discovery of becoming, of development was an important discovery of Hegel's. The unity of being and nonentity gives rise to becoming, to development. Development in the world presupposes nonentity. But with Hegel there is no end, nor any eschatology in the true sense of the word. The dialectic of the finite and the infinite is continually resolved, but never consummated. That is why it was possible for him to accept even so scandalous an end as that which made the Prussian State into an absolute monarchy. The two European philosophers of the greatest genius, Kant and Hegel, provide no solution to the dialectic of contradictions, for they have no doctrine of the end of things. This is provided only by prophetic religious experience, and that was outside the purview of both of them. There was partial truth both in Kant and in Hegel and they help one to comprehend the philosophical problem of the end of the world and of history, a problem which had hitherto been expressed in religious phraseology only.[2] It is not true to say that Hegel's dialectic is simply a matter of logic. It follows from his recognition of the identity of thought and being that the logical dialectic becomes a dialectic of being. It might be said, using the terminology of some of the movements in philosophical thought at the present time, that in Hegel there was an existential dialectic.[3] His theory of mas-

---

[2] See my book, *Creativeness and Objectivization.*
[3] Wahl has interpreted him in this way; and so has Netty Nadler. See her book, *Der dialektische Widerspruch in Hegels Philosophie und das Paradox des Christentums.*

ter and slave, and of the unhappy consciousness are of that kind.

We do not acknowledge the identity of being and thought; for us, therefore, the dialectic is different in character, and is connected with religious spiritual experience. There is a paradox in the fact that when there is no envisagement of an end everything becomes finite. Eternity is revealed only in the prospect of an end. The dialectic of antinomies is not resolved within the confines of our world æon, which bears all over it the impress of objectivization. Here Kant is more right than Hegel. But Hegel was more right than Kant in his recognition of development through contradiction, although the development does not arrive at any solution. There is a paradox in thinking of the end of time, the end of history, as occurring actually within this time. This is what makes the interpretation of the Apocalypse so difficult. One cannot think of the end of history either as happening within the limits of our vitiated time, as an event which belongs to this world, or as taking place outside historical time, as an event which belongs to the next world. The end is the conquest of both cosmic time and historical time. There will be no more time. This is not an end in time but an end of time. But existential time, which has its roots in eternity, remains, and it is in existential time that the end of things takes place. This will be the entrance into a new æon. This is not yet eternity, which men still try to objectivize. The sharp line which marks the frontier between the here and the beyond will be obliterated.

But there is a further aspect of the paradox of time. It lies in the fact that a mysterious coincidence of past and future is possible, a coincidence of origins and end. The eschatological problem is the fundamental metaphysical problem. Philosophers have given very little attention to it, almost none at all, because they have separated philosophical cognition from religious experience. And this is a false separation, it is a wrong interpretation of the antinomies of cognition. The world ought to end and history ought to end; otherwise everything is devoid of meaning. The end is the triumph of meaning. It is the union of the divine and human, and the eschatological consummation of the existential dialectic of the divine and the human. We ought to move forward, and it may be that we are already moving forward, into the time of the end, which will be of infinite continuance.

From the philosophical point of view the end of the world and history is above all the triumph over objectivization, that is to say triumph over the world of alienation, necessity, impersonality, and hostility. It is the formation of a world of objects which is the source of all the misfortunes of man. The object is alien and intolerable to me.[4] Hegel too connected the unhappy consciousness with relation to the object, with dichotomy and disruption. Consciousness is always dichotomy and disruption; it presupposes an opposition between subject and object that always involves unhappiness. The overcoming of dichotomy and objectivization, the way of escape from slavery to the world, to objects, may be called the awakening of superconsciousness or of the higher consciousness. Objectivization is always a cooling of the creative fire. In history there is a cooling development. It is what Péguy called 'politics' as distinct from 'mysticism'. The fate of monasteries, revolutions, communist colonies, Tolstoyans, Dukhobors, the fate of love ('only the morning of love is good'), the posthumous fate of men of genius, all tell of chilling objectivization. It is impossible to expect the final solution of world

---

[4] Sartre, whose philosophy is fashionable nowadays, a gifted man, and very characteristic of our time, is in fact the slave of objectivity, the world of things, the world of phenomena, which has no reality in itself. It is a profound truth that reality depends upon the creative activity of man. But Sartre would think that behind the apparent there is nothing, there is no mystery. See his book, *L'Être et le Néant*, and mine, *Solitude and Society*.

history along this line. Classical culture would seek to petrify the world, to fix it in rigid forms, whereas the world
ought in fact to be fused and molten in the fire. 'I am come
to send fire on the earth; and what will I, if it be already
kindled?' These words have been forgotten in objectivized,
cooled, Christianity. Man is crushed between two sinister
infinities, and being in that position, desires so to order himself that he may not feel its tragedy.

The endless expanse of alien space filled Pascal with
terror, but the endlessness of time in past and future is just
as frightening. This double sinister infinity expresses itself
in an existence which is projected into the external, that is
to say in objectivized existence which is ever more and
more disrupted from its noumenal core. In his discontent
with the present man turns either to the memory of a golden
age in the past or to the expectation of a golden age in the
future. Man is capable of imagining a better, and fairer,
a more truthful and just life than this unpleasing life. But
whence does he get power for such imagining? Nor in any
case will this power of imagination that he possesses van-
quish the power of time, that fateful power of time, which
holds sway even in his very conception of the golden age.
Man materializes the thousand years' reign. The prophetic
idea of the thousand years' reign is foreign to St Augustine.
In his view the thousand years' reign was already realized
in the historical Church. This left him in the power of objectivization. But historical Christianity is coming to an end
in its fated way, and the inevitable transition to eschatological Christianity is taking place. Rays of light shine from the
future. The final future unites with the sources of the past.
There are three stages of revelation: revelation in nature,
revelation in history, and eschatological revelation. It is only
in this last that God finally and fully reveals Himself. This
stage is preceded by a state of Godforsakenness, by yearning anguish, by the mechanization and devastation of na-

ture, by the mechanization and secularization of history, and by transition through a period of godlessness.

Eschatological revelation is also revelation in Spirit and in Truth, which is eternal revelation. There is a tragic clash between Truth and the world. Pure undistorted Truth burns up the world. The goal is the attainment of wholeness, the overcoming of disruption, the surmounting of false antinomies in thoughts, dreams, passions, emotions, desires. There may be suffering in the dissevered parts of the soul, whereas in other parts of it there may not be. It is only because suffering does not grip the whole soul that man can exist, but his existence is unhappy. Universal history recalls to the mind not only tragedy but comedy also, and comedy always comes to an end in the same way. It is the fatal failure of history about which I have already spoken. All efforts to create a new life, whether in historical Christianity, by social revolutions, or by the formation of sects and so forth, alike end in objectivization, and adaptation to dull, everyday normality. The old rises in new forms, the old inequality, love of power, luxury, schisms and the rest. Life in our æon is only a testing and a pathway, but the testing has a meaning and the path leads to a consummating end. It would become easier for man if he were aware of the fact that a further revelation of the unknown is at hand, a revelation not only of the Holy Spirit but of a new man and a new cosmos.

A passive and an active eschatology are both possible. In the majority of cases the apocalyptic frame of mind has led to a passive waiting for the end, and a refusal to face the problems of history. Such was *The Story of Antichrist* by Vladimir Solovëv. Apocalyptic time is interpreted as a time of mere waiting for, and submitting to, the action of divine and diabolic powers. This is a decadent temper of mind. But an active eschatology is possible; and that imposes a knowledge of self which answers to the dignity of man as free spirit. It asserts the need to strengthen human

activity and human creativeness when the end comes. The
thought of the end must be grasped not in a passive and
negative attitude of mind but creatively and positively. I
have already said that every creative act of man is eschatological in character and brings this world to an end. The
end is interpreted in different ways according to whether
man looks at it from the point of view of historical Christianity, or from that of the more complete revelation of the
Spirit. In the latter case man is a subject not an object, and
he is a creative subject. Christian consciousness has reflected
too little upon the fact that the race of mankind will come
to an end if all men become completely Christian, absolutely continent, or monks. Here the eschatological depth
of the problem of sex comes into view. It is commonly said
that the end of marriage is the begetting of children and
that that is the supreme good. But at the same time it is
thought that this supreme good is the result of what is considered vicious and sinful. Rosanov exposes very acutely and
vigorously the hypocrisy which results from this inconsist-
ency. Solovëv and Kierkegaard alone thought that in the
actual begetting of children there is something vicious and
sinful.

The metaphysics of sex has an immediate connection
with the problem of the end. When the end comes something will be changed in the life of sex. After the submer-
gence of this side of life in horrifying darkness and dissolution enlightenment must come. Love can transfigure the old
sexual life and direct the energy of sex which holds man in
bondage, into creative channels. We are aware of the possibility of such sublimation of energy. Love will be given
a central position in the religion of the Spirit, the religion
of the end, love which is creative and transfiguring. Both
eros-love and agape-love will play such a part. But before
entering upon the higher epoch and reaching unity man
will have to follow to the end the path of dichotomy and
the way of suffering which is scarcely to be borne. It must

always be remembered that at the end of His path Jesus cried, 'My God, My God, why hast Thou forsaken Me?' There was a man who at the end of a long historical path also experienced abandonment, Godforsakenness, of another sort, and that was Nietzsche. The world process is tragic in character; it cannot be understood as a continuous progressive movement forward. The evil results of the world process, for all that they may even increase, are thrown out into non-being, but men and women, living creatures, cannot be finally cast into non-being. There is only one thing which perhaps earns the eternal pains of hell and that is the too insistent defence of them, accompanied by a feeling of satisfaction.

The greatest religious and moral truth to which man must grow, is that we cannot be saved individually. My salvation presupposes the salvation of others also, the salvation of my neighbour, it presupposes universal salvation, the salvation of the whole world, the transfiguration of the world. The very idea of salvation arises from the oppressed condition of man; and it is associated with a forensic conception of Christianity. This ought to be replaced by the idea of creative transformation and enlightenment, by the idea of perfecting all life. 'Behold I make all things new.' It is not only God Who makes all things new, it is man too. The period of the end is not only a period of destruction, but also a period of divine-human creativeness, a new life and a new world. The Church of the New Testament was a symbolic image of the eternal Church of the Spirit. In the Church of the Spirit the eternal Gospel will be read. When we draw near to the eternal Kingdom of the Spirit the torturing contradictions of life will be overcome and sufferings which towards the end will be increased, will pass into their antithesis, into joy. And this will be the case not only for the future but also for the past, for there will be a reversal of time and all living things will share in the end.

MARTIN BUBER

�֎ ✖ ✖ ✖

MARTIN BUBER

Martin Buber, the celebrated Jewish religious philosopher, was born in Vienna in 1878, but until the age of fourteen was brought up in the Galician home of his grandfather, Solomon Buber, a distinguished scholar. There he received a thorough Jewish education in the traditional style, and first came into contact with Hasidism, which was to become one of the great formative influences of his life and thought. At the universities of Vienna and Berlin, he pursued "secular" studies, particularly philosophy and the history of art, with great distinction.

While still a student in his early twenties, he joined the emerging Zionist movement and in 1901 became editor of the Zionist periodical *Die Welt*. Buber's Zionism, however, soon revealed its basic differences with the purely political Zionism associated with the name of Theodor Herzl. His Zionism was cultural and spiritual, involving primarily an effort to encourage a renascence of total Jewish existence. *Der Jude*, which he founded and edited from 1916 to 1924, was the protagonist of this idea, and quickly became the leading organ of German-speaking Jewry. From 1926 to 1930 he published, jointly with the Catholic theologian,

Joseph Wittig, and the Protestant physician and psycho-
therapist, Viktor von Weizsäcker, the journal *Die Kreatur*,
devoted to social and pedagogical problems in relation to
religion.

Meanwhile, Buber was pursuing his philosophical, cultural, and religious studies. His thinking at first had a de-
cidedly mystical cast, and indeed some of his early writing
was devoted to presenting and interpreting the classics of
mysticism, Western and Oriental. Gradually, however, his
outlook shifted, and the change was speeded, according to
Buber's own account,[1] by a shattering experience which
completed the conversion from the mystical (Buber calls
it the "religious") to the "everyday." In *Daniel*, published
in 1913, a distinctly existential view comes to the fore.
Men, Buber finds, are capable of a twofold relation to their
experience and environment—"orientation" and "realization." "Orientation" is the "objective" attitude that orders
the environment for knowledge and use; "realization" is the
approach that brings out the inner meaning of life in intensified perception and existence (what German philosophy was beginning to call *Existenz*). The first draft of *I and
Thou* was, according to Buber, made in 1916, though he
did not, he says, attain "decisive clarity" until 1919. In *I
and Thou*, as published in 1923, the existential has already
given way to the dialogical approach, which governs all
of Buber's subsequent work. Basically, each of the stages is
subsumed in its successors: one aspect of the mystical reap-
pears in the existential, and the existential is fulfilled and
deepened in the dialogical.

Soon after the First World War, Buber became acquainted with Franz Rosenzweig, with whom he collabo-
rated in a fruitful series of literary and educational enterprises that left their mark on a generation of German Jews.
The most important of these joint ventures was the Buber-

[1] See Martin Buber, *Between Man and Man* (Macmillan,
1948; Beacon, 1955), pp. 13–14.

Rosenzweig translation of the Hebrew Bible, and the Freies Jüdisches Lehrhaus (Jewish Academy) in Frankfurt, a unique institution that achieved an enduring intellectual influence. For some years after 1923 Buber was professor at the University of Frankfurt. After the triumph of the Nazis he took over direction of the educational activities of the hard-pressed Jewish community, and strove mightily to build up its inner strength and spiritual resources.

In 1938, at the age of sixty, Buber left for Palestine to become professor of social philosophy at the Hebrew University. His new life was no more sheltered and academic than his old life in Germany had been. His brand of religio-cultural Zionism had all along been frowned upon by the "politicals" in the Zionist movement, and now in Palestine itself he developed a viewpoint which threw him into sharp opposition to the dominant ideology. Along with Judah L. Magnes, Ernst Simon, and others, he advocated a program of Jewish-Arab understanding on the basis of a binational state. The movement made little headway in the heavily charged atmosphere of the Jewish community, but it did at least raise another and dissident voice against the prevailing orthodoxy. All these activities Buber combined with extensive lecture tours throughout western Europe. In 1951, upon his retirement from his professorship at the Hebrew University at the age of seventy-three, Buber visited the United States and lectured at many universities and seminaries. He made a deep impression upon large segments of the American intellectual community. In 1957 he returned to this country briefly to deliver the William Alanson White Lectures at the Washington School of Psychiatry, and to conduct seminars at several institutions of learning. He plans to come back for a few months' stay at Princeton in 1958.

Until 1953 Buber directed the Institute of Adult Studies of the Hebrew University which he had founded in 1949 for the training of teachers who would work in the immi-

gration camps to help integrate the vast numbers of new
arrivals into the life of the community. Adult education has
always been one of his abiding concerns.

Buber's interests have throughout been broad and varied,
embracing philosophy, theology, biblical scholarship, psychology, education, and social thought. From early manhood Buber has been a socialist of the "communitarian"
(small community) school—the program of which he has
documented and expounded in *Paths in Utopia*—and his
whole teaching has been an effort to combine this concept
with his cultural Zionism and his existential (or dialogical)
Judaism. He has striven for genuine unity of thought and
action, commitment and performance, in a life that has
never been confined to the academic.

The sources of Martin Buber's thought are many, but the
authentic Jewish note of existential "realization" is never
hard to detect, whatever the combination. His thinking has
developed in fruitful dialogue with the men of his age and
of ages past. He was early influenced by the giants of German idealism and romanticism, and by the German mystics,
Meister Eckhart and Jakob Boehme. Hasidism, in both its
mystical and existential strains, has permeated his thinking
from his youth. But of all nineteenth-century figures, it was
Kierkegaard, Dostoevsky, and Nietzsche who, by his own
account, meant most to him, and with them, too, his intellectual relations have been complex and many-sided. He
has always closely followed the thought of his day, and his
comments on Scheler, Heidegger, Sartre, Jung, Bergson,
and Simone Weil, to mention but a few of the names
that occur in his more recent writings, are among the most
illuminating in contemporary criticism. But fundamentally
Buber's thinking has been his own in a way that can be
said of few other men; everything that comes from him
bears the mark of his unique personality and life experience. In him the word and the deed have indeed been fused
into the authentic unity of the lived life.

SELECTED BIBLIOGRAPHY

WORKS BY BUBER

(A full bibliography of writings by, about, and relating to Martin Buber will be found in Maurice S. Friedman, *Martin Buber: The Life of Dialogue* [University of Chicago Press, 1955], pp. 283–98. In the list below, only books available in English are given.)

I and Thou. Scribner's, 1937.

Mamre: Essays in Religion. Melbourne University Press, 1946.

Moses. Oxford: East and West Library, 1946.

Tales of the Hasidim: The Early Masters. Schocken, 1947.

Tales of the Hasidim: The Later Masters. Schocken, 1948.

Israel and the World: Essays in a Time of Crisis. Schocken, 1948.

Between Man and Man. Macmillan, 1948; Beacon, 1955.

Hasidism. Philosophical Library, 1948.

The Prophetic Faith. Macmillan, 1949.

Paths in Utopia. London: Routledge and Kegan Paul, 1949.

At the Turning: Three Addresses on Judaism. Farrar, Straus, and Young, 1952.

Eclipse of God: Studies in the Relation Between Religion and Philosophy. Harper, 1952.

Israel and Palestine: The History of an Idea. London: East and West Library, 1952.

Two Types of Faith. Macmillan, 1952.

Right and Wrong: An Interpretation of Some Psalms. London: SCM, 1952.

"The Suspension of Ethics," in Ruth Nanda Anshen, ed., *Moral Principles of Action.* Harper, 1952.

For the Sake of Heaven. Harper, 1953.

Good and Evil: Two Interpretations. Scribner's, 1953.

The Legend of the Baal-Shem. Harper, 1955.

The Tales of Rabbi Nachman. Horizon, 1956.

"Existence and Relation," "Elements of the Interhuman," "Guilt and Guilt Feelings" (The William Alanson White Memorial Lectures, Fourth Series), *Psychiatry*, Vol. XX, no. 2, May 1957.

Pointing the Way: Collected Essays. Harper, 1957.

WORKS ABOUT BUBER

Agus, Jacob B., *Modern Philosophies of Judaism,* pp. 213–79. Behrman's, 1941.

Cohen, Arthur A., *Martin Buber.* Hillary House, 1957.

Friedman, Maurice S., *Martin Buber: The Life of Dialogue.* University of Chicago Press, 1955.

Herberg, Will, ed., *The Writings of Martin Buber.* Meridian, 1956.

Pfuetze, Paul E., *The Social Self.* Bookman Associates, 1954.

Tillich, Paul, "Martin Buber and Christian Thought," *Commentary,* June 1948.

Dialogue

SECTION ONE: DESCRIPTION

SETTING OF THE QUESTION

The life of dialogue is not limited to men's traffic with one another; it is, it has shown itself to be, a relation of men to one another that is only represented in their traffic.

Accordingly, even if speech and communication may be dispensed with, the life of dialogue seems, from what we may perceive, to have inextricably joined to it as its minimum constitution one thing, the mutuality of the inner action. Two men bound together in dialogue must obviously be turned to one another, they must therefore—no matter with what measure of activity or indeed of consciousness of activity—have turned to one another.

It is good to put this forward so crudely and formally. For behind the`formulating question about the limits of a category under discussion is hidden a question which bursts all formulas asunder.

(From Martin Buber, *Between Man and Man* [Macmillan, 1947; Beacon, 1955], Chap. I, pp. 8–39.)

OBSERVING, LOOKING ON, BECOMING AWARE

We may distinguish three ways in which we are able to perceive a man who is living before our eyes. (I am not thinking of an object of scientific knowledge, of which I do not speak here.) The object of our perception does not need to know of us, of our being there. It does not matter at this point whether he stands in a relation or has a standpoint towards the perceiver.

The *observer* is wholly intent on fixing the observed man in his mind, on "noting" him. He probes him and writes him up. That is, he is diligent to write up as many "traits" as possible. He lies in wait for them, that none may escape him. The object consists of traits, and it is known what lies behind each of them. Knowledge of the human system of expression constantly incorporates in the instant the newly appearing individual variations, and remains applicable. A face is nothing but physiognomy, movements nothing but gestures of expression.

The *onlooker* is not at all intent. He takes up the position which lets him see the object freely, and undisturbed awaits what will be presented to him. Only at the beginning may he be ruled by purpose, everything beyond that is involuntary. He does not go around taking notes indiscriminately, he lets himself go, he is not in the least afraid of forgetting something ("Forgetting is good," he says). He gives his memory no tasks, he trusts its organic work which preserves what is worth preserving. He does not bring in the grass as green fodder, as the observer does; he turns it over and lets the sun shine on it. He pays no attention to traits ("Traits lead astray," he says). What stands out for him from the object is what is not "character" and not "expression" ("The interesting is not important," he says). All great artists have been onlookers.

But there is a perception of a decisively different kind.

The onlooker and the observer are similarly orientated, in that they have a position, namely, the very desire to perceive the man who is living before our eyes. Moreover, this man is for them an object separated from themselves and their personal life, who can in fact for this sole reason be "properly" perceived. Consequently what they experience in this way, whether it is, as with the observer, a sum of traits, or, as with the onlooker, an existence, neither demands action from them nor inflicts destiny on them. But rather the whole is given over to the aloof fields of æsthesis.

It is a different matter when in a receptive hour of my personal life a man meets me about whom there is something, which I cannot grasp in any objective way at all, that "says something" to me. That does not mean, says to me what manner of man this is, what is going on in him, and the like. But it means, says something *to me*, addresses something to me, speaks something that enters my own life. It can be something about this man, for instance that he needs me. But it can also be something about myself. The man himself in his relation to me has nothing to do with what is said. He has no relation to me, he has indeed not noticed me at all. It is not he who says it to me, as that solitary man silently confessed his secret to his neighbour on the seat; but *it* says it.

To understand "say" as a metaphor is not to understand. The phrase "that doesn't say a thing to me" is an outworn metaphor; but the saying I am referring to is real speech. In the house of speech are many mansions, and this is one of the inner.

The effect of having this said to me is completely different from that of looking on and observing. I cannot depict or denote or describe the man in whom, through whom, something has been said to me. Were I to attempt it, that would be the end of saying. This man is not my object; I have got to do with him. Perhaps I have to accomplish something about him; but perhaps I have only to learn something, and it is only a matter of my "accepting". It may be that I have to answer at once, to this very man before me; it may be that the saying has a long and manifold transmission before it, and that I am to answer some other person at some other time and place, in who knows what kind of speech, and that it is now only a matter of taking the answering on myself. But in each instance a word demanding an answer has happened to me.

We may term this way of perception *becoming aware*.

It by no means needs to be a man of whom I become aware. It can be an animal, a plant, a stone. No kind of appearance or event is fundamentally excluded from the series of the things through which from time to time something is said to me. Nothing can refuse to be the vessel for the Word. The limits of the possibility of dialogue are the limits of awareness.

THE SIGNS

Each of us is encased in an armour whose task is to ward off signs. Signs happen to us without respite, living means being addressed, we would need only to present ourselves and to perceive. But the risk is too dangerous for us, the soundless thunderings seem to threaten us with annihilation, and from generation to generation we perfect the defence apparatus. All our knowledge assures us, "Be calm, everything happens as it must happen, but nothing is directed at you, you are not meant; it is just 'the world', you can experience it as you like, but whatever you make of it in yourself proceeds from you alone, nothing is required of you, you are not addressed, all is quiet."

Each of us is encased in an armour which we soon, out of familiarity, no longer notice. There are only moments which penetrate it and stir the soul to sensibility. And when such a moment has imposed itself on us and we then take notice and ask ourselves, "Has anything particular taken place?

Was it not of the kind I meet every day?" then we may reply to ourselves, "Nothing particular, indeed, it is like this every day, only we are not there every day."

The signs of address are not something extraordinary, something that steps out of the order of things, they are just what goes on time and again, just what goes on in any case, nothing is added by the address. The waves of the æther roar on always, but for most of the time we have turned off our receivers.

What occurs to me addresses me. In what occurs to me the world-happening addresses me. Only by sterilizing it, removing the seed of address from it, can I take what occurs to me as a part of the world-happening which does not refer to me. The interlocking sterilized system into which all this only needs to be dovetailed is man's titanic work. Mankind has pressed speech too into the service of this work.

From out of this tower of the ages the objection will be levelled against me, if some of its doorkeepers should pay any attention to such trains of thought, that it is nothing but a variety of primitive superstition to hold that cosmic and telluric happenings have for the life of the human person a direct meaning that can be grasped. For instead of understanding an event physically, biologically, sociologically (for which I, inclined as I always have been to admire genuine acts of research, think a great deal, when those who carry them out only know what they are doing and do not lose sight of the limits of the realm in which they are moving), these keepers say, an attempt is being made to get behind the event's alleged significance, and for this there is no place in a reasonable world continuum of space and time.

Thus, then, unexpectedly I seem to have fallen into the company of the augurs, of whom, as is well-known, there are remarkable modern varieties.

But whether they haruspicate or cast a horoscope their signs have this peculiarity that they are in a dictionary, even if not necessarily a written one. It does not matter how esoteric the information that is handed down: he who searches out the signs is *well up in* what life's juncture this or that sign means. Nor does it matter that special difficulties of separation and combination are created by the meeting of several signs of different kinds. For you can "look it up in the dictionary". The common signature of all this business is that it is for all time: things remain the same, they are discovered once for all, rules, laws, and analogical conclusions may be employed throughout. What is commonly termed superstition, that is, perverse faith, appears to me rather as perverse knowledge. From "superstition" about the number 13 an unbroken ladder leads into the dizziest heights of gnosis. This is not even the aping of a real faith.

Real faith—if I may so term presenting ourselves and perceiving—begins when the dictionary is put down, when you are done with it. What occurs to me says something to me, but what it says to me cannot be revealed by any esoteric information; for it has never been said before nor is it composed of sounds that have ever been said. It can neither be interpreted nor translated, I can have it neither explained nor displayed; it is not a *what* at all, it is said into my very life; it is no experience that can be remembered independently of the situation, it remains the address of that moment and cannot be isolated, it remains the question of a questioner and will have its answer.

(It remains the question. For that is the other great contrast between all the business of interpreting signs and the speech of signs which I mean here: this speech never gives information or appeasement.)

Faith stands in the stream of "happening but once" which is spanned by knowledge. All the emergency structures of analogy and typology are indispensable for the work of the human spirit, but to step on them when the question of the questioner steps up to you, to me, would be running away. Lived life is tested and fulfilled in the stream alone.

With all deference to the world continuum of space and time I know as a living truth only concrete world reality which is constantly, in every moment, reached out to me. I can separate it into its component parts, I can compare them and distribute them into groups of similar phenomena, I can derive them from earlier and reduce them to simpler phenomena; and when I have done all this I have not touched my concrete world reality. Inseparable, incomparable, irreducible, now, happening once only, it gazes upon me with a horrifying look. So in Stravinsky's ballet the director of the wandering marionette show wants to point out to the people at the annual fair that a pierrot who terrified them is nothing but a wisp of straw in clothes: he tears it asunder—and collapses, gibbering, for on the roof of the booth the *living* Petrouchka sits and laughs at him.

The true name of concrete reality is the creation which is entrusted to me and to every man. In it the signs of address are given to us.

A CONVERSION

In my earlier years the "religious" was for me the exception. There were hours that were taken out of the course of things. From somewhere or other the firm crust of everyday was pierced. Then the reliable permanence of appearances broke down; the attack which took place burst its law asunder. "Religious experience" was the experience of an otherness which did not fit into the context of life. It could begin with something customary, with consideration of some familiar object, but which then became unexpectedly mysterious and uncanny, finally lighting a way into the lightning-pierced darkness of the mystery itself. But also, without any intermediate stage, time could be torn apart—

first the firm world's structure, then the still firmer self-assurance flew apart and you were delivered to fulness. The "religious" lifted you out. Over there now lay the accustomed existence with its affairs, but here illumination and ecstasy and rapture held, without time or sequence. Thus your own being encompassed a life here and a life beyond, and there was no bond but the actual moment of the transition.

The illegitimacy of such a division of the temporal life, which is streaming to death and eternity and which only in fulfilling its temporality can be fulfilled in face of these, was brought home to me by an everyday event, an event of judgment, judging with that sentence from closed lips and an unmoved glance such as the ongoing course of things loves to pronounce.

What happened was no more than that one forenoon, after a morning of "religious" enthusiasm, I had a visit from an unknown young man, without being there in spirit. I certainly did not fail to let the meeting be friendly, I did not treat him any more remissly than all his contemporaries who were in the habit of seeking me out about this time of day as an oracle that is ready to listen to reason. I conversed attentively and openly with him—only I omitted to guess the questions which he did not put. Later, not long after, I learned from one of his friends—he himself was no longer alive—the essential content of these questions; I learned that he had come to me not casually, but borne by destiny, not for a chat but for a decision. He had come to me, he had come in this hour. What do we expect when we are in despair and yet go to a man? Surely a presence by means of which we are told that nevertheless there is meaning.

Since then I have given up the "religious" which is nothing but the exception, extraction, exaltation, ecstasy; or it has given me up. I possess nothing but the everyday out of which I am never taken. The mystery is no longer disclosed, it has escaped or it has made its dwelling here where everything happens as it happens. I know no fulness but each mortal hour's fulness of claim and responsibility. Though far from being equal to it, yet I know that in the claim I am claimed and may respond in responsibility, and know who speaks and demands a response.

I do not know much more. If that is religion then it is just *everything*, simply all that is lived in its possibility of dialogue. Here is space also for religion's highest forms. As when you pray you do not thereby remove yourself from this life of yours but in your praying refer your thought to it, even though it may be in order to yield it; so too in the unprecedented and surprising, when you are called upon from above, required, chosen, empowered, sent, you with this your mortal bit of life are referred to, this moment is not extracted from it, it rests on what has been and beckons to the remainder which has still to be lived, you are not swallowed up in a fulness without obligation, you are willed for the life of communion.

WHO SPEAKS?

In the signs of life which happens to us we are addressed. Who speaks?

It would not avail us to give for reply the word "God", if we do not give it out of that decisive hour of personal existence when we had to forget everything we imagined we knew of God, when we dared to keep nothing handed down or learned or self-contrived, no shred of knowledge, and were plunged into the night.

When we rise out of it into the new life and there begin to receive the signs, what can we know of that which—of him who gives them to us? Only what we experience from time to time from the signs themselves. If we name the speaker of this speech God, then it is always the God of a moment, a moment God.

I will now use a *gauche* comparison, since I know no right one.

When we really understand a poem, all we know of the poet is what we learn of him in the poem—no biographical wisdom is of value for the pure understanding of what is to be understood: the *I* which approaches us is the subject of this single poem. But when we read other poems by the poet in the same true way their subjects combine in all their multiplicity, completing and confirming one another, to form the one polyphony of the person's existence.

In such a way, out of the givers of the signs, the speakers of the words in lived life, out of the moment Gods there arises for us with a single identity the Lord of the voice, the One.

ABOVE AND BELOW

Above and below are bound to one another. The word of him who wishes to speak with men without speaking with God is not fulfilled; but the word of him who wishes to speak with God without speaking with men goes astray.

There is a tale that a man inspired by God once went out from the creaturely realms into the vast waste. There he wandered till he came to the gates of the mystery. He knocked. From within came the cry: "What do you want here?" He said, "I have proclaimed your praise in the ears of mortals, but they were deaf to me. So I come to you that you yourself may hear me and reply." "Turn back," came the cry from within. "Here is no ear for you. I have sunk my hearing in the deafness of mortals."

True address from God directs man into the place of lived speech, where the voices of the creatures grope past one another, and in their very missing of one another succeed in reaching the eternal partner.

RESPONSIBILITY

The idea of responsibility is to be brought back from the province of specialized ethics, of an "ought" that swings free in the air, into that of lived life. Genuine responsibility exists only where there is real responding.

Responding to what?

To what happens to one, to what is to be seen and heard and felt. Each concrete hour allotted to the person, with its content drawn from the world and from destiny, is speech for the man who is attentive. Attentive, for no more than that is needed in order to make a beginning with the reading of the signs that are given to you. For that very reason, as I have already indicated, the whole apparatus of our civilization is necessary to preserve men from this attentiveness and its consequences. For the attentive man would no longer, as his custom is, "master" the situation the very moment after it stepped up to him: it would be laid upon him to go up to and into it. Moreover, nothing that he believed he possessed as always available would help him, no knowledge and no technique, no system and no programme; for now he would have to do with what cannot be classified, with concretion itself. This speech has no alphabet, each of its sounds is a new creation and only to be grasped as such.

It will, then, be expected of the attentive man that he faces creation as it happens. It happens as speech, and not as speech rushing out over his head but as speech directed precisely at him. And if one were to ask another if he too heard and he said he did, they would have agreed only about an experiencing and not about something experienced.

But the sounds of which the speech consists—I repeat it in order to remove the misunderstanding, which is perhaps still possible, that I referred to something extraordinary and larger than life—are the events of the personal everyday life. In them, as they now are, "great" or "small", we are addressed, and those which count as great, yield no greater signs than the others.

Our attitude, however, is not yet decided through our becoming aware of the signs. We can still wrap silence about us—a reply characteristic of a significant type of the age—or we can step aside into the accustomed way; although both times we carry away a wound that is not to be forgotten in any productivity or any narcotism. Yet it can happen that we venture to respond, stammering perhaps—the soul is but rarely able to attain to surer articulation—but it is an honest stammering, as when sense and throat are united about what is to be said, but the throat is too horrified at it to utter purely the already composed sense. The words of our response are spoken in the speech, untranslatable like the address, of doing and letting—whereby the doing may behave like a letting and the letting like a doing. What we say in this way with the being is our entering upon the situation, into the situation, which has at this moment stepped up to us, whose appearance we did not and could not know, for its like has not yet been.

Nor are we now finished with it, we have to give up that expectation: a situation of which we have become aware is never finished with, but we subdue it into the substance of lived life. Only then, true to the moment, do we experience a life that is something other than a sum of moments. We respond to the moment, but at the same time we respond on its behalf, we answer for it. A newly-created concrete reality has been laid in our arms; we answer for it. A dog has looked at you, you answer for its glance, a child has clutched your hand, you answer for its touch, a host of men moves about you, you answer for their need.

MORALITY AND RELIGION

Responsibility which does not respond to a word is a metaphor of morality. Factually, responsibility only exists when the court is there to which I am responsible, and "self-responsibility" has reality only when the "self" to which I am responsible becomes transparent into the absolute. But he who practises real responsibility in the life of dialogue does not need to name the speaker of the word to which he is responding—he knows him in the word's substance which presses on and in, assuming the cadence of an inwardness, and stirs him in his heart of hearts. A man can ward off with all his strength the belief that "God" is there, and he tastes him in the strict sacrament of dialogue.

Yet let it not be supposed that I make morality questionable in order to glorify religion. Religion, certainly, has this advantage over morality, that it is a phenomenon and not a postulate, and further that it is able to include composure as well as determination. The reality of morality, the demand of the demander, has a place in religion, but the reality of religion, the unconditioned being of the demander, has no place in morality. Nevertheless, when religion does itself justice and asserts itself, it is much more dubious than morality, just because it is more actual and inclusive. Religion as risk, which is ready to give itself up, is the nourishing stream of the arteries; as system, possessing, assured and assuring, religion which believes in religion is the veins' blood, which ceases to circulate. And if there is nothing that can so hide the face of our fellow-man as morality can, religion can hide from us as nothing else can the face of God. Principle there, dogma here, I appreciate the "objective" compactness of dogma, but behind both there lies in wait the—profane or holy—war against the situation's power of dialogue, there lies in wait the "once-for-all" which resists the unforeseeable moment. Dogma, even when its claim of origin remains uncontested, has become the most exalted form of invulnerability against revelation. Revelation will tolerate no perfect tense, but man with the arts of his craze for security props it up to perfectedness.

SECTION TWO: LIMITATION

THE REALMS

The realms of the life of dialogue and the life of monologue do not coincide with the realms of dialogue and monologue even when forms without sound and even without gesture are included. There are not merely great spheres of the life of dialogue which in appearance are not dialogue, there is also dialogue which is not the dialogue of life, that is, it has the appearance but not the essence of dialogue. At times, indeed, it seems as though there were only this kind of dialogue.

I know three kinds. There is genuine dialogue—no matter whether spoken or silent—where each of the participants really has in mind the other or others in their present and particular being and turns to them with the intention of establishing a living mutual relation between himself and them. There is technical dialogue, which is prompted solely by the need of objective understanding. And there is monologue disguised as dialogue, in which two or more men, meeting in space, speak each with himself in strangely tortuous and circuitous ways and yet imagine they have escaped the torment of being thrown back on their own resources. The first kind, as I have said, has become rare; where it arises, in no matter how "unspiritual" a form, witness is borne on behalf of the continuance of the organic substance of the human spirit. The second belongs to the inalienable sterling quality of "modern existence". But

real dialogue is here continually hidden in all kinds of odd
corners and, occasionally in an unseemly way, breaks surface surprisingly and inopportunely—certainly still oftener
it is arrogantly tolerated than downright scandalizing—as in
the tone of a railway guard's voice, in the glance of an old
newspaper vendor, in the smile of the chimney-sweeper.
And the third. . . .

A *debate* in which the thoughts are not expressed in the
way in which they existed in the mind but in the speaking
are so pointed that they may strike home in the sharpest
way, and moreover without the men that are spoken to being regarded in any way present as persons; a *conversation*
characterized by the need neither to communicate something, nor to learn something, nor to influence someone, nor
to come into connexion with someone, but solely by the
desire to have one's own self-reliance confirmed by marking
the impression that is made, or if it has become unsteady
to have it strengthened; a *friendly chat* in which each regards himself as absolute and legitimate and the other as
relativized and questionable; a *lovers' talk* in which both
partners alike enjoy their own glorious soul and their pre-
cious experience—what an underworld of faceless spectres
of dialogue!

The life of dialogue is not one in which you have much to
do with men, but one in which you really have to do with
those with whom you have to do. It is not the solitary man
who lives the life of monologue, but he who is incapable of
making real in the context of being the community in which,
in the context of his destiny, he moves. It is, in fact, solitude
which is able to show the innermost nature of the contrast.
He who is living the life of dialogue receives in the ordinary
course of the hours something that is said and feels himself
approached for an answer. But also in the vast blankness of,
say, a companionless mountain wandering that which confronts him, rich in change, does not leave him. He who is
living the life of monologue is never aware of the other as

something that is absolutely not himself and at the same time something with which he nevertheless communicates. Solitude for him can mean mounting richness of visions and thoughts but never the deep intercourse, captured in a new depth, with the incomprehensibly real. Nature for him is either an *état d'âme*, hence a "living through" in himself, or it is a passive object of knowledge, either idealistically brought within the soul or realistically alienated. It does not become for him a word apprehended with senses of beholding and feeling.

Being, lived in dialogue, receives even in extreme dereliction a harsh and strengthening sense of reciprocity; being, lived in monologue, will not, even in the tenderest intimacy, grope out over the outlines of the self.

This must not be confused with the contrast between "egoism" and "altruism" conceived by some moralists. I know people who are absorbed in "social activity" and have never spoken from being to being with a fellow-man. I know others who have no personal relation except to their enemies, but stand in such a relation to them that it is the enemies' fault if the relation does not flourish into one of dialogue.

Nor is dialogic to be identified with love. I know no one in any time who has succeeded in loving every man he met. Even Jesus obviously loved of "sinners" only the loose, lovable sinners, sinners against the Law; not those who were settled and loyal to their inheritance and sinned against him and his message. Yet to the latter as to the former he stood in a direct relation. Dialogic is not to be identified with love. But love without dialogic, without real outgoing to the other, reaching to the other, and companying with the other, the love remaining with itself—this is called Lucifer.

Certainly in order to be able to go out to the other you must have the starting place, you must have been, you must be, with yourself. Dialogue between mere individuals is only a sketch, only in dialogue between persons is the sketch filled in. But by what could a man from being an individual so really become a person as by the strict and sweet experiences of dialogue which teach him the boundless contents of the boundary?

What is said here is the real contrary of the cry, heard at times in twilight ages, for universal unreserve. He who can be unreserved with each passer-by has no substance to lose; but he who cannot stand in a direct relation to each one who meets him has a fulness which is futile. Luther is wrong to change the Hebrew "companion" (out of which the Seventy had already made one who is near, a neighbour) into "nearest." If everything concrete is equally near, equally nearest, life with the world ceases to have articulation and structure, it ceases to have human meaning. But nothing needs to mediate between me and one of my companions in the companionship of creation, whenever we come near one another, because we are bound up in relation to the same centre.

THE BASIC MOVEMENTS

I term basic movement an essential action of man (it may be understood as an "inner" action, but it is not there unless it is there to the very tension of the eyes' muscles and the very action of the foot as it walks), round which an essential attitude is built up. I do not think of this happening in time, as though the single action preceded the lasting attitude; the latter rather has its truth in the accomplishing, over and over again, of the basic movement, without forethought but also without habit. Otherwise the attitude would have only æsthetic or perhaps also political significance, as a beautiful and as an effective lie. The familiar maxim, "An attitude must first be adopted, the rest follows of itself" ceases to be true in the circle of essential action and essential attitude—that is, where we are concerned with the wholeness of the person.

The basic movement of the life of dialogue is the turning towards the other. That, indeed, seems to happen every hour and quite trivially. If you look at someone and address him you turn to him, of course with the body, but also in the requisite measure with the soul, in that you direct your attention to him. But what of all this is an essential action, done with the essential being? In this way, that out of the incomprehensibility of what lies to hand this one person steps forth and becomes a presence. Now to our perception the world ceases to be an insignificant multiplicity of points to one of which we pay momentary attention. Rather it is a limitless tumult round a narrow breakwater, brightly outlined and able to bear heavy loads—limitless, but limited by the breakwater, so that, though not engirdled, it has become finite in itself, been given form, released from its own indifference. And yet none of the contacts of each hour is unworthy to take up from our essential being as much as it may. For no man is without strength for expression, and our turning towards him brings about a reply, however imperceptible, however quickly smothered, in a looking and sounding forth of the soul that are perhaps dissipating in mere inwardness and yet do exist. The notion of modern man that this turning to the other is sentimental and does not correspond to the compression of life today is a grotesque error, just as his affirmation that turning to the other is impractical in the bustle of this life today is only the masked confession of his weakness of initiative when confronted with the state of the time. He lets it dictate to him what is possible or permissible, instead of stipulating, as an unruffled partner, what is to be stipulated to the state of *every* time, namely, what space and what form it is bound to concede to creaturely existence.

The basic movement of the life of monologue is not turning away as opposed to turning towards; it is "reflexion".

When I was eleven years of age, spending the summer on my grandparents' estate, I used, as often as I could do it unobserved, to steal into the stable and gently stroke the neck of my darling, a broad dapple-grey horse. It was not a casual delight but a great, certainly friendly, but also deeply stirring happening. If I am to explain it now, beginning from the still very fresh memory of my hand, I must say that what I experienced in touch with the animal was the Other, the immense otherness of the Other, which, however, did not remain strange like the otherness of the ox and the ram, but rather let me draw near and touch it. When I stroked the mighty mane, sometimes marvellously smooth-combed, at other times just as astonishingly wild, and felt the life beneath my hand, it was as though the element of vitality itself bordered on my skin, something that was not I, was certainly not akin to me, palpably the other, not just another, really the Other itself; and yet it let me approach, confided itself to me, placed itself elementally in the relation of *Thou* and *Thou* with me. The horse, even when I had not begun by pouring oats for him into the manger, very gently raised his massive head, ears flicking, then snorted quietly, as a conspirator gives a signal meant to be recognizable only by his fellow-conspirator; and I was approved. But once—I do not know what came over the child, at any rate it was childlike enough—it struck me about the stroking, what fun it gave me, and suddenly I became conscious of my hand. The game went on as before, but something had changed, it was no longer the same thing. And the next day, after giving him a rich feed, when I stroked my friend's head he did not raise his head. A few years later, when I thought back to the incident, I no longer supposed that the animal had noticed my defection. But at the time I considered myself judged.

Reflexion is something different from egoism and even from "egotism". It is not that a man is concerned with himself, considers himself, fingers himself, enjoys, idolizes and bemoans himself; all that can be added, but it is not integral to reflexion. (Similarly, to the turning towards the

other, completing it, there can be added the realizing of
the other in his particular existence, even the encompassing
of him, so that the situations common to him and oneself
are experienced also from his, the other's, end.) I term it
reflexion when a man withdraws from accepting with his
essential being another person in his particularity—a particularity which is by no means to be circumscribed by the
circle of his own self, and though it substantially touches
and moves his soul is in no way immanent in it—and lets
the other exist only as his own experience, only as a "part
of myself". For then dialogue becomes a fiction, the mysterious intercourse between two human worlds only a game,
and in the rejection of the real life confronting him the essence of all reality begins to disintegrate.

THE WORDLESS DEPTHS

Sometimes I hear it said that every *I and Thou* is only
superficial, deep down word and response cease to exist,
there is only the one primal being unconfronted by another. We should plunge into the silent unity, but for the
rest leave its relativity to the life to be lived, instead of imposing on it this absolutized *I* and absolutized *Thou* with
their dialogue.

Now from my own unforgettable experience I know well
that there is a state in which the bonds of the personal nature of life seem to have fallen away from us and we experience an undivided unity. But I do not know—what the
soul willingly imagines and indeed is bound to imagine
(mine too once did it)—that in this I had attained to a
union with the primal being or the godhead. That is an
exaggeration no longer permitted to the responsible understanding. Responsibly—that is, as a man holding his ground
before reality—I can elicit from those experiences only that
in them I reached an undifferentiable unity of myself
without form or content. I may call this an original pre-

biographical unity and suppose that it is hidden unchanged
beneath all biographical change, all development and com-
plication of the soul. Nevertheless, in the honest and sober
account of the responsible understanding this unity is nothing but the unity of this soul of mine, whose "ground" I
have reached, so much so, beneath all formations and contents, that my spirit has no choice but to understand it as
the groundless. But the basic unity of my own soul is certainly beyond the reach of all the multiplicity it has hitherto
received from life, though not in the least beyond individuation, or the multiplicity of all the souls in the world of
which it is one—existing but once, single, unique, irreducible, this creaturely one: one of the human souls and not
the "soul of the All"; a defined and particular being and
not "Being"; the creaturely basic unity of a creature, bound
to God as in the instant before release the creature is to the
creator spiritus, not bound to God as the creature to the
creator spiritus in the moment of release.

The unity of his own self is not distinguishable in the
man's feeling from unity in general. For he who in the
act or event of absorption is sunk beneath the realm of all
multiplicity that holds sway in the soul cannot experience
the cessation of multiplicity except as unity itself. That is,
he experiences the cessation of his own multiplicity as the
cessation of mutuality, as revealed or fulfilled absence of
otherness. The being which has become one can no longer
understand itself on this side of individuation nor indeed
on this side of *I and Thou.* For to the border experience
of the soul "one" must apparently mean the same as "the
One".

But in the actuality of lived life the man in such a moment is not above but beneath the creaturely situation,
which is mightier and truer than all ecstasies. He is not
above but beneath dialogue. He is not nearer the God who
is hidden above *I and Thou,* and he is farther from the God
who is turned to men and who gives himself as the *I* to a

Thou and the *Thou* to an *I*, than that other who in prayer
and service and life does not step out of the position of
confrontation and awaits no wordless unity, except that
which perhaps bodily death discloses.

Nevertheless, even he who lives the life of dialogue
knows a lived unity: the unity of *life,* as that which once
truly won is no more torn by any changes, not ripped asunder into the everyday creaturely life and the "deified" exalted hours; the unity of unbroken, raptureless persever-
ance in concreteness, in which the word is heard and a
stammering answer dared.

OF THINKING

To all unprejudiced reflection it is clear that all *art* is
from its origin essentially of the nature of dialogue. All
music calls to an ear not the musician's own, all sculpture
to an eye not the sculptor's, architecture in addition calls
to the step as it walks in the building. They all say, to him
who receives them, something (not a "feeling" but a perceived mystery) that can be said only in this one language.
But there seems to cling to *thought* something of the life of
monologue to which communication takes a second, secondary place. Thought seems to arise in monologue. Is it
so? Is there here—where, as the philosophers say, pure subject separates itself from the concrete person in order to
establish and stabilize a world for itself—a citadel which
rises towering over the life of dialogue, inaccessible to it, in
which man-with-himself, the single one, suffers and tri-
umphs in glorious solitude?

Plato has repeatedly called thinking a voiceless colloquy
of the soul with itself. Everyone who has really thought
knows that within this remarkable process there is a stage
at which an "inner" court is questioned and replies. But
that is not the arising of the thought but the first trying
and testing of what has arisen. The arising of the thought

does not take place in colloquy with oneself. The character of monologue does not belong to the insight into a basic relation with which cognitive thought begins; nor to the grasping, limiting and compressing of the insight; nor to its moulding into the independent conceptual form; nor to the reception of this form, with the bestowal of relations, the dovetailing and soldering, into an order of conceptual forms; nor, finally, to the expression and clarification in language (which till now had only a technical and reserved symbolic function). Rather are elements of dialogue to be discovered here. It is not himself that the thinker addresses in the stages of the thought's growth, in their answerings, but as it were the basic relation in face of which he has to answer for his insight, or the order in face of which he has to answer for the newly arrived conceptual form. And it is a misunderstanding of the dynamic of the event of thought to suppose that these apostrophizings of a being existing in nature or in ideas are "really" colloquies with the self.

But also the first trying and testing of the thought, when it is provisionally completed, before the "inner" court, in the platonic sense the stage of monologue, has besides the familiar form of its appearance another form in which dialogue plays a great part, well-known to Plato if to anyone. There he who is approached for judgment is not the empirical self but the *genius,* the spirit I am intended to become, the image-self, before which the new thought is borne for approval, that is, for taking up into its own consummating thinking.

And now from another dimension which even this lease of power does not satisfy there appears the longing for a trying and testing in the sphere of pure dialogue. Here the function of receiving is no longer given over to the *Thou-I* but to a genuine *Thou* which either remains one that is thought and yet is felt as supremely living and "other", or else is embodied in an intimate person. "Man", says Wilhelm von Humboldt in his significant treatise on *The Dual Number* (1827), "longs even for the sake of his mere thinking for a *Thou* corresponding to the *I*. The conception appears to him to reach its definiteness and certainty only when it reflects from another power of thought. It is produced by being torn away from the moving mass of representation and shaped in face of the subject into the object. But the objectivity appears in a still more complete form if this separation does not go on in the subject alone, if he really sees the thought outside himself; and this is possible only in another being, representing and thinking like himself. And between one power of thought and another there is no other mediator but speech." This reference, simplified to an aphorism, recurs with Ludwig Feuerbach in 1843: "True dialectic is not a monologue of the solitary thinker with himself, it is a dialogue between *I* and *Thou*."

But this saying points beyond that "reflecting" to the fact that even in the original stage of the proper act of thought the inner action might take place in relation to a genuine and not merely an "inward" (Novalis) *Thou*. And where modern philosophy is most earnest in the desire to ask its questions on the basis of human existence, situation and present, in some modifications an important further step is taken. Here it is certainly no longer just that the *Thou* is ready to receive and disposed to philosophize along with the *I*. Rather, and pre-eminently, we have the *Thou* in opposition because we truly have the other who thinks other things in another way. So, too, it is not a matter of a game of draughts in the tower of a castle in the air, but of the binding business of life on the hard earth, in which one is inexorably aware of the otherness of the other but does not at all contest it without realizing it; one takes up its nature into one's own thinking, thinks in relation to it, addresses it in thought.

This man of modern philosophy, however, who in this way no longer thinks in the untouchable province of pure ideation, but thinks in reality—does he think in reality? Not solely in a reality framed by thought? Is the other, whom he accepts and receives in this way, not solely the other framed by thought, and therefore unreal? Does the thinker of whom we are speaking hold his own with the bodily fact of otherness?

If we are serious about thinking between *I* and *Thou* then it is not enough to cast our thoughts towards the other subject of thought framed by thought. We should also, with the thinking, precisely with the thinking, live towards the other man, who is not framed by thought but bodily present before us; we should live towards his concrete life. We should live not towards another thinker of whom we wish to know nothing beyond his thinking but, even if the other is a thinker, towards his bodily life over and above his thinking—rather, towards his person, to which, to be sure, the activity of thinking also belongs.

When will the action of thinking endure, include, and refer to the presence of the living man facing us? When will the dialectic of thought become dialogic, an unsentimental, unrelaxed dialogue in the strict terms of thought with the man present at the moment?

EROS

The Greeks distinguished between a powerful, world-begetting Eros and one which was light and whose sphere was the soul; and also between a heavenly and a profane Eros. Neither seems to me to indicate an absolute distinction. For the primal god Desire from whom the world is derived, is the very one who in the form of a "tender elfin spirit" (Jacob Grimm) enters into the sphere of souls and in an arbitrary daimonic way carries out here, as mediator of the pollination of being, his cosmogonic work: he is the great pollen-bearing butterfly of psychogenesis. And the Pandemos (assuming it is a genuine Eros and not a Priapos

impudently pretending to be the higher one) needs only to
stir his wings to let the primal fire be revealed in the body's
games.

Of course, the matter in question is whether Eros has
not forfeited the power of flight and is now condemned to
live among tough mortals and govern their mortality's
paltry gestures of love. For the souls of lovers do to one
another what they do; but lame-winged beneath the rule of
the lame-winged one (for his power and powerlessness are
always shown in theirs) they cower where they are, each
in his den, instead of soaring out each to the beloved partner
and there, in the beyond which has come near, "knowing".

Those who are loyal to the strong-winged Eros of dialogue know the beloved being. They experience his particular life in simple presence—not as a thing seen and touched,
but from the innervations to his movements, from the
"inner" to his "outer". But by this I mean nothing but the
bipolar experience, and—more than a swinging over and
away in the instant—a contemporaneity at rest. That inclination of the head over there—you feel how the soul enjoins it on the neck, you feel it not on your neck but on
that one over there, on the beloved one, and yet you yourself are not as it were snatched away, you are here, in the
feeling self-being, and you receive the inclination of the
head, its injunction, as the answer to the word of your own
silence. In contemporaneity at rest you make and you experience dialogue. The two who are loyal to the Eros of
dialogue, who love one another, receive the common event
from the other's side as well, that is, they receive it from
the two sides, and thus for the first time understand in a
bodily way what an event is.

The kingdom of the lame-winged Eros is a world of mirrors and mirrorings. But where the winged one holds sway
there is no mirroring. For there I, the lover, turn to this
other human being, the beloved, in his otherness, his independence, his self-reality, and turn to him with all the

power of intention of my own heart. I certainly turn to him as to one who is there turning to me, but in that very reality, not comprehensible by me but rather comprehending me, in which I am there turning to him. I do not assimilate into my own soul that which lives and faces me, I vow it faithfully to myself and myself to it, I vow, I have faith.

The Eros of dialogue has the simplicity of fulness; the Eros of monologue is manifold. Many years I have wandered through the land of men, and have not yet reached an end of studying the varieties of the "erotic man" (as the vassal of the broken-winged one at times describes himself). There a lover stamps around and is in love only with his passion. There one is wearing his differentiated feelings like medal-ribbons. There one is enjoying the adventures of his own fascinating effect. There one is gazing enraptured at the spectacle of his own supposed surrender. There one is collecting excitement. There one is displaying his "power". There one is preening himself with borrowed vitality. There one is delighting to exist simultaneously as himself and as an idol very unlike himself. There one is warming himself at the blaze of what has fallen to his lot. There one is experimenting. And so on and on—all the manifold monologists with their mirrors, in the apartment of the most intimate dialogue!

I have spoken of the small fry, but I have had more in mind the leviathans. There are some who stipulate to the object they propose to devour that both the doing as a holy right and the suffering as a sacred duty are what is to be called heroic love. I know of "leaders" who with their grip not only cast into confusion the plasma of the growing human being but also disintegrate it radically, so that it can no longer be moulded. They relish this power of their influence, and at the same time deceive themselves and their herd into imagining they are moulders of youthful souls, and call on Eros, who is inaccessible to the *profanum vulgus*, as the tutelary god of this work.

They are all beating the air. Only he who himself turns
to the other human being and opens himself to him receives
the world in him. Only the being whose otherness, accepted by my being, lives and faces me in the whole compression of existence, brings the radiance of eternity to me.
Only when two say to one another with all that they are,
"It is *Thou*", is the indwelling of the Present Being between
them.

COMMUNITY

In the view customary to-day, which is defined by politics, the only important thing in groups, in the present as in
history, is what they aim at and what they accomplish.
Significance is ascribed to what goes on within them only
in so far as it influences the group's action with regard to
its aim. Thus it is conceded to a band conspiring to conquer the state power that the comradeship which fills it is
of value, just because it strengthens the band's reliable as-
sault power. Precise obedience will do as well, if enthusiastic
drill makes up for the associates remaining strangers to one
another; there are indeed good grounds for preferring the
rigid system. If the group is striving even to reach a higher
form of society then it can seem dangerous if in the life of
the group itself something of this higher form begins to be
realized in embryo. For from such a premature seriousness
a suppression of the "effective" impetus is feared. The opinion apparently is that the man who whiles away his time
as a guest on an oasis may be accounted lost for the project
of irrigating the Sahara.

By this simplified mode of valuation the real and individual worth of a group remains as uncomprehended as
when we judge a person by his effect alone and not by his
qualities. The perversion of thought grows when chatter is
added about sacrifice of being, about renunciation of self-
realization, where possible with a reference to the favourite

metaphor of the dung. Happiness, possession, power, authority, life can be renounced, but sacrifice of being is a sublime absurdity. And no moment, if it has to vouch for its relation to reality, can call upon any kind of later, future moments for whose sake, in order to make them fat, it has remained so lean.

The feeling of community does not reign where the desired change of institutions is wrested in common, but without community, from a resisting world. It reigns where the fight that is fought takes place from the position of a community struggling for its own reality as a community. But the future too is decided here at the same time; all political "achievements" are at best auxiliary troops to the effect which changes the very core, and which is wrought on the unsurveyable ways of secret history by the moment of realization. No way leads to any other goal but to that which is like it.

But who in all these massed, mingled, marching collectivities still perceives what that is for which he supposes he is striving—what community is? They have all surrendered to its counterpart. Collectivity is not a binding but a bundling together: individuals packed together, armed and equipped in common, with only as much life from man to man as will inflame the marching step. But community, growing community (which is all we have known so far) is the being no longer side by side but *with* one another of a multitude of persons. And this multitude, though it also moves towards one goal, yet experiences everywhere a turning to, a dynamic facing of, the other, a flowing from *I* to *Thou*. Community is where community happens. Collectivity is based on an organized atrophy of personal existence, community on its increase and confirmation in life lived towards one other. The modern zeal for collectivity is a flight from community's testing and consecration of the person, a flight from the vital dialogic, demanding the staking of the self, which is in the heart of the world.

The men of the "collective" look down superciliously on the "sentimentality" of the generation before them, of the age of the "youth movement". Then the concern, wide-ranging and deeply-pondered, was with the problem of all life's relations, "community" was aimed at and made a problem at the same time. They went round in circles and never left the mark. But now there is commanding and marching, for now there is the "cause". The false paths of subjectivity have been left behind and the road of objectivism, going straight for its goal, has been reached. But as there existed a pseudo-subjectivity with the former, since the elementary force of being a subject was lacking, so with the latter there exists a pseudo-objectivism, since one is here fitted not into a world but into a worldless faction. As in the former all songs in praise of freedom were sung into the void, because only freeing from bonds was known, but not freeing to responsibility, so in the latter even the noblest hymns on authority are a misunderstanding. For in fact they strengthen only the semblance of authority which has been won by speeches and cries; behind this authority is hidden an absence of consistency draped in the mighty folds of the attitude. But genuine authority, celebrated in those hymns, the authority of the genuine charismatic in his steady re-sponse to the lord of Charis, has remained unknown to the political sphere of the present. Superficially the two gen-erations are different in kind to the extent of contradiction, in truth they are stuck in the same chaotic condition. The man of the youth movement, pondering his problems, was concerned (whatever the particular matter at different times) with his very own share in it, he "experienced" his *I* without pledging a self—in order not to have to pledge a self in response and responsibility. The man of the collective undertaking, striding to action, succeeded beforehand in getting rid of himself and thus radically escaping the ques-tion of pledging a self. Progress is nevertheless to be re-corded. With the former monologue presented itself as dialogue. With the latter it is considerably simpler, for the life of monologue is by their desire driven out from most men, or they are broken of the habit; and the others, who give the orders, have at least no need to feign any dialogic.

Dialogue and monologue are silenced. Bundled together, men march without *Thou* and without *I*, those of the left who want to abolish memory, and those of the right who want to regulate it: hostile and separated hosts, they march into the common abyss.

SECTION THREE: CONFIRMATION

CONVERSATION WITH THE OPPONENT

I hope for two kinds of readers for these thoughts: for the *amicus* who knows about the reality to which I am pointing with a finger I should like to be able to stretch out like Grünewald's Baptist; and for the *hostis* or *adversarius* who denies this reality and therefore contends with me, because I point to it (in his view misleadingly) as to a reality. Thus he takes what is said here just as seriously as I myself do, after long waiting writing what is to be written—just as seriously, only with the negative sign. The mere *inimicus*, as which I regard everyone who wishes to relegate me to the realm of ideology and there let my thoughts count, I would gladly dispense with.

I need say nothing at this point to the *amicus*. The hour of common mortality and the common way strikes in his and in my ears as though we stood even in the same place with one another and knew one another.

But it is not enough to tell the *adversarius* here what I am pointing at—the hiddenness of his personal life, his secret, and that, stepping over a carefully avoided threshold, he will discover what he denies. It is not enough. I dare not turn aside his gravest objection. I must accept it, as and where it is raised, and must answer.

So now the *adversarius* sits, facing me in his actual form as he appears in accordance with the spirit of the time, and speaks, more above and beyond me than towards and to me, in accents and attitude customary in the universal duel, free of personal relation.

"In all this the actuality of our present life, the conditioned nature of life as a whole, is not taken into account. All that you speak of takes place in the never-never-land, not in the social context of the world in which we spend our days, and by which if by anything our reality is defined. Your 'two men' sit on a solitary seat, obviously during a holiday journey. In a big city office you would not be able to let them sit, they would not reach the 'sacramental' there. Your 'interrupted conversation' takes place between intellectuals who have leisure a couple of months before the huge mass event to spin fantasies of its prevention through a spiritual influence. That may be quite interesting for people who are not taken up with any duty. But is the business employee to 'communicate himself without reserve' to his colleagues? Is the worker at the conveyor belt to 'feel himself addressed in what he experiences'? Is the leader of a gigantic technical undertaking to 'practise the responsibility of dialogue'? You demand that we enter into the situation which approaches us, and you neglect the enduring situation in which every one of us, so far as we share in the life of community, is elementally placed. In spite of all references to concreteness, all that is pre-war individualism in a revised edition."

And I, out of a deep consciousness of how almost impossible it is to think in common, if only in opposition, where there is no common experience, reply.

Before all, dear opponent, if we are to converse with one another and not at and past one another, I beg you to notice that I do not demand. I have no call to that and no authority for it. I try only to say that there is something, and to indicate how it is made: I simply record. And how could the life of dialogue be demanded? There is no ordering of dialogue. It is not that you *are* to answer but that you *are able*.

You are really able. The life of dialogue is no privilege of intellectual activity like dialectic. It does not begin in the upper story of humanity. It begins no higher than where humanity begins. There are no gifted and ungifted here, only those who give themselves and those who withhold themselves. And he who gives himself to-morrow is not noted to-day, even he himself does not know that he has it in himself, that we have it in ourselves, he will just find it, "and finding be amazed".

You put before me the man taken up with duty and business. Yes, precisely him I mean, him in the factory, in the shop, in the office, in the mine, on the tractor, at the printing-press: man. I do not seek for men. I do not seek men out for myself, I accept those who are there, I have them, I have him, in mind, the yoked, the wheel-treading, the conditioned. Dialogue is not an affair of spiritual luxury and spiritual luxuriousness, it is a matter of creation, of the creature, and he is that, the man of whom I speak, he is a creature, trivial and irreplaceable.

In my thoughts about the life of dialogue I have had to choose the examples as "purely" and as much in the form of paradigm as memory presented them to me in order to make myself intelligible about what has become so unfamiliar, in fact so sunk in oblivion. For this reason I appear to draw my tales from the province which you term the "intellectual", in reality only from the province where things succeed, are rounded off, in fact are exemplary. But I am not concerned with the pure; I am concerned with the turbid, the repressed, the pedestrian, with toil and dull contraryness—and with the break-through. With the break-through and not with a perfection, and moreover with the

break-through not out of despair with its murderous and re-
newing powers; no, not with the great catastrophic break-
through which happens once for all (it is fitting to be silent
for a while about that, even in one's own heart), but with
the breaking through from the status of the dully-tempered
disagreeableness, obstinacy, and contraryness in which the
man, whom I pluck at random out of the tumult, is living
and out of which he can and at times does break through.

Whither? Into nothing exalted, heroic or holy, into no
Either and no Or, only into this tiny strictness and grace of
every day, where I have to do with just the very same
"reality" with whose duty and business I am taken up in
such a way, glance to glance, look to look, word to word,
that I experience it as reached to me and myself to it, it as
spoken to me and myself to it. And now, in all the clank-
ing of routine that I called my reality, there appears to me,
homely and glorious, the effective reality, creaturely and
given to me in trust and responsibility. We do not find
meaning lying in things nor do we put it into things, but
between us and things it can happen.

It is not sufficient, dear opponent, first of all to ascribe to
me the pathos of "all or nothing" and then to prove the
impossibility of my alleged demand. I know neither what all
nor what nothing is, the one appears to me to be as inhu-
man and contrived as the other. What I am meaning is the
simple *quantum satis* of that which this man in this hour
of his life is able to fulfil and to receive—if he gives himself. That is, if he does not let himself be deceived by the
compact plausibility that there are places excluded from
creation, that he works in such a place and is able to return to creation when his shift is over; or that creation is
outstripped, that it once was but is irrevocably over, now
there is business and now it is a case of stripping off all
romanticism, gritting the teeth and getting through with
what is recognized as necessary. I say—if he does not let
himself be deceived.

No factory and no office is so abandoned by creation that a creative glance could not fly up from one working-place to another, from desk to desk, a sober and brotherly glance which guarantees the reality of creation which is happening—*quantum satis*. And nothing is so valuable a service of dialogue between God and man as such an unsentimental and unreserved exchange of glances between two men in an alien place.

But is it irrevocably an alien place? Must henceforth, through all the world's ages, the life of the being which is yoked to business be divided in two, into alien "work" and home "recovery"? More, since evenings and Sundays cannot be freed of the workday character but are unavoidably stamped with it, must such a life be divided out between the business of work and the business of recovery without a remainder of directness, of unregulated surplus—of freedom? (And the freedom I mean is established by no new order of society.)

Or does there already stir, beneath all dissatisfactions that can be satisfied, an unknown and primal and deep dissatisfaction for which there is as yet no recipe of satisfaction anywhere, but which will grow to such mightiness that it dictates to the technical leaders, the promoters, the inventors, and says, "Go on with your rationalizing, but humanize the rationalizing *ratio* in yourselves. Let it introduce the living man into its purposes and its calculations, him who longs to stand in a mutual relation with the world." Dear opponent, does the longing already stir in the depths—an impulse to great construction or a tiny spark of the last revolution—to fill business with the life of dialogue? That is, in the formulation of the *quantum satis*, the longing for an order of work in which business is so continually soaked in vital dialogic as the tasks to be fulfilled by it allow? And of the extent to which they can allow it there is scarcely an inkling to-day, in an hour when the question which I put is at the mercy of the fanatics, blind to reality, who conform to the time, and of the heralds, blind to possibility, of the impervious tragedy of the world.

Be clear what it means when a worker can experience even his relation to the machine as one of dialogue, when, for instance, a compositor tells that he has understood the machine's humming as "a merry and grateful smile at me for helping it to set aside the difficulties and obstructions which disturbed and bruised and pained it, so that now it could run free". Must even you not think then of the story of Androcles and the Lion?

But when a man draws a lifeless thing into his passionate longing for dialogue, lending it independence and as it were a soul, then there may dawn in him the presentiment of a world-wide dialogue, a dialogue with the world-happening that steps up to him even in his environment, which consists partly of things. Or do you seriously think that the giving and taking of signs halts on the threshold of that business where an honest and open spirit is found?

You ask with a laugh, can the leader of a great technical undertaking practise the responsibility of dialogue? He can. For he practises it when he makes present to himself in its concreteness, so far as he can, *quantum satis,* the business which he leads. He practises it when he experiences it, instead of as a structure of mechanical centres of force and their organic servants (among which latter there is for him no differentiation but the functional one), as an association of persons with faces and names and biographies, bound together by a work that is represented by, but does not consist of, the achievements of a complicated mechanism. He practises it when he is inwardly aware, with a latent and disciplined fantasy, of the multitude of these persons, whom naturally he cannot separately know and remember as such; so that now, when one of them for some reason or other steps really as an individual into the circle of his vision and the realm of his decision, he is aware of him without strain not as a number with a human mask but as a person. He practises it when he comprehends and handles these persons as persons—for the greatest part necessarily indirectly, by means of a system of mediation which varies according to the extent, nature and structure of the undertaking, but also directly, in the parts which concern him by way of organization. Naturally at first both camps, that of capital and that of the proletariat, will decry his masterly attitude of fantasy as fantastic nonsense and his practical attitude to persons as dilettantist. But just as naturally only until his increased figures of production accredit him in their eyes. (By this of course is not to be implied that those increases necessarily come to pass: between truth and success there is no pre-stabilized harmony.) Then, to be sure, something worse will follow. He will be pragmatically imitated, that is, people will try to use his "procedure" without his way of thinking and imagining. But this demoniac element inherent in spiritual history (think only of all the magicizing of religion) will, I think, shipwreck here on the power of discrimination in men's souls. And meanwhile it is to be hoped that a new generation will arise, learning from what is alive, and will take all this in real seriousness as he does.

Unmistakably men are more and more determined by "circumstances". Not only the absolute mass but also the relative might of social objectives is growing. As one determined partially by them the individual stands in each moment before concrete reality which wishes to reach out to him and receive an answer from him; laden with the situation he meets new situations. And yet in all the multiplicity and complexity he has remained Adam. Even now a real decision is made in him, whether he faces the speech of God articulated to him in things and events—or escapes. And a creative glance towards his fellow-creature can at times suffice for response.

Man is in a growing measure sociologically determined. But this growing is the maturing of a task not in the "ought" but in the "may" and in "need", in longing and in grace. It is a matter of renouncing the pantechnical mania or habit with its easy "mastery" of every situation; of taking everything up into the might of dialogue of the genuine life, from the trivial mysteries of everyday to the majesty of destructive destiny.

The task becomes more and more difficult, and more and more essential, the fulfilment more and more impeded and more and more rich in decision. All the regulated chaos of the age waits for the break-through, and wherever a man perceives and responds, he is working to that end.

The Dialogue between Heaven and Earth

The most important of all that the biblical view of existence has opened up for all times is clearly recognized by a comparison of Israel's Holy Writ with those holy books of the nations that originated independently of it. None of those books is, like it, full of a dialogue between Heaven and earth. It tells us how again and again God addresses man and is addressed by him. God announces to man what plan He has for the world; as the earliest of the book prophets puts it (Amos 4.13), God lets him know "his soliloquy," He discloses to him His will and calls upon him to take part in its realization. But man is no blind tool, he was created as a free being, free also vis-à-vis God, free to surrender to Him or to refuse himself to Him. To God's sovereign address, man gives his autonomous answer; if he remains silent, his silence, too, is an answer. Very often we hear God's voice alone, as in the prophetical books, for the most part, where only in isolated cases—in certain accounts of visions, or in the diary-like records of Jeremiah—the prophet's reply becomes articulate, and sometimes these records actually

(From Martin Buber, *At the Turning: Three Addresses on Judaism* [Farrar, Straus, and Young, 1952], Third Address, pp. 47–62.)

assume a dialogic form; but even in all those passages where God alone speaks we are made to feel that the person addressed by Him answers with his wordless soul, that is to say, that he stands in the dialogic situation. And again, very often we hear the voice of man alone, as generally in the Psalms, where only in isolated cases the worshipper indicates the divine reply; but here, too, the dialogic situation is apparent; it is apparent to us that man, lamenting, suppliant, thanksgiving, praise-singing man, experiences himself as heard and understood, accepted and confirmed, by Him to Whom he addresses himself. The basic doctrine which fills the Hebrew Bible is that our life is a dialogue between the above and the below.

But does this still apply to our present-day life? Believers and unbelievers deny it. A view common among believers is that though everything contained in Scripture is literally true, though God did certainly speak to the men chosen by Him, yet, since then, the holy spirit has been taken from us, heaven is silent to us, and only through the books of the written and oral tradition is God's will made known to us as to what we shall do or not do; certainly, even today, the worshipper stands immediately before his Creator, but how could he dare, like the Psalmist, to report to the world words of personal reply, of personal granting as spoken immediately to him? And as for the unbelievers, it goes without saying that the atheists need not be mentioned at all, but only the adherents of a more or less philosophic God-concept, with which they cannot reconcile the idea of God's addressing, and being addressed by, man; to them, the entire dialogics of Scripture is nothing but a mythical figment, instructive from the point of view of the history of the human mind, but inapplicable to our life.

As against either opinion, a faithful and unprepossessed reader of Scripture must endorse the view he has learnt from it: what happened once happens now and always, and the fact of its happening to us is a guarantee of its having happened. The Bible has, in the form of a glorified remembrance, given vivid, decisive expression to an ever-recurrent happening. In the infinite language of events and situations, eternally changing, but plain to the truly attentive, transcendence speaks to our hearts at the essential moments of personal life. And there is a language in which we can answer it; it is the language of our actions and attitudes, our reactions and our abstentions; the totality of these answers is what we may call our answering-for-ourselves in the most proper sense of the expression. This fundamental interpretation of our existence we owe to the Hebrew Bible; and whenever we truly read it, our self-understanding is renewed and deepened.

II

But in Scripture, not only the individual, the community too, is addressed from above, in such a manner as is found in no other of the holy books of mankind.

Here the people, as a people, confronts God and receives, as a people, His never-ceasing instruction. It, too, like the individual, is called upon to participate in the realization of the divine will on earth. Just as the individual is to hallow himself in his personal life, the people is to hallow itself in its communal life; it is to become a "holy people." Like the individual, it is free as to its answer to the divine call, free to say yes or no to God by its doing and its not-doing. The people is not a sum of individuals addressed by God, it is something existent beyond that, something essential and irreplaceable, meant by God as such, claimed by Him as such, and answerable to Him as such. God leads it and requires it to follow his sole leadership. He has created not only man as an individual, men as individuals, but also the human peoples; and He uses them, like the former, for His purpose, for the completion of His world-creation. He takes care of them in their history; not only Israel but all peoples are, as the prophet proclaims, led by Him to freedom when enslaved by other peoples, and in freedom they shall serve Him, as peoples, each in its own way and according to its own character. Though He reprimands Israel with especial severity because, contrary to its mandate, it has not fulfilled divine justice in the life of the community, yet He reprimands the other peoples as well, because they, who are also His children, do not act toward each other as brothers should. Some day, however, so the prophecy runs (Isa. 2), the representatives of all of them will crowd round Mount Moriah and there, as Israel once did, alone, at Mount Sinai, receive that divine instruction on the great peace between the peoples. "The noble ones of the peoples are gathered together," so the Psalmist says (Ps. 47.10), "as the people of the God of Abraham"—of Abraham, who is called "the father of a multitude of nations," a description meaning more than genealogy. Since world history is the advance of the peoples toward this goal, it is, essentially, holy history.

This is also why in Scripture the divine voice addresses man not as an isolated individual but always as an individual member of the people. Even before there is a people of Israel, its father-to-be, Abraham, is addressed as such: he is to become "a blessing" in his seed. And in the legislation, both in the Decalogue and in the injunctions supplementing it, God again and again addresses Himself to a "thou" which is certainly the "thou" of each individual in each generation of the people, but as conceived in his connection with the people, at whose communal life that legislation is aimed, so that everyone, when a commandment conveys to him the will of God with regard to his own life, conceives himself as the individual condensation of the people. This basic view unfolds itself up to the highest level of human existence: "Thou art my servant, the Israel in whom I will be glorified," says God (Isa. 49) to His elect:

the man who fulfills the mandate given to the people em-
bodies the truth of the people's existence.

From here, modern life, both of peoples and of persons,
is judged and its sentence passed. This life is split in two:
what is thought reprehensible in the relations between persons is thought commendable in the relations between peoples. This is contrary to the prophetic demand: the prophet
(Amos 1.2) accuses a people of sinning against another
people because it "remembered not the brotherly cove-
nant." But that split naturally continues into the life of
modern man as an individual: his existence is divided into
a private and a public one, which are governed by very
different laws. What he disapproves, in his fellow man and
in himself, in the former sphere, he approves, in his fellow
man and in himself, in the latter: lying degrades the private
person, but it well befits the political partisan, provided that
it is practiced skillfully and successfully. This duality of
moral values is intolerable from the point of view of biblical
faith: here, deceit is under all circumstances regarded as
disgraceful (also, e.g., in the case of the patriarchs, as we
see from the prophetical criticism of Jacob and from some
other indications), even if it is prompted by a desire to promote the cause of justice; in fact, in the latter case, it is the
more pernicious, since it poisons and disintegrates the good
which it is supposed to serve.

If the first biblical axiom is: "Man is addressed by God
in his life," the second is: "The life of man is meant by
God as a unit."

III

As we have seen, in the biblical conception of existence
God addresses the human person and the human people
with a view to what shall be, what shall be realized through
this person, through this people. This means that man is
placed in freedom and that every hour in which he, in his

current situation, feels himself to be addressed is an hour of genuine decision. In the first instance, of course, he decides only upon his own behavior, but by doing so he participates, in a measure which he is neither able nor authorized to determine, in the decision upon what the next hour will be like, and through this upon what the future generally will be like.

It is from here that the great biblical phenomenon of prophecy must be understood. The essential task of the prophets of Israel was not to foretell an already determined future, but to confront man and people in Israel, at each given moment, with the alternative that corresponded to the situation. It was not announced what would happen under any circumstances, but what would happen if the hearers of the message realized God's will, and what would happen if they refused themselves to its realization. The divine voice chose the prophet, as it were, for its "mouth," in order to bring home to man again and again, in the most immediate fashion, his freedom and its consequences. Even when the prophet did not speak in alternative form, but announced unconditionally that after such and such a time the catastrophe would happen, this announcement—as we learn from the paradigmatic Book of Jonah—nevertheless contained a hidden alternative: the people is driven into despair, but in precisely this state kindles the spark of "turning": the people turns to God—and is saved. By an extreme threat to existence, man is stirred to the depths of his soul and brought to a radical decision for God, but this his decision is at the same time a fateful decision in the strictest sense.

Postbiblical thinkers have pondered how the freedom of the human will and the resultant indetermination of the future can be reconciled with divine foresight and predetermination. Outstanding among all that has been said in the effort to overcome this contradiction is the well-known saying of Akiba's ("All is surveyed, and the power is given"), whose meaning is that to God, Who sees them together, the times do not appear in succession but in progress-less eternity, while in the progression of times, in which man lives, freedom reigns, at any given time, in the concrete moment of decision; beyond that, human wisdom has not attained. In the Bible itself, there is no pondering; it does not deal with the essence of God but with His manifestation to mankind; the reality of which it treats is that of the human world, and in it, the immutable truth of decision applies.

For guilty man, this means the decision to turn from his wrong way to the way of God. Here we see most clearly what it means in the biblical view that our answering-for-ourselves is essentially our answering to a divine address. The two great examples are Cain and David. Both have murdered (for so the Bible understands also David's deed, since it makes God's messenger say to him that he "slew Uriah the Hittite with the sword,") and both are called to account by God. Cain attempts evasion: "Am I my brother's keeper?" He is the man who shuns the dialogue with God. Not so David. He answers: "I have sinned against the Lord." This is the true answer: whomsoever one becomes guilty against, in truth one becomes guilty against God. David is the man who acknowledges the relation between God and himself, from which his answerability arises, and realizes that he has betrayed it.

The Hebrew Bible is concerned with the terrible and merciful fact of the *immediacy* between God and ourselves. Even in the dark hour after he has become guilty against his brother, man is not abandoned to the forces of chaos. God Himself seeks him out, and even when He comes to call him to account, His coming is salvation.

IV

But there is, in the biblical view, a third, widest sphere
of divine utterance. God speaks not only to the individual
and to the community, within the limits and under the conditions of a particular biographical or historical situation.
Everything, being and becoming, nature and history, is essentially a divine pronouncement, an infinite context of signs
meant to be perceived and understood by perceiving and
understanding creatures.

But here, a fundamental difference exists between nature
and human history. Nature, as a whole and in all its elements, enunciates something that may be regarded as an
indirect self-communication of God to all those ready to
receive it. This is what the psalm means that makes Heaven
and earth "declare," wordlessly, the glory of God. Not so
human history—not only because mankind, being placed in
freedom, co-operates incessantly in shaping its course, but
quite especially because, in nature, it is God the Creator
who speaks, and His creative act is never interrupted; in
history, on the other hand, it is the revealing God that
speaks, and revelation is essentially not a continuous process, but breaks in again and again upon the course of events
and irradiates it. Nature is full of God's utterance, if one
but hears it, but what is said here is always that one,
though all-inclusive, something, that which the psalm calls
the glory of God; in history however, times of great utterance, when the mark of divine direction is recognizable in
the conjunction of events, alternate with, as it were, mute
times, when everything that occurs in the human world and
pretends to historical significance appears to us as empty of
God, with nowhere a beckoning of His finger, nowhere a
sign that He is present and acts upon this our historical
hour. In such times it is difficult for the individual, and the
more for the people, to understand themselves as addressed

by God; the experience of concrete answerability recedes more and more, because, in the seemingly Godforsaken space of history, man unlearns from taking the relationship between God and himself seriously in the dialogic sense.

In an hour when the exiles in Babylon perceived God's passage through world history, in the hour when Cyrus was about to release them and send them home, the anonymous prophet of the exile, who like none before him felt called upon to interpret the history of peoples, in one of his pamphlets (Isa. 48.16) made God say to Israel: "Never from the beginning have I spoken in secrecy." God's utterance in history is unconcealed, for it is intended to be heard by the peoples. But Isaiah, to whose book the pronouncements of the anonymous prophet have been attached, not only speaks (8.17) of a time when God "hideth His face from the house of Jacob," but he also knows (28.21) that there are times when we are unable to recognize and acknowledge God's own deeds in history as His deeds, so uncanny and "barbarous" do they seem to us. And the same chapter of the prophet of the exile (45) in which God says (v. 11): "Ask me of the things to come," states (v. 14 ff.) that in the hour of the liberation of peoples the masses whom Egypt put to forced labor and Ethiopia sold as slaves will immediately, with the chains of serfdom still on their bodies, as it were, turn to God, throw themselves down, and pray: "Verily Thou art a God That hideth Himself, O God of Israel, Saviour!" During the long periods of enslavement it seemed to them as though there were nothing divine any more and the world were irretrievably abandoned to the forces of tyranny; only now do they recognize that there is a Saviour, and that He is *one*—the Lord of History. And now they know and profess: He is a God That hides Himself, or more exactly: the God That hides Himself and reveals Himself.

The Bible knows of God's hiding His face, of times when the contact between Heaven and earth seems to be interrupted. God seems to withdraw Himself utterly from the earth and no longer to participate in its existence. The space of history is then full of noise, but, as it were, empty of the divine breath. For one who believes in the living God, who knows about Him, and is fated to spend his life in a time of His hiddenness, it is very difficult to live.

There is a Psalm, the 82nd, in which life in a time of God's hiddenness is described in a picture of startling cruelty. It is assumed that God has entrusted the government of mankind to a host of angels and commanded them to realize justice on earth and to protect the weak, the poor, and the helpless from the encroachments of the wrongdoers. But they "judge unjustly" and "lift up the face of the wicked." Now the Psalmist envisions how God draws the unfaithful angels before His seat, judges them, and passes sentence upon them: they are to become mortal. But the Psalmist awakes from his vision and looks about him: iniquity still reigns on earth with unlimited power. And he cries to God: "Arise, O God, judge the earth!"

This cry is to be understood as a late, but even more powerful, echo of that bold speech of the patriarch arguing with God: "The judge of all the earth, will he not do justice?!" It reinforces and augments that speech; its implication is: will he allow injustice to reign further? And so the cry transmitted to us by Scripture becomes our own cry, which bursts from our hearts and rises to our lips in a time of God's hiddenness. For this is what the biblical word does to us: it confronts us with the human address as one that is heard and may look forward to an answer.

In this our own time, one asks again and again: how is a Jewish life still possible after Oswiecim? I would like to frame this question more correctly: how is a life with God still possible in a time in which there is an Oswiecim? The estrangement has become too cruel, the hiddenness too deep. One can still "believe" in the God who allowed those things to happen, but can one still speak to Him? Can one still hear His word? Can one still, as an individual and as a people, enter at all into a dialogic relationship with Him? Can one still call to Him? Dare we recommend to the survivors of Oswiecim, the Job of the gas chambers: "Call to Him, for He is kind, for His mercy endurest forever"?

But how about Job himself? He not only laments, but he charges that the "cruel" (30.21) God has "removed his right" from him (27.2) and thus that the judge of all the earth acts against justice. And he receives an answer from God. But what God says to him does not answer the charge; it does not even touch upon it. The true answer that Job receives is God's appearance only, only this that distance turns into nearness, that "his eye sees Him," (42.5) that he knows Him again. Nothing is explained, nothing adjusted; wrong has not become right, nor cruelty kindness. Nothing has happened but that man again hears God's address.

The mystery has remained unsolved, but it has become his, it has become man's.

And we?

We—by that is meant all those who have not got over what happened and will not get over it. How is it with us? Do we stand overcome before the hidden face of God as the tragic hero of the Greeks before faceless fate? No, rather even now we contend, we too, with God, even with Him, the Lord of Being, Whom we once, we here, chose for our Lord. We do not put up with earthly being, we struggle for its redemption, and struggling we appeal to the help of our Lord, Who is again and still a hiding one. In such a state we await His voice, whether it come out of the storm or out of a stillness which follows it. Though His coming appearance resembles no earlier one, we shall recognize again our cruel and merciful Lord.

The Question to the
Single One

Only by coming up against the category of the "Single One", and by making it a concept of the utmost clarity, did Søren Kierkegaard become the one who presented Christianity as a paradoxical problem for the single "Christian". He was only able to do this owing to the radical nature of his solitariness. His "single one" cannot be understood without his solitariness, which differed in kind from the solitariness of one of the earlier Christian thinkers, such as Augustine or Pascal, whose name one would like to link with his. It is not irrelevant that beside Augustine stood a mother and beside Pascal a sister, who maintained the organic connexion with the world as only a woman as the envoy of elemental life can; whereas the central event of Kierkegaard's life and the core of the crystallization of his thought was the renunciation of Regina Olsen as representing woman and the world. Nor may this solitariness be compared with that of a monk or a hermit: for him the renunciation stands essentially only at the beginning, and even if it must be ever anew achieved and practised, it is not that which is the life theme, the basic problem, and the stuff out

(From Martin Buber, *Between Man and Man* [Macmillan, 1947; Beacon, 1955], Chap. II, pp. 40–58.)

of which all teaching is woven. But for Kierkegaard this is just what renunciation is. It is embodied in the category of the single one, "the category through which, from the religious standpoint, time and history and the race must pass" (Kierkegaard, 1847).

By means of an opposition we can first of all be precisely aware what the single one, in a special and specially important sense, is not. A few years before Kierkegaard outlined his *Report to History* under the title *The Point of View for my Work as an Author,* in whose *Two Notes* the category of the Single One found its adequate formulation, Max Stirner published his book about "The Unique One". This too is a border concept like the single one, but one from the other end. Stirner, a pathetic nominalist and unmasker of ideas, wanted to dissolve the alleged remains of German idealism (as which he regarded Ludwig Feuerbach) by raising not the thinking subject nor man but the concrete present individual as "the exclusive I" to be the bearer of the world, that is, of "his" world.

Here this Unique One "consuming himself" in "self-enjoyment" is the only one who has primary existence; only the man who comes to such a possession and consciousness of himself has primary existence—on account of the "unity and omnipotence of our I that is sufficient to itself, for it lets nothing be but itself". Thus the question of an essential relation between him and the other is eliminated as well. He has no essential relation except to himself (Stirner's alleged "living participation" "in the person of the other" is without essence, since the other has in his eyes no primary existence). That is, he has only that remarkable relation with the self which does not lack certain magical possibilities (since all other existence becomes the haunting of ghosts that are half in bonds, half free), but is so empty of any genuine power to enter into relation that it is better to describe as a relation only that in which not only *I* but also *Thou* can be said. This border product of a German

Protagoras is usually underrated: the loss of reality which responsibility and truth have suffered in our time has here if not its spiritual origin certainly its exact conceptual prediction. "The man who belongs to himself alone . . . is by origin free, for he acknowledges nothing but himself," and "True is what is Mine" are formulas which forecast a congealing of the soul unsuspected by Stirner in all his rhetorical assurance. But also many a rigid collective *We*, which rejects a superior authority, is easily understood as a translation from the speech of the Unique One into that of the *Group-I* which acknowledges nothing but itself—carried out against Stirner's intention, who hotly opposes any plural version.

Kierkegaard's Single One has this in common with its counterpoint, Stirner's Unique One, that both are border categories; it has no more in common than this, but also it has no less.

The category of the Single One, too, means not the subject or "man", but concrete singularity; yet not the individual who is detecting his existence, but rather the person who is finding himself. But the finding himself, however primally remote from Stirner's "utilize thyself", is not akin either to that "know thyself" which apparently troubled Kierkegaard very much. For it means a becoming, and moreover in a weight of seriousness that only became possible, at least for the West, through Christianity. It is therefore a becoming which (though Kierkegaard says that his category was used by Socrates "for the dissolution of heathendom") is decisively different from that effected by the Socratic "delivery". "No-one is excluded from being a Single One except he who excludes himself by wishing to be 'crowd'." Here not only is "Single One" opposed to "crowd", but also becoming is opposed to a particular mode of being which evades becoming. That may still be in tune with Socratic thought. But what does it mean, to become a Single One? Kierkegaard's account shows clearly that the nature of his category is no longer Socratic. It runs, "to fulfil the first condition of all religiosity" is "to be a single man". It is for this reason that the "Single One" is "the category through which, from the religious standpoint, time and history and the race must pass".

Since the concept of religiosity has since lost its definiteness, what Kierkegaard means must be more precisely defined. He cannot mean that to become a Single One is the presupposition of a condition of the soul, called religiosity. It is not a matter of a condition of the soul but a matter of existence in that strict sense in which—precisely by fulfilling the personal life—it steps in its essence over the boundary of the person. Then being, familiar being, becomes unfamiliar and no longer signifies my being but my participation in the Present Being. That this is what Kierkegaard means is expressed in the fundamental word that the Single One "corresponds" to God. In Kierkegaard's account, then, the concept "of all religiosity" has to be more precisely defined by "of all religious reality". But since this also is all too exposed to the epidemic sickening of the word in our time, by which every word is at once covered with the leprosy of routine and changed into a slogan, we must go further, as far as possible, and, giving up vexatious "religion", take a risk, but a necessary risk, and explain the phrase as meaning "of all real human dealings with God". That Kierkegaard means this is shown by his reference to a "speaking with God". And indeed a man can have dealings with God only as a Single One, as a man who has become a Single One. This is so expressed in the Old Testament, though there a people too meets the Godhead as a people, that it time and again lets only a named person, Enoch, Noah, "have dealings with Elohim". Not before a man can say *I* in perfect reality—that is, finding himself—can he in perfect reality say *Thou*—that is, to God. And even if he does it in a community he can only do it "alone". "As the 'Single One' he [every man] is alone, alone in the whole world, alone before God." That is—what Kierkegaard, strangely, does not think of—thoroughly un-Socratic: in the words "the divine gives me a sign" Socrates's "religiosity" is represented, significant for all ages; but the words "I am alone before God" are unthinkable as coming from him. Kierkegaard's "alone" is no longer of Socrates; it is of Abraham—Genesis 12. 1 and 22. 2, alike demand in the same "Go before thee" the power to free oneself of all bonds, the bonds to the world of fathers and to the world of sons; and it is of Christ.

Clarity demands a further twofold distinction. First, with respect to mysticism. It too lets the man be alone before God but not as the Single One. The relation to God which it thinks of is the absorption of the *I*, and the Single One ceases to exist if he cannot—even in devoting himself—say *I*. As mysticism will not permit God to assume the servant's form of the speaking and acting person, of a creator, of a revealer, and to tread the way of the Passion through time as the partner of history, suffering along with it all destiny, so it forbids man, as the Single One persisting as such, from really praying and serving and loving such as is possible only by an *I* to a *Thou*. Mysticism only tolerates the Single One in order that he may radically melt away. But Kierkegaard knows, at any rate in relation to God, what love is, and thus he knows that there is no self-love that is not self-deceit (since he who loves—and it is he who matters—loves only the other and essentially not himself), but that without being and remaining oneself there is no love.

The second necessary distinction is with respect to Stirner's "Unique One". (For the sake of conceptual precision this expression is to be preferred to the more humanistic ones, such as Stendhal's *égotiste*.)

A preliminary distinction must be made with respect to so-called individualism, which has also produced a "religious" variety. The Single One, the person ready and able for the "standing alone before God", is the counterpart of what still, in no distant time, was called—in a term which is treason to the spirit of Goethe—personality, and man's becoming a Single One is the counterpart of "personal development". All individualism, whether it is styled æsthetic or ethical or religious, has a cheap and ready pleasure in man provided he is "developing". In other words, "ethical" and "religious" individualism are only inflexions of the "æsthetic" (which is as little genuine *æsthesis* as those are genuine *ethos* and genuine *religio*).

Morality and piety, where they have in this way become an autonomous aim, must also be reckoned among the show-pieces and shows of a spirit that no longer knows about Being but only about its mirrorings.

Where individualism ceases to be wanton Stirner begins. He is also, it is true, concerned with the "shaping of free personality", but in the sense of a severance of the "self" from the world: he is concerned with the tearing apart of his existential bindings and bonds, with breaking free from all ontic otherness of things and of lives, which now may only serve as "nourishment" of his selfhood. The contrapuntal position of Stirner's Unique One to Kierkegaard's Single One becomes clearest when the questions of responsibility and truth are raised.

For Stirner both are bound to be false questions. But it is important to see that intending to destroy both basic ideas he has destroyed only their routine forms and thus, contrary to his whole intention, has prepared for their purification and renewal. Historically-minded contemporaries have spoken disparagingly of him as a modern sophist; since then the function of the sophists, and consequently of their like, of dissolving and preparing, has been recognized. Stirner may have understood Hegel just as little as Protagoras did Heraclitus; but even as it is meaningless to reproach Protagoras with laying waste the gardens of the great cosmologist, so Stirner is untouched by being ridiculed as the unsuspecting and profane interloper in the fields of post-

Kantian philosophy. Stirner is not, any more than the sophists are, a curious interlude in the history of human
thought. Like them he is an *epeisódion* in the original
sense. In his monologue the action secretly changes, what
follows is a new thing—as Protagoras leads towards his contemporary Socrates, Stirner leads towards his contemporary
Kierkegaard.

Responsibility presupposes one who addresses me primarily, that is, from a realm independent of myself, and to
whom I am answerable. He addresses me about something
that he has entrusted to me and that I am bound to take
care of loyally. He addresses me from his trust and I respond in my loyalty or refuse to respond in my disloyalty,
or I had fallen into disloyalty and wrestle free of it by the
loyalty of the response. To be so answerable to a trusting
person about an entrusted matter that loyalty and disloyalty
step into the light of day (but both are not of the same
right, for now loyalty, born again, is permitted to conquer
disloyalty)—this is the reality of responsibility. Where no
primary address and claim can touch me, for everything is
"My property", responsibility has become a phantom. At
the same time life's character of mutuality is dissipated. He
who ceases to make a response ceases to hear the Word.

But this reality of responsibility is not what is questioned
by Stirner; it is unknown to him. He simply does not know
what of elemental reality happens between life and life, he
does not know the mysteries of address and answer, claim
and disclaim, word and response. He has not experienced
this because it can only be experienced when one is not
closed to the otherness, the ontic and primal otherness of
the other (to the primal otherness of the other, which of
course, even when the other is God, must not be confined
to a "wholly otherness"). What Stirner with his destructive
power successfully attacks is the substitute for a reality that
is no longer believed: the fictitious responsibility in face of
reason, of an idea, a nature, an institution, of all manner of

illustrious ghosts, all that in its essence is not a person and hence cannot really, like father and mother, prince and master, husband and friend, like God, make you answerable. He wishes to show the nothingness of the word which has decayed into a phrase; he has never known the living word, he unveils what he knows. Ignorant of the reality whose appearance is appearance, he proves its nature to be appearance. Stirner dissolves the dissolution. "What you call responsibility is a lie!" he cries, and he is right: it is a lie. But there is a truth. And the way to it lies freer after the lie has been seen through.

Kierkegaard means true responsibility when, rushing in a parabola past Stirner, he speaks thus of the crowd and the Single One: "Being in a crowd either releases from repentance and responsibility or weakens the responsibility of the Single One, since the crowd leaves only a fragment of responsibility to him." These words, to which I intend to return, no longer have in view any illusion of a responsibility without a receiver, but genuine responsibility, recognized once more, in which the demander demands of me the entrusted good and I must open my hands or they petrify.

Stirner has unmasked as unreal the responsibility which is only ethical by exposing the non-existence of the alleged receivers as such. Kierkegaard has proclaimed anew the responsibility which is in faith.

And as with responsibility so with truth itself: here the parabolic meeting becomes still uncannier.

"Truth . . . exists only—in your head." "The truth is a—creature." "For Me there is no truth, for nothing passes beyond Me." "So long as you believe in the truth you do not believe in yourself. . . . You alone are the truth." What Stirner undertakes here is the dissolution of *possessed* truth, of "truth" as a general good that can be taken into possession and possessed, that is at once independent of and accessible to the person. He does not undertake this like the sophists and other sceptics by means of epistemology. He

does not seem to have been acquainted with the epistemo-
logical method; he is as audaciously naive in his behaviour
as though Hume and Kant had never lived. But neither
would the epistemology have achieved for him what he
needed; for it, and the solipsist theory as well, leads only to
the knowing subject and not to the concrete human person
at which Stirner aims with undeviating fanaticism. The
means by which he undertakes the dissolution of possessed
truth is the demonstration that it is conditioned by the person. "True is what is Mine." There already lies hidden the
fundamental principle of our day, "What I take as true is
defined by what I am". To this two sentences may be taken
as alternatives or as a combination—to Stirner's horror, certainly, but in logical continuation as an inseparable exposition—first the sentence "And what I am is conditioned by
my complexes", and second the sentence "And what I am
is conditioned by the class I belong to", with all its variants.
Stirner is the involuntary father of modern psychological
and sociological relativizings which for their part (to antici-
pate) are at once true and false.

But again Stirner is right, again he dissolves the dissolution. *Possessed* truth is not even a creature, it is a ghost, a
succubus with which a man may succeed in effectively imagining he is living, but with which he cannot live. You
cannot devour the truth, it is not served up anywhere in
the world, you cannot even gape at it, for it is not an object.
And yet there does exist a participation in the being of inaccessible truth—for the man who stands its test. There exists a real relation of the whole human person to the unpos-
sessed, unpossessable truth, and it is completed only in
standing its test. This real relation, whatever it is called, is
the relation to the Present Being.

The re-discovery of truth, which has been disenthroned
in the human world by the semblance of truth, but which
is in truth eternally irremovable, which cannot be possessed
but which can be served, and for which service can be given

by perceiving *and* standing test, is accomplished by Kierkegaard in a paradoxical series of sentences. It begins with
the words, "He who communicates it [the truth] is only a
Single One. And then its communication is again only for
the Single One; for this view of life, 'the Single One', is the
very truth." You must listen carefully. Not that the Single
One exists and not that he should exist is described as the
truth, but "this view of life" which consists in the Single
One's existing, and which is hence also simply identified
with him. To be the Single One is the communication of
the truth, that is, the human truth. "The crowd," says
Kierkegaard, "produces positions of advantage in human
life," which "overlook in time and the world the eternal
truth—the Single One." "You alone are the truth" is what
Stirner says. "The Single One is the truth," is what is said
here. That is the uncanny parabolic phenomenon of words
to which I have referred. In "a time of dissolution" (Kierkegaard) there is the blank point at which the No and the Yes
move up to and past one another with all their power, but
purely objectively and without consciousness. Now Kierkegaard continues: "The truth cannot be communicated and
received except as it were before God's eyes, by God's help;
so that God is there, is the medium as he is the truth. . . .
For God is the truth and its medium." Thus "'The Single
One' is the truth" and "God is the truth". That is true because the Single One "corresponds" to God. Hence Kierkegaard can say that the category of the "Single One" is and
remains "the fixed point which can resist pantheist confusion". The Single One corresponds to God. For "man is
akin to the Godhead". In Old Testament language, the Single One realizes the "image" of God precisely through having become a Single One. In the language in which alone a
generation, wrestling with the problem of truth, succumb-
ing to it, turning from it, but also exploring it ever anew,
can understand the conquest, the Single One existentially
stands the test of the appearing truth by "the personal ex-

istence expressing what is said" [I would say "what is un-said"]. There is this human side of truth—in human exist-ence. God is the truth because he is, the Single One is the truth because he reaches his existence.

Stirner has dissolved the truth which is only noetic, and against all his knowledge and desire cleared a space into which Kierkegaard's believed and tested truth has stepped, the truth which can no longer be obtained and possessed by the *noesis* alone, but which must be existentially realized in order to be inwardly known and communicated.

But there is still a third and last contact and repulsion. For Stirner every man is the Unique One if only he discards all ideological ballast (to which for him the religious be-longs) and settles down as owner of his world-property. For Kierkegaard "every, absolutely every man" "can and ought" to be "the Single One"—only he must . . . what, indeed, must he? He must become a Single One. For "the matter is thus: this category cannot be taught by precept; it is something that you can *do*, it is an *art* . . . and moreover an art whose practice could cost the artist, in time, his life". But when we investigate closely to see if there is a nearer definition anywhere, even if not precisely one that can be taught by precept, one will be found—no more than one, no more than a single word, but it is found: it is "obey". It is at any rate what is under all circumstances prohibited to Stirner's Unique One by his author. It is easy to discover that behind all Stirner's prohibitions to his Unique One this stands as the real, comprehensive and decisive prohibition. With this one verb Kierkegaard finally thrusts off the spirit which, without either of them knowing, had approached so near, too near, in the time of dissolution.

And yet—the illumination of our time makes it visible—the two, primally different, primally strange to one another, concerning one another in nothing but with one another concerning us, work together, not a hundred years ago but to-day, the one announcing decay as decay, the other proving the eternal structure to be inviolable. To renounce obedience to any usurping lord is Stirner's demand; Kierkegaard has none of his own—he repeats the ancient, misused, desecrated, outworn, inviolable "obey the Lord". If a man becomes the Single One "then the obedience is all right" even in the time of dissolution, where otherwise the obedience is not all right.

Stirner leads out of all kinds of alleys into the open country where each is the Unique One and the world is his property. There they bustle in futile and noncommittal life, and nothing comes of it but bustle, till one after the other begins to notice what this country is called. Kierkegaard leads to a "narrow pass"; his task is "where possible to induce the many, to invite them, to stir them to press through this narrow pass, 'the Single One', through which, note well, none passes unless he becomes 'the Single One', since in the concept itself the opposite is excluded". I think, however, that in actual history the way to this narrow pass is through that open country that first is called individual egoism and then collective egoism and, finally, by its true name, despair.

But is there really a way through the narrow pass? Can one really become the Single One?

"I myself do not assert of myself," says Kierkegaard, "that I am that one. For I have indeed fought for it, but have not yet grasped it, and am in the continued fight continually reminded that it is beyond human strength to be 'the Single One' in the highest sense."

"In the highest sense"—that is spoken with a Christian and a christological reference, it manifests the paradox of the Christian task. But it is also convincing to the non-Christian. It has in it the assertion that no man can say of himself that he has become the Single One, since a higher sense of the category always remains unfulfilled beyond him; but it also has in it the assertion that every man can nevertheless become a Single One. Both are true.

"The eternal, the decisive, can be worked for only where one man is; and to become this one man, which all men can, means to let oneself be helped by God." This is a way.

And yet it is not the way; for reasons of which I have not spoken in this section and of which I now have to speak.

THE SINGLE ONE AND HIS THOU

Kierkegaard's "to become a Single One" is, as we have seen, not meant Socratically. The goal of this becoming is not the "right" life, but the entry into a relation. "To become" means here to become *for* something, "for" in the strict sense which simply transcends the circle of the person himself. It means to be made ready for the one relation which can be entered into only by the Single One, the one; the relation for whose sake man exists.

This relation is an exclusive one, the exclusive one, and this means, according to Kierkegaard, that it is the excluding relation, excluding all others; more precisely, that it is the relation which in virtue of its unique, essential life expels all other relations into the realm of the unessential.

"Everyone should be chary about having to do with 'the others', and should essentially speak only with God and with himself," he says in the exposition of the category. Everyone, so it is to be understood, because everyone can be the one.

The joining of the "with God" with the "with himself" is a serious incompatibility that nothing can mitigate. All the enthusiasm of the philosophers for monologue, from Plato to Nietzsche, does not touch the simple experience of faith that speaking with God is something *toto genere* different from "speaking with oneself"; whereas, remarkably, it is not something *toto genere* different from speaking with another human being. For in the latter case there is common the fact of being approached, grasped, addressed, which cannot be anticipated in any depth of the soul; but in the former case it is not common in spite of all the soul's adventures in doubling roles—games, intoxications, dreams, visions, surprises, overwhelmings, overpowerings—in spite of all tensions and divisions, and all the noble and strong images for traffic with oneself. "Then one became two"— that can never become *ontically* true, just as the reverse "one and one at one" of mysticism can never be ontically true. Only when I have to do with another essentially, that is, in such a way that he is no longer a phenomenon of my *I*, but instead is my *Thou*, do I experience the reality of speech with another—in the irrefragable genuineness of mutuality. *Abyssus abyssum clamat*—what that means the soul first experiences when it reaches its frontier and finds itself faced by one that is simply not the soul itself and yet is a self.

But on this point Kierkegaard seems to correct himself. In the passage in his *Journals* where he asks the question, "And how does one become a Single One?" the answer begins with the formulation, obviously more valid in the problem under discussion, that one should be, "regarding the highest concerns, related solely to God".

If, in this sentence, the word "highest" is understood as imiting in its content, then the phrase is self-evident: the highest concerns can be put only to the highest. But it cannot be meant in this way; this is clear from the other sentence, "Everyone should. . . ." If both are held together, then Kierkegaard's meaning is evident that the Single One has to do *essentially* (is not "chary") only with God.

But thereby the category of the Single One, which has scarcely been properly discovered, is already fatefully misunderstood.

Kierkegaard, the Christian concerned with "contemporaneity" with Jesus, here contradicts his master.

To the question—which was not merely aimed at "tempting" him, but was rather a current and significant controversial question of the time—which was the all-inclusive and fundamental commandment, the "great" commandment, Jesus replied by connecting the two Old Testament commandments between which above all the choice lay: "love God with all your might" and "love your neighbour as one like yourself". Both are to be "loved", God and the "neighbour" (i.e., not man in general, but the man who meets me time and again in the context of life), but in different ways. The neighbour is to be loved "as one like myself" (not "as I love myself"; in the last reality one does not love oneself, but one should rather learn to love oneself through love of one's neighbour), to whom, then, I should show love as I wish it may be shown to me. But God is to be loved with all my soul and all my might. By connecting the two Jesus brings to light the Old Testament truth that God and man are not rivals. Exclusive love to God ("with *all* your heart") is, *because he is God,* inclusive love, ready to accept and include all love. It is not himself that God creates, not himself he redeems, even when he "reveals himself" it is not himself he reveals: his revelation does not have himself as object. He limits himself in all his limitlessness, he makes room for the creatures, and so, in love to him, he makes room for love to the creatures.

"In order to come to love," says Kierkegaard about his renunciation of Regina Olsen, "I had to remove the object". That is sublimely to misunderstand God. Creation is not a hurdle on the road to God, it is the road itself. We are created along with one another and directed to a life with one another. Creatures are placed in my way so that I, their fellow-creature, by means of them and with them find the way to God. A God reached by their exclusion would not be the God of all lives in whom all life is fulfilled. A God in whom only the parallel lines of single approaches intersect is more akin to the "God of the philosophers" than to the "God of Abraham and Isaac and Jacob". God wants us to come to him by means of the Reginas he has created and not by renunciation of them. If we remove the object, then—we have removed the object altogether. Without an object, artificially producing the object from the abundance of the human spirit and calling it God, this love has its being in the void.

"The matter must be brought back to the monastery from which Luther broke out." So Kierkegaard defines the task of the time. "Monastery" can here mean only the institutional safeguarding of man from an essential relation, inclusive of his whole being, to any others but God. And certainly to one so safeguarded the orientation towards the point called God is made possible with a precision not to be attained otherwise. But what "God" in this case means is in fact only the end-point of a human line of orientation. But the real God lets no shorter line reach him than each man's longest, which is the line embracing the world that is accessible to this man. For he, the real God, is the creator, and all beings stand before him in relation to one another in his creation, becoming useful in living with one another for his creative purpose. To teach an acosmic relation to God is not to know the creator. Acosmic worship of a God of whom one knows, along with Kierkegaard, that it is of his grace "that he wills to be a person in relation to you", is Marcionism, and not even consistent Marcionism; for this worship does not separate the creator and the redeemer as it would have to do if it were consistent.

But one must not overlook the fact that Kierkegaard is not at all concerned to put Luther breaking out of the monastery in the wrong. On one occasion he treats Luther's marriage as something removed from all natural personal life, all directness between man and wife, as a symbolic action, a deed representing and expressing the turning-point of the spiritual history of the west. "The most important thing," he makes Luther say, "is that it becomes notorious that I am married." But behind Luther's marrying Katharina there emerges, unnamed but clear, Kierkegaard's not marrying Regina. "Put the other way round, one could say . . . in defiance of the whole nineteenth century I cannot marry." Here there is added as a new perspective the qualitative difference between historical epochs. Certainly, on Kierkegaard's view it is true for both ages that the Single One should not have to do essentially with any others but God, and according to him, then, Luther speaks not essentially but only symbolically with Katharina; though bound to the world he remains essentially worldless and "alone before God". But the symbolic actions are opposed: by the one the word of a new bond with the world—even if perhaps in the end a bond that is not binding—is spoken to the one century; by the other the word of a new and in any event binding renunciation is spoken to the other century. What is the reason? Because the nineteenth century has given itself up to the "crowd", and "the crowd is untruth".

But now two things are possible. Either the bond with the world preached with his life by Luther is in Kierkegaard's view not binding or "essential" or necessary for the leading of Luther's age to God. But that would make Luther one who lets what is not binding be effective as something that is binding, who has a different thing to say for men than he has for God, and who treats the sacrament as though it were fulfilled outside God; it would make Luther one in whose symbolic action no authority could reside. Or else on the other hand the bond with the world preached with his life by Luther is in Kierkegaard's view binding and essential and necessary for leading to God. Then the difference between the two epochs, which is for the rest indubitably a qualitative one, would have a say in what is basically independent of history, more so than birth and death—the relation of the Single One to God. For the essential quality of this relation cannot be of one kind in the former century and of another in the latter; it cannot in the one go right through the world and in the other go over and beyond the world. Human representations of the relation change, the truth of the relation is unchangeable because it stands in eternal mutuality; it is not man who defines his approach to it but the creator who in the unambiguity of man's creation has instituted the approach.

It is certainly not possible to speak of God other than dialectically, for he does not come under the principle of contradiction. Yet there is a limit of dialectic where assertion ceases but where there is knowledge. Who is there who confesses the God whom Kierkegaard and I confess, who could suppose in decisive insight that God wants *Thou* to be truly said only to him, and to all others only an unessential and fundamentally invalid word—that God demands of us to choose between him and his creation? The objection is raised that the world as a fallen world is not to be identified with the creation. But what fall of the world could be so mighty that it could *for him* break it away from being his creation? That would be to make the action of the world into one more powerful than God's action and into one compelling him.

The essential is not that we should see things as standing out from God nor as being absorbed in him, but that we should "see things in God", the things themselves. To apply this to our relations with creatures: only when all relations, uncurtailed, are taken into the one relation, do we set the ring of our life's world round the sun of our being.

Certainly that is the most difficult thing, and man in order to be able to do it must let himself be helped from time to time by an inner-worldly "monastery". Our relations to creatures incessantly threaten to get incapsulated. As the world itself is sustained in its independence as the world through striving to be closed to God, though as creation it is open to him, so every great bond of man—though in it he has perceived his connexion with the infinite—defends itself vigorously against continually debouching into the infinite. Here the monastic forms of life in the world, the loneliness in the midst of life into which we turn as into hostelries, help us to prevent the connexion between the conditioned bonds and the one unconditioned bond from slackening. This too, if we do not wish to see our participation in the Present Being dying off, is an imperative interchange, the systole to the diastole of the soul; and the loneliness must know the quality of strictness, of a monastery's strictness, in order to do its work. But it must never wish to tear us away from creatures, never refuse to dismiss us to them. By that it would act contrary to its own law and would close us, instead of enabling us, as is its office, to keep open the gates of finitude.

Kierkegaard does not conceal from us for a moment that his resistance to a bond with the world, his religious doctrine of loneliness, is based on personal nature and personal destiny. He confesses that he "ceased to have common speech" with men. He notes that the finest moment in his life is in the bathhouse, before he dives into the water: "I have nothing more to do with the world". He exposes before our eyes some of the roots of his "melancholy". He knows precisely what has brought him to the point of being chary about having to do with others and of essentially speaking only with God and with himself. And yet, as soon as he begins with the "direct" language, he expresses it as an imperative: let *everyone* do so. Continually he points to his own shadow—and wants to leap across it. He is a being excepted and exposed, and certainly so are we all, for so is man as man. But Kierkegaard has moved to the fringe of being excepted and exposed, and maintains equilibrium only by means of the unheard-of balance of his "author's" reticently communicative existence with the complicated safeguards of all the "pseudonyms"; whereas we are not on the fringe, and that is no "not yet" nor any sort of compromising, no shirking of melancholy; it is organic continuance and grace of preservation and significant for the future of the spirit. Kierkegaard behaves in our sight like a schizophrenist, who tries to win over the beloved individual into "his" world as if it were the true one. But it is not the true one. We, ourselves wandering on the narrow ridge, must not shrink from the sight of the jutting rock on which he stands over the abyss; nor may we step on it. We have much to learn from him, but not the final lesson.

Our rejection can be supported by Kierkegaard's own teaching. He describes "the ethical" as "the only means by which God communicates with 'man'" (1853). The context of the teaching naturally keeps at a distance the danger of understanding this in the sense of an absolutizing of the ethical. But it must be understood so that not merely an autarkic ethic but also an autarkic religion is inadmissible; so that as the ethical cannot be freed from the religious neither can the religious from the ethical without ceasing to do justice to the present truth. The ethical no longer appears here, as in Kierkegaard's earlier thought, as a "stage" from which a "leap" leads to the religious, a leap by which a level is reached that is quite different and has a different meaning; but it dwells in the religious, in faith and service. This ethical can no longer mean a morality belonging to a realm of relativity and time and again overtaken and invalidated by the religious; but it means an *essential* action and suffering in relation to men, which are co-ordinated with the essential relation to God. But only he who has to do with men essentially can essentially act and suffer in relation to them. If the ethical is the only means by which God communicates with man then I am forbidden to speak essentially only with God and myself. And so indeed it is. I do not say that Kierkegaard on his rock, alone with the mercy of the Merciful, is forbidden. I say only that you and I are forbidden.

Kierkegaard is deeply conscious of the dubiousness which arises from the negativizing extension of the category of the Single One. "The frightful thing," he writes in his Journal, and we read it, as he wrote it, with fear and trembling, "is that precisely the highest form of piety, to let everything earthly go, can be the highest egoism." Here obviously a distinction is made according to motives, and the idea of egoism used here is an idea of motivation. If we put in its place an objective idea, an idea of a state of affairs, the sentence is changed to a still more frightful one: "Precisely what appears to us as the highest form of piety—to let everything earthly go—is the highest egoism."

Is it true that the Single One "corresponds" to God? Does he realize the "image" of God solely by having become a Single One? One thing is lacking for that to be—and it is the decisive thing.

"Certainly," says Kierkegaard, "God is no egoist, but he is the infinite Ego." Yet thereby too little is said of the God whom we confess—if one dares to say anything at all. He hovers over his creation not as over a chaos, he embraces it. He is the infinite *I* that makes every *It* into his *Thou*.

The Single One corresponds to God when he in his human way embraces the bit of the world offered to him as God embraces his creation in his divine way. He realizes the image when, as much as he can in a personal way, he says *Thou* with his being to the beings living round about him.

No-one can so refute Kierkegaard as Kierkegaard himself. Reasoning with and judging himself, he corrects his own spirit from its depths, often before it has uttered itself. In 1843 Kierkegaard enters this unforgettable confession in his Journal: "Had I had faith I would have stayed with Regina." By this he means, "If I had really believed that 'with God all things are possible', hence also the resolution of this—my melancholy, my powerlessness, my fear, my alienation, fraught with destiny, from woman and from the world—then I would have stayed with Regina." But while meaning this he says something different, too, namely, that the Single One, if he really believes, and that means if he is really a Single One (which, as we saw, he has become for the one relation of faith), can and may have to do essentially with another. And behind this there lurks the extreme that he who can and may also *ought to* do this. "The only means by which God communicates with man is the ethical." But the ethical in its plain truth means to help God by loving his creation in his creatures, by loving it towards him. For this, to be sure, one must let oneself be helped by him.

"The Single One is the category through which, from the religious standpoint, time and history and the race must pass." What is this "religious standpoint"? One beside others? The standpoint towards God, gained by standing aside from all others? God one object beside other objects, the chosen one beside the rejected ones? God as Regina's successful rival? Is that still God? Is that not merely an object adapted to the religious genius? (Note that I am not speaking of true holiness for which, as it hallows *everything*, there is no "religious standpoint".) Religious genius? Can there be religious geniuses? Is that not a *contradictio in adiecto*? Can the religious be a specification? "Religious geniuses" are theological geniuses. Their God is the God of the theologians. Admittedly, that is not the God of the philosophers, but neither is it the God of Abraham and Isaac and Jacob. The God of the theologians, too, is a logicized God, and so is even the God of a theology which will speak only dialectically and makes light of the principle of contradiction. So long as they practise theology they do not get away from religion as a specification. When Pascal in a volcanic hour made that stammering distinction between God and God he was no genius but a man experiencing the primal glow of faith; but at other times he was a theological genius and dwelt in a specifying religion, out of which the happening of that hour had lifted him.

Religion as a specification misses its mark. God is not an object beside objects and hence cannot be reached by renunciation of objects. God, indeed, is not the cosmos, but far less is he Being *minus* cosmos. He is not to be found by subtraction and not to be loved by reduction.

The Suspension of Ethics

The first book by Kierkegaard that I read as a young man was *Fear and Trembling*. This is built entirely upon the Biblical narrative of the sacrifice of Isaac. I still think of that hour today because it was then that I received the impulse to reflect upon the categories of ethics and religion in their relation to each other.

Through the example of the temptation of Abraham, this book sets forth the idea that there is a "teleological suspension of the ethical," that the validity of a moral duty can be at times suspended in accordance with the purpose of a higher—of the highest—duty. When God commands one to murder his son, the immorality of the immoral is suspended for the duration of this situation. What is more, that which is otherwise purely evil is for the duration of this situation purely good because it has become pleasing to God. In the place of the universal and the universally valid there is something which is founded exclusively on the personal relation between God and the "Single One." But just through this the ethical—the universal and the universally valid—is relativized. Its values and laws are banished from

(From Ruth Nanda Anshen, ed., *Moral Principles of Action* [Harper, 1952], Chap. XIII, pp. 223–27.)

the absolute into the relative; for no absoluteness belongs any longer to that which is a duty in the sphere of the ethical conscience as soon as it is confronted with the absolute duty toward God. "But what then is duty?" asks Kierkegaard. "Duty is, to be sure, just a synonym for God's will!" In other words: God establishes the order of good and evil —and breaks through it where he wishes, and does so from person to person, that is, in direct personal relation with the individual.

On the deadly seriousness of this "from person to person" Kierkegaard has, it is true, laid the greatest possible stress. He has declared most clearly that this trial will only be laid upon one who is worthy of being called God's chosen one. "But who," he asks, "is such a one?" In particular, he assures us time and again that he himself does not have this courage of faith which is necessary to plunge confidently, with closed eyes, into the absurd. It is impossible for him to perform the paradoxical movement of faith that Abraham performed. One must keep in mind, however, the fact that Kierkegaard also states that he has fought to become "the Single One" in the strictest sense of the term but has not attained it, and that he nonetheless once considered having the words "that Single One" placed upon his grave. There are many indications that when he described how Abraham gave up his son and nonetheless believed that he would not lose him (so Kierkegaard understood the event), he had in mind the day, a little more than a year before, when he himself broke his engagement with his beloved and yet thought that he would be able to preserve it in a higher, incomprehensible dimension. In the way of this union (he once explained) "there stood a godly protest,"[1] though he had, to be sure, no lasting confidence in this idea —so little, in fact, that in the year of the publication of *Fear*

[1] She also stated once, much later, that he had sacrificed her to God.

and Trembling he was able to set down the sentence, "Had I had faith, I would have remained with her."

The event is here removed out of the situation between Abraham and God, in which God breaks through the ethical order that he himself established, into a sphere where what happens takes place in a much less unequivocal fashion than in the Biblical narrative. "That which the Single One is to understand by Isaac," says Kierkegaard, "can be decided only by and for himself." This means, clearly and precisely, that he does not learn it, at least not unmistakably, from God. God demands a sacrifice of him, but it is left to the Single One to interpret what that sacrifice is, and his interpretation will always be determined by his life-circumstances in this hour. How differently the Biblical voice speaks here! "Thy son, thine only one, whom thou lovest, Isaac." There is nothing here to interpret. The man who hears learns entirely what is demanded of him; the God who speaks proposes no riddles.

But we still have not arrived at the decisive problematic position. This first appears to us when Kierkegaard compares his Abraham with Agamemnon, who is preparing to sacrifice Iphigenia. Agamemnon is the tragic hero, who is called upon by the "universal" to make the sacrifice for the welfare of his people. He, therefore, "remains within the borders of the ethical," which Abraham, "the knight of faith," crosses over. Everything depends upon this: that Abraham crosses over them with the paradoxical movement of faith; for otherwise all becomes a "temptation," the readiness to sacrifice becomes the readiness to murder, and "Abraham is lost." This also is decided in "absolute isolation." "The knight of faith," says Kierkegaard, "is left to his own resources, single and alone, and therein lies the dreadful."

This is true in so far as there is no one on earth who can help him to come to a decision and to perform "the movement of infinity." But Kierkegaard here takes for granted something that cannot be taken for granted even in the world of Abraham, much less in ours. He does not take into consideration the fact that the problematic position of the decision of faith is preceded by the problematic situation of the hearing itself: Who is it whose voice one hears? For Kierkegaard it is self-evident because of the Christian tradition in which he grew up that he who demands the sacrifice is none other than God. But for the Bible, at least for the Old Testament, it is not, without further question, self-evident. Indeed a certain "instigation" to a forbidden action is even ascribed in one place to God (II Samuel 24:1) and in another to Satan (I Chronicles 21:1).

Abraham, to be sure, could not confuse with another the voice which once bade him leave his homeland and which he at that time recognized as the voice of God without the speaker's saying to him who he was. And God did indeed "tempt" him; that is, through the extremest demand he drew forth the innermost readiness to sacrifice out of the depths of Abraham's being, and he allowed this readiness to grow to the full intention to commit the act. He thus made it possible for Abraham's relation to Him, God, to become wholly real. But then, when no further hindrance stood between the intention and the deed, he contented himself with Abraham's fulfilled readiness and prevented the action.

It can happen, however, that a sinful man is uncertain whether or not he has to sacrifice his (perhaps also very beloved) son to God for his sins (Micah 6:7). For Moloch imitates the voice of God. In contrast to this, God himself demands of this man nothing more than justice and love, and that he "walk humbly" with Him, with God (Micah 6:8)—in other words, not much more than that which is fundamentally ethical.

Where, therefore, the "suspension" of the ethical conscience is concerned, the question of questions which takes

precedence over every other is: Are you really addressed by
the Absolute or by one of his apes? It should be noted in
this connection that, according to the report of the Bible,
the divine voice which speaks to the Single One is the "voice
of a thin silence" (I Kings 19:21).[2] The voice of Moloch,
in contrast, usually prefers a mighty roaring. However, in
our age especially, it appears to be extremely difficult to
distinguish the one from the other.

Ours is an age in which the suspension of the ethical
conscience fills the world in a caricatured form. The apes
of the Absolute, to be sure, have always in the past bustled
about on earth. Over and over again men are commanded
from out of the darkness to sacrifice their Isaac, and *here*
it is true: "That which the Single One is to understand by
Isaac, can be decided only by and for himself." But stored
away in men's hearts, there were in all those times images
of the Absolute—partly pallid, partly crude, altogether false
and yet true, fleeting as an image in a dream yet verified
in eternity. Inadequate as this presence certainly was, in
so far as one bore it concretely in mind one only needed
to call on it in order not to succumb to the deception of
the voices.

That is no longer so, since, in Nietzsche's words, "God
is dead," that is, realistically speaking, since the image-
making power of the human heart has been in decline—
since the spiritual man can no longer catch a glimpse of
the appearance of the Absolute. False absolutes rule over
the soul, which is no longer able to put them to flight
through the image of the true Absolute. Everywhere, over
the whole surface of the human world—in the East and in
the West, from the left and from the right, they pierce un-
hampered through the level of the ethical conscience and
demand of you "the sacrifice." Time and again, when I ask

[2] A bold visual metaphor for an acoustical reality: it is a
silence, but not a thick and solid one, rather one that is of such
veil-like thinness that the Word shines through it.

well-intentioned young souls: "Why do you give up your dearest possession, your personal integrity?" they answer me: "Even this, this most difficult sacrifice, is the thing that is needed in order that . . ."—it makes no difference, "in order that equality may come" or "in order that freedom may come" or "in order that the Kingdom may come," it makes no difference! And they bring the sacrifice faithfully: in the realm of Moloch honest men lie and compassionate men torture. And they really and truly believe that brother-murder will prepare the way for brotherhood! There appears to be no escape from the most evil of all idolatry.

There is no escape from it until the new conscience of men has arisen that will summon them to guard, with the innermost power of their souls, against the confusion of the relative with the Absolute, that will enable them to see through illusion and to recognize this confusion for what it is. To penetrate again and again into the false absolute with an incorruptible, probing glance—until one has discovered its limits, its limitedness—this is today perhaps the only way to reawaken the power of man to glimpse the never-vanishing appearance of the Absolute.

PAUL TILLICH

PAUL TILLICH

Paul J. Tillich, one of the most distinguished contemporary Protestant theologians and religious philosophers, was born in August 1886, in Starzeddel, in the Prussian province of Brandenburg, near the Silesian border. His father, a minister of the Prussian Territorial Church (Lutheran) in that town, was a man of intellectual distinction and strong character who rose to occupy an important place in local church affairs. His mother came from the Rhineland; she too, with a different religious tradition, possessed a strong personality. When he was twelve the boy was sent to a humanistic Gymnasium not far from home, where he remained for two years until the family moved to Berlin.

To his early environment Tillich traces the beginnings of what he calls the "romantic" trend in his feeling and thinking, his "aesthetic-meditative" attitude toward nature and his sense of history. These influences were intensified, Tillich believes, by his "actual communication with nature" throughout his life; by the "impact of [German] poetry . . . full of expressions of nature mysticism"; and by his Lutheran background, where a certain "nature mysticism was possible," as it was not in Calvinism.[1] This early bias has

[1] Paul Tillich, "Autobiographical Reflections," in Kegley,

apparently remained potent throughout his life, and has contributed to what some critics have regarded as the pantheistic strain in his philosophy.

In 1900, with the removal of the family, Tillich transferred to the Friedrich Wilhelm Gymnasium in Berlin, and four years later matriculated in the theological faculties of Berlin, Tübingen, and Halle. Receiving his doctorate of philosophy in Breslau in 1911 and his theological degree in Halle a year later, he was ordained minister in the latter year, and served briefly as vicar in Moabit. Then came the First World War.

The war and its aftermath proved a crucial period in Tillich's life. At home, because of the traditional authoritarian atmosphere in which he was immersed, he had already begun to feel a certain sense of "narrowness and restrictedness" in his environment, and expressed his autonomous strivings by taking an independent philosophical position in his discussions with his father. The war experience—he served as chaplain from 1914 to 1918—impelled him to extend both his resistance to authority and his strivings for autonomy to the social and political sphere. The situation that led to the German Revolution in 1918 also produced the religious-socialist movement, with which Tillich became closely identified and in which he was one of the leading spirits. It was a situation of *kairos*, he felt, a situation of "fulfilled time," big with creative possibilities; and this *kairos* he attempted to interpret and serve in his speaking and writing, particularly through the periodical *Blätter für religiösen Sozialismus*, founded close upon the end of the war. In this period, too, he more clearly defined his attitude to Marx as a "dialectical Yes and No," corresponding to the "dialectical Yes and No" directed to Nietzsche, despite the "use and abuse" of the former by the Communists and of the latter by the Nazis.

Charles W., and Robert W. Bretall, eds., *The Theology of Paul Tillich* (Macmillan, 1952), pp. 4–5.

Meanwhile, Tillich pursued his academic life, as privat-dozent of theology in the University of Berlin from 1919 to 1924, where he became interested in a "theology of culture"; as professor of systematic theology at Marburg in 1924 (where he came face to face with theological neo-orthodoxy in its "radical effects" and with Heidegger's existentialism); as professor of religion at the technical *Hochschule* in Dresden in 1925; as professor of theology at Leipzig in 1928; and finally as professor of philosophy at the University of Frankfurt-am-Main from 1929 to 1933. His interests throughout were at least as much philosophical and cultural as theological.

The rising Hitler movement confronted German "religious socialism" with a serious problem, for some (among them Emanuel Hirsch) saw in nazism a new and engrossing expression of the *kairos*. Tillich categorically rejected this interpretation, and when Hitler took power, he was quickly dismissed.

Reinhold Niebuhr happened to be in Germany during the summer of 1933, and he promptly invited Tillich to come to Union Theological Seminary in New York. Tillich, with his family, arrived in November of that year, and began an association with Union Seminary as professor of philosophical theology that lasted till his retirement in 1954. Upon his retirement from Union, he was appointed University Professor at Harvard, where he continues the lecturing, teaching, and writing that have made him such a powerful intellectual force in Europe and America. For though he became an American citizen in 1940, he has maintained his connections with the Old World, returning to Germany several times since the end of the Second World War.

Tillich's early "romanticism" was strengthened by his thorough initiation into German classical philosophy, particularly Schelling. Schelling was the subject of his earliest philosophical writing, and in Schelling's so-called "second period" he saw "the beginning of that movement which today is called Existentialism."[2] Just before the First World War he discovered Kierkegaard, whose influence became very powerful in the Germany of the 1920s. The mystical side of the Lutheran tradition, particularly Jakob Boehme, has always been congenial to him, and has entered significantly into his theological system.

From his postwar days in Berlin, Tillich has been preoccupied with bringing religion into relation with politics, art, philosophy, depth psychology, and sociology. These interests he continued in the United States, although the concentration here has been more on philosophy (ontology) and depth psychology (*The Courage to Be; Love, Power, and Justice*). Some of the most important of his German writings were published in English soon after his arrival in this country in *The Religious Situation*, and *The Interpretation of History*, and (later) in *The Protestant Era*. His *Systematic Theology*, on which he says he was already at work in the 1920s, finally began to appear in 1951.

Tillich, as he himself has frequently asserted, stands "at the frontier": it is often hard to determine whether he is essentially a theologian, a philosopher, or a critic of culture. It is equally difficult to place him theologically, for though he is certainly associated with the "neo-orthodox" trend in recent Protestant thinking, he exhibits a synthesizing, mediating spirit, and a sympathy for Schleiermacher, quite alien to this movement. His political outlook, too, remains difficult to define, for although he insists that "religious socialism" has perennial significance, he nevertheless recognizes that the present is a period in which socialist programs seem to have lost their relevance.

Particularly in the past ten years Tillich's influence has grown mightily in this country, extending far beyond the church and the circle of the religious. He has always found the face-to-face encounter involved in lecturing and teach-

[2] Paul Tillich, "Autobiographical Reflections," in Kegley, Charles W., and Robert W. Bretall, eds., *op. cit.*, p. 11.

ing a source of "the greatest anxiety and the greatest happiness";[3] on their part, the audiences he reaches, undergraduates, theologians, philosophers, and lay people alike, find in their encounter with him a memorable event, as exhilarating as it is shattering.

[3] Paul Tillich, "Autobiographical Reflections," in Kegley, Charles W., and Robert W. Bretall, eds., *op. cit.*, p. 15.

SELECTED BIBLIOGRAPHY

WORKS BY TILLICH

(A comprehensive bibliography of writings by Paul Tillich through 1952 will be found in Charles W. Kegley and Robert W. Bretall, eds., *The Theology of Paul Tillich* [Macmillan, 1952], pp. 353–62.)

The Religious Situation. Holt, 1932; Meridian, 1956.

The Interpretation of History. Scribner's, 1936.

The Protestant Era. University of Chicago Press, 1948.

The Shaking of the Foundations. Scribner's, 1948.

Systematic Theology, Vol. I, 1951; Vol. II, 1957. University of Chicago Press.

The Courage to Be. Yale University Press, 1952.

"Being and Love," in Ruth Nanda Anshen, ed., *Moral Principles of Action.* Harper, 1952.

Love, Power, and Justice. Oxford University Press, 1954.

Biblical Religion and the Search for Ultimate Reality. University of Chicago Press, 1955.

The New Being. Scribner's, 1955.

"Existential Analyses and Religious Symbols," in Harold A. Basilius, ed., *Contemporary Problems in Religion.* Wayne University Press, 1956.

The Dynamics of Faith. Harper, 1957.

WORKS ABOUT TILLICH

Adams, James Luther, *Paul Tillich's Philosophy of Culture, Science, and Religion.* University of Chicago Library,

Department of Photographic Reproductions (microfilm), 1947.

Cochrane, Arthur C., *The Existentialists and God*, pp. 77–99. Westminster, 1956.

Kegley, Charles W., and Robert W. Bretall, eds., *The Theology of Paul Tillich*. Macmillan, 1952.

Killen, R., *The Ontological Theology of Paul Tillich*. Kampen (The Netherlands): J. H. Kok, 1956.

Soper, David W., *Major Voices in American Theology*, pp. 107–152. Westminster, 1953.

Weigel, Gustave, "Contemporaneous Protestantism and Paul Tillich," *Theological Studies*. June 1950.

The Problem
of Theological Method

I. METHOD AND REALITY

Method is the systematic way of doing something, especially of gaining knowledge. No method can be found in separation from its actual exercise; methodological considerations are abstractions from methods actually used. Descartes's *Discours de la méthode* followed Galileo's application of the method of mathematical physics and brought it to general consciousness and philosophical definiteness. Schleiermacher's method, as used in the *Glaubenslehre*, followed the mystical-romantic reinterpretation of religion and established a methodology of inner experience. The methodological remarks made in this paper describe the method actually used in my attempts to elaborate a theology of "self-transcending Realism" (*gläubiger Realismus*), which is supposed to overcome supra-naturalism as well as its naturalistic counterpart.

It is not a sound procedure to borrow a method for a special realm of inquiry from another realm in which this method has been successfully used. It seems that the emphasis on the so-called "empirical" method in theology has not grown out of actual theological demands but has been

(From *The Journal of Religion*, Vol. XXVII, no. 1, January 1947.)

imposed on theology under the pressure of a "methodological imperialism," exercised by the pattern of natural sciences. This subjection of theology to a strange pattern has resulted in an undue extension of the concept "empirical" and the lack of a clear distinction between the different meanings of "experience" in the theological enterprise. For some it is the general human experience on the basis of which they try to approach inferentially the religious objects; for others it is the religious experience of mankind, empathically interpreted. Sometimes it is the religious experience of the theologian and the group to which he belongs that gives the material for an "empirical" theology. Sometimes an ontological intuition is called "experience." Certainly, every concrete reality is open to many methods, according to its different "levels" or "functional potentialities." And each of the ways mentioned (besides some others) can contribute something to the investigation of a phenomenon as complex as religion. But the confusing term "empirical" should not be imposed on all of them; nor should the attempt be made to establish a methodological monism which includes chemistry as well as theology. Reality itself makes demands, and the method must follow; reality offers itself in different ways, and our cognitive intellect must receive it in different ways. An exclusive method applied to everything closes many ways of approach and impoverishes our vision of reality. A world construed according to the model of classical mechanics or Hegelian dialectics or behavioristic protocols is not the cognitive fulfilment of the potentialities of reality. In this respect a genuine pragmatism which refuses to close any door is much more realistic than a dogmatic empiricism with which it is sometimes confused—even by its own followers.

We encounter reality—or reality imposes itself upon us—sometimes in a more complex way, sometimes in definite and distinguishable elements and functions. Whenever we encounter reality in the one or the other way, it challenges our cognitive power and brings it into action. The way in which the cognitive power works is dependent on three factors: its own structure, the structure of the reality it encounters, and the relation of the two structures. In a methodical approach these three factors are noticed, analyzed, and evaluated. But the *prius* of all this is the encounter itself; and nothing is more destructive for knowledge than the establishment of methods which, by their very nature, prevent the actual encounter or prejudice its interpretation. (It is my opinion that the term "encounter" is more adequate for our pre-theoretical relation to reality than the term "experience," which has lost so much of its specific meaning that it needs to be "saved," namely, restricted to a theoretically interpreted encounter.)

The presupposition of theology is that there is a special encounter with reality—or a special way in which reality imposes itself on us—which is ordinarily called "religious." And it is the presupposition of this paper that "having a religious encounter with reality" means "being ultimately concerned about reality."

II. THEOLOGY AND PHILOSOPHY OF RELIGION

The ultimate concern or the religious encounter with reality can be considered in two ways. It can be looked at as an event beside other events, to be observed and described in theoretical detachment; or it can be understood as an event in which he who considers it is "existentially" involved. In the first case the philosopher of religion is at work, in the second the theologian speaks. The philosopher of religion notices the ultimate concern, which he cannot help finding in the history of religion as a quality of practically all representative personalities, symbols, and activities that are called "religious." But in his dealing with this characteristic of religion he himself is only theoretically, but not existentially, concerned. The religious concern is not his concern in so far as he is a philosopher of religion. He points to it, he explains it, but his work is not an expression of the religious encounter with reality. This is different in the theologian. He applies his ultimate concern to everything, as an *ultimate* concern demands—even to his theoretical interpretation of the religious encounter. For the theologian the interpretation of the ultimate concern is itself a matter of ultimate concern, a *religious* work.

But this distinction is not unambiguous. There is an element in every philosophy (not only in every philosopher) which is "existential," i.e., which has the character of an ultimate decision about the meaning of reality. The less technical and the more creative a philosophy is, the more it shows, at least implicitly, an ultimate concern. No creative philosophy can escape its religious background. This is the reason for the tremendous influence that philosophy has had not only on theology but also on the history of religion and vice versa; for, as the philosopher cannot escape his theological background, so the theologian cannot escape his philosophical tool. Those who try to do so deceive themselves: their language, which is shaped through philosophy, betrays them (as even Barth has admitted).

Nevertheless, the distinction between theology and philosophy of religion is valid and cannot be obliterated without dangerous consequences. It is very unfortunate that the so-called "Continental" theology has brought into disregard the function of an independent philosophy of religion, thus creating an intolerable theological absolutism; and it is equally unfortunate that American (nonfundamentalistic) theology was not able to protect itself from being dissolved into a general philosophy of religion, thus producing a self-destructive relativism.

Theology is the existential and, at the same time, methodical interpretation of an ultimate concern. The interpretation of an ultimate concern is "existential" if it is done in the situation of concern. The interpretation of an ultimate concern is methodical if it relates the concern rationally to the whole of experience. Theology, literally and historically, unites these two elements. Theological propositions, therefore, are propositions which deal with an object in so far as it is related to an ultimate concern. No object is excluded from theology if this criterion is applied, not even a piece of stone; and no object is in itself a matter of theology, not even God as an object of inference. This makes theology absolutely universal, on the one hand, and absolutely definite, on the other hand. Theology has to deal with everything, but only under the theological criterion, the ultimate concern.

The concept "ultimate concern" is itself the result of a theological procedure. It expresses two sides of the religious experience: (1) The one side is the absolute or unconditional or ultimate element in religious experience. Every religious relation, attitude, symbol, and action is unconditionally *serious; decisive* in an absolute sense; *transcending* any preliminary, transitory, and dependent value. The whole history of religion confirms this side of religious experience. Where there is a living religion, it makes an absolute claim; it claims the "whole heart"; it does not admit anything ultimate besides itself. (2) The other side is the dynamic presence of the "ultimate" as a continuous, never ceasing, concrete, and universal concern, always demanding and giving, always threatening and promising. As an actual concern it expresses itself in the actualities of life, qualifying every section of existence and using every section of existence for its own embodiment in symbols and actions; for the religious or ultimate concern refers to the ultimate foundation of our being and the ultimate meaning of our existence. Therefore, we can formulate the abstract criterion of every theological work in this way: Those propositions are theological which deal with a subject in so far as it belongs to the foundation of our being and in so far as the meaning of our existence depends on it.

III. THE POSITIVE ELEMENT IN THE
THEOLOGICAL METHOD

The ultimate concern is a concrete concern; otherwise it could not be a concern at all. Even mysticism lives in concrete traditions and symbols in order to express, in action and thought, that which transcends everything concrete. Theology, therefore, must interpret the totality of symbols, institutions, and ideas in which an ultimate concern has embodied itself; theology is, first of all, *positive*. It works on the basis, in the material, and for the purpose of an actual religion. The participation in a religious reality is a presupposition of all theology. You have to be within the circle of a concrete religion in order to interpret it existentially. This is the "theological circle" which theology cannot (and never should try to) escape. This circle is not vicious, but its denial is dishonest, for it could be denied only in the name of an assumedly higher ultimate, which immediately would establish the same circle.

Traditionally, the theological circle has been expressed in the assertion that faith is the precondition of theology. (*Pistis* precedes *gnosis*, as the Alexandrians said; *credo ut intelligam*, as Anselm, following Augustine, formulated it.) Faith, in this context, means a convinced and active participation in the life of a religious group, its traditions, its tensions, its activities. It is not the individual belief of the theologian to which they refer (as we are inclined to misinterpret the *credo ut intelligam*); but it is the spiritual substance out of which a theologian must create, even if he is aware of the weakness of his personal faith (otherwise there would be no honest theologian).

The ultimate concern out of which *we* are working as theologians is embodied in Christianity. If a Christian theologian says that for him Christianity is one among other elements in the religion he intends to interpret, this can mean two things—either that he is not a theologian but a philosopher of religion or that he belongs to a new religious synthesis which is, like everything concrete, inclusive and exclusive at the same time and which therefore establishes a theological circle, just as Christianity does. Since such a concrete synthesis has not yet appeared within my own theological circle and since I am convinced that Christianity is able to take all possible elements of religious truth into itself without ceasing to be Christianity, I am going to speak now about Christian theology, as the only one which is within my existential reach.

Christian theology is a work of the Christian church. The theological function is one of its essential functions, which never can be lost so long as there is the church. Christian theology, moreover, cannot be carried on except by the church. The positive character of the ultimate concern makes "individual theology" impossible. The individual theologian can and should find more adequate methods of interpretation. But he cannot find that which he is asked to interpret. Concretely speaking: Christian theology is the interpretation of the message that Jesus is the Christ, and of the symbols and institutions based on this message. Theology is the methodical self-interpretation of the Christian church (1) in the direction of its foundation, the "new reality" which has become manifest in Jesus as the Christ, and (2) in the direction of the life, past and present, which is determined by this new reality. The original document of the new reality is the Bible; the expression of the life determined by this new reality is the Tradition.

IV. THE THEOLOGICAL METHOD WITH RESPECT TO BIBLE AND TRADITION

Bible and Tradition give the material in which the theologian works. The Bible implies three elements which have different impacts on the theological method. First, and

basically, it contains the decisive manifestation of what
concerns us ultimately, in the picture of Jesus as the Christ.
This is the criterion of all Christian theology, the criterion
also of the theological use of the Bible, for the Bible contains, second, the reception of this manifestation in the
original church. Every biblical writer is, at the same time,
a witness to the new reality in Jesus as the Christ and a
witness of the way in which he and the group to which
he belongs have received the new reality. In the latter sense
they have started the Tradition. In the first sense they point
to that which judges the Tradition, including their own
contribution to it. (This is the meaning of Luther's statement that the Bible is the "Word of God" in so far as it
Christum treibet; in the power of this criterion he himself
judged the canon.) From this it follows that not the Bible
as such, as a part of the history of religion, is the norm of
Christian theology but the Bible in so far as it is the genuine witness to the new reality. It is the permanent task of
Christian theology (in unity with the developing religious
and historical understanding of the Bible) to elaborate the
norm of Christian theology out of the whole of the biblical
material and to apply the norm equally to Bible and Tradition. The third element in the biblical literature that is
important for theological method is the preparation for the
decisive manifestation of the new reality and for its reception by the church. In the Old as well as in the New
Testament we find in language, rites, and ideas a large
element of general revelation as it has occurred and continuously occurs within human religion generally. Our eyes
have been opened to this element by the work of the *reli-
gionsgeschichtliche Schule* in historical theology. So far as
method goes, this means that in every theological statement
we must take into consideration the religious substance
which is transformed and purified in the prophetic and
apostolic message. Only in this sense, but in this sense definitely, the *history of religion* belongs to the positive element

in Christian theology. The universality of the Christian claim implies that there is no religion, not even the most primitive, which has not contributed or will not contribute to the preparation and reception of the new reality in history. In this sense the theologian always must be a "pagan" and a "Jew" and a "Greek" (humanist) and bring their spiritual substance under the criterion of the theological norm. For instance, the terms "Son of Man," "Messiah," "Son of God," "Kyrios," "Logos," appear in the history of religion; and, if they are used for the interpretation of the new reality, they contribute to it with their previous connotations, but in such a way that their meaning is judged and saved at the same time. This method of *judging and saving the history of religion* is exercised by all the biblical writers. It must be done methodically and creatively by the theologian.

Methodologically, the Tradition (the beginning of which is the biblical literature) is not normative but *guiding*. This is a rejection of the Roman Catholic point of view; just as the subordination of the biblical literature to the theological norm implied in it is a rejection of orthodox Protestantism. Tradition cannot be normative in Christian theology because there is always an element in Tradition which must be judged and cannot be the judge itself. But Tradition can and must be guiding for the theologian, because it is the expression of the continuous reception of the new reality in history and because, without tradition, no theological existence is possible. It is rather a naïve illusion of some Protestants to believe that by jumping over two thousand years of Christian tradition they can come into a direct and existential (more than philological) relation to the biblical texts. The guiding function of the Tradition has a positive and a negative side. Positively, the Tradition shows the questions implied in the Christian message, the main possibilities of answers, and the points in which Christians have agreed and have disagreed. Negatively, the Tradition shows answers which have generally been avoided and, above all, answers which have been characterized by the church as "heretical." He who takes the Tradition seriously must take heresies seriously. He knows that a heresy is supposed to be, not a deviating opinion, but an existential attack on, or a distortion of, the theological norm in the name of theology. He will not easily—not without the consciousness that he risks his participation in the new reality—promote a view which has been characterized as heretical by the church as a whole. This, of course, should not prevent anyone from following his theological conscience (as Luther did in Worms); but it should sharpen that conscience.

The positive element in theological method is historically given. But nothing is more ambiguous than the concept "historical." When the Anglican church accepted the apostolic succession as one of its basic doctrines, it meant to emphasize the historical continuity of the manifestation of the new reality in history. In this sense the doctrine emphasized the historical element in church and theology. But when Anglican theologians, answering Roman attacks, tried to justify the apostolic character of their episcopate by an 8,000 to 1 documentary probability that there was a real apostolic succession, they introduced another meaning of "historical," namely, the probabilities (which never can become religious certainties) of historical research. In that moment their religious position was scientifically undermined because they confused the two meanings of "historical." The same is true of biblical criticism. If the Christian faith is based even on a 100,000 to 1 probability that Jesus has said or done or suffered this or that; if Christianity is based on possible birth-registers of Nazareth or crime-registers of Pontius Pilate, then it has lost its foundation completely. Then the historical event, that a new reality has appeared in mankind and the world (a reality which is reflected in the picture of Jesus as the Christ), has become a matter of empirical verification, ideally through a competent reporter, armed with a camera, phonograph, and psychograph. Since such a reporter, unfortunately, was not available in the year A.D. 30, we have to replace him by more or less probable conjectures. But this is not the historical character of Jesus as the Christ. It is regrettable that one of the greatest events in the history of religion— the radical criticism of the holy legend of Christianity by Christian theologians, which destroyed a whole system of pious superstition—has been abused for the purpose of giving a pseudo-scientific foundation to the Christian faith. The historical foundation of theological method does not mean that the theologian has to wait, with fear and trembling, for the next mail which may bring him a new, more critical, or more conservative statement about some important facts of the "life of Jesus" according to which he has to change his faith and his theology. But is does mean that his theology is determined by the event of the appearance of the new reality in history, as reflected in the *full* biblical picture of Jesus as the Christ and as witnessed by all biblical writers and by the whole tradition of Christianity.

V. THE ELEMENT OF IMMEDIACY IN THE THEOLOGICAL METHOD

The positive element in theology, as discussed above, gives the *content* of theological work; the rational element, to be discussed later, gives the *form* of theological work; and the element of immediacy, to be discussed now, gives the *medium* of theological work. Without participation in the reality within which theology speaks, no theology is possible; it is the air in which theology breathes. We call this participation "experience" in the larger sense of the word, in which it covers the mere encounter as well as the cognitively conscious encounter. "Experience" in both senses is the medium, the element in which theology lives. But the religious experience of the theologian is not a positive source and not a norm of systematic theology. Everybody's religious experience is shaped by the denominational group to which he belongs. The education in his own church opened the door to religious reality for every theologian. Later he has personal experiences which confirm or transform his earlier ones. But his intention should never be to make his earlier or later experiences the content of his theology; they certainly will enter into it, but this is an event, not an intention. It is the function of the medium to mediate, not to hold fast. It was the danger of Schleiermacher's theology that his concept of "religious consciousness" became confused with "experience." But it contradicts the basic principle of the Reformation to look at one's self instead of looking beyond one's self at the new reality which liberates man from himself. Our experience is changing and fragmentary; it is not the source of truth, although without it no truth can become *our* truth.

It might be said that the whole history of religion, including the biblical religion and the development of Christianity, is the reservoir of man's religious experience and that the positive element of theology is identical with the contents of this experience. Such a statement is correct, but ambiguous. A content, e.g., of the experience of the prophet Isaiah, is the paradoxical acting of God in history. This divine acting transcends every immediate experience. It has become manifest to the prophet in a situation which we should call "revelation." Of course, the prophet is aware of this situation, and to that extent it is an "experience." Not the experiential side, however, is significant for the prophet and for the theologian, but the revelatory side. The word "revelation" has been distorted into "supra-natural communication of knowledge"; it is hard to save the word (and many others) from this state of corruption into which it has been brought by both supra-naturalism and naturalism. Nevertheless, "revelation" points to something for which no other adequate word is available—certainly not "religious experience." Revelation is the manifestation of the ultimate ground and meaning of human existence (and implicitly of all existence). It is not a matter of objective knowledge, of empirical research or rational inference. It is a matter of ultimate concern; it grasps the total personality and is effective through a set of symbols. Revelation is not restricted to a special period of history, to special personalities or writings. It occurs wherever it "wills." But we can speak of it only if it has become revelation *for us,* if we have experienced it existentially. Not experience, but revelation received *in* experience, gives the content of every theology.

There is, however, one point (which is only a point, without length or breadth) in which medium and content are identical, because in this point subject and object are identical: It is the awareness of the ultimate itself, the *esse ipsum,* which transcends the difference between subject and object and lies, as the presupposition of all doubts, beyond doubt; it is the *veritas ipsa,* as Augustine has called it. It is wrong to call this point "God" (as the ontological argument does), but it is necessary to call it "that in us which makes it impossible for us to escape God." It is the presence of the element of "ultimacy" in the structure of our existence, the basis of religious experience. It has been called "religious *a priori*"; but if we use this phrase (in the sense of *anima naturaliter religiosa*), we must remove every content from it and reduce it to the pure potentiality of having experiences with the character of "ultimate concern." Every content of such an experience is dependent on revelation, namely, on the special way, form, and situation in which this potentiality is actualized by a concern which is concrete and ultimate at the same time. While the certainty of the pure ultimacy is ultimate, conditioned by nothing, its concrete embodiment in symbols and acts is a matter of destiny and venturing faith. Whenever we speak of religious experience, it is important to distinguish these (inseparable) elements: (1) the "point" of immediate awareness of the unconditional which *is* empty but unconditionally certain; and (2) the "breadth" of a concrete concern which is full of content but has the conditional certainty of venturing faith. Theology deals with the second element, while presupposing the first and measuring every theological statement by the standard of the ultimacy of the ultimate concern.

VI. THE ELEMENT OF RATIONALITY IN THE THEOLOGICAL METHOD

Theology is the rational "word" about God; it is the methodical interpretation of our ultimate concern. The rational element is not a source of theology. It does not give the content. But it gives the form; and the relation between form and content is extremely complex and demands careful analysis.

Theology is often identified with systematic theology. Although this terminology is bad, because it excludes historical and practical theology from their full part in the whole world of theology, it indicates that theology is essentially systematic. The word "system" has a narrower and a larger meaning. In its narrower sense the word points to the ideal of a deductive method in which a whole of interdependent presuppositions is derived from highest principles. Attempts have been made to develop such a system in the history of Christian thought. But the positive element in theology utterly resists a "system" in this sense; it includes openness and undermines a closed system. But "system" has also a larger sense. It designates a whole of propositions which are consistent, interdependent, and developed according to a definite method. In this sense all classical theology was systematic, and no theology, however fragmentary its actual work may be, can surrender the systematic idea. Every meaningful fragment is an implicit system, as every system is an explicit fragment; for man, and especially the theologian, lives in fragments, in reality as well as in thought.

It is obvious that the positive character of theology excludes a rational or natural theology, if these terms mean that, without existential participation in an ultimate concern, a detached analysis of reality can produce theological propositions. Even the rational substructure on which, according to scholasticism, the revealed superstructure is built, has convincing power only in the situation of faith. Even if (with Thomas and against Duns Scotus) the logical necessity and correctness of the arguments of natural theology are acknowledged, their existential significance without revelation is not asserted.

The terms "natural religion" or "natural revelation" or "natural theology" are extremely misleading. If religion is the state of being grasped by an ultimate concern, "natural religion" can only mean that the ultimate concern is experienced in an encounter with nature. This, of course, is not only possible and real, but it is a necessary part of every ultimate concern; but it cannot be separated from other elements which also belong to every ultimate concern, such as personal and social elements. The concepts "natural revelation" and "natural theology" are often used for a knowledge of God which is inferentially derived from the structure of reality. But, whether such conclusions are valid or not, in neither case have they the character of "revelation," and they should not be called "theological," for there is no meaningful speaking of God if he is taken as an object which is not, at the same time, the ground of the speaking about him. There is no meaningful speaking of God except in an existential attitude or in the situation of revelation. In any other attitude the religious word "God" is used after it has been deprived of its genuine, namely, its religious, meaning. So we can say: There *is* revelation through nature; but there is no natural (rational) revelation. And there *is* theology dealing with nature; but there is no natural theology. Reason elaborates but does not produce theological propositions.

But the question arises as to whether the "elaboration" of the positive element in theology does not introduce a rational element into the substance itself. The urgency of this question is obvious when we look at the large number of philosophical concepts which have been used for theological purposes throughout the whole history of Christian thought.

It is possible to make a distinction between two types of theology, the *kerygmatic* and the *apologetic* type. In the kerygmatic type the kerygma—the message—is reproduced, interpreted, and organized either in predominantly biblical terms or in terms taken from the classical tradition. In the apologetic type the kerygma is related to the prephilosophical and the philosophical interpretations of reality. An apology "makes answer"—answers the questions asked of, and the criticisms directed against, a concrete religion. But an answer is possible only if there is a common ground between the one who asks and the one who answers. Apologetic theology presupposes the idea of a universal revelation, to which reference can be made because it is acknowledged by both sides. Here the rational element in theological method becomes most important and most intimately connected with the positive element. The way in which this connection has been and should be carried through can be called the "method of correlation."

VII. THE METHOD OF CORRELATION

Wherever theology is understood in "existential" terms, all theological statements have the character of "correlation." Luther has expressed this principle very often and very strongly: "As you believe, so you have." This does not mean that the belief produces its contents; such an idea would have been utterly blasphemous for Luther. But it does mean that the objective and the subjective side of faith are interrelated, for faith is the expression of the impact of an ultimate concern on the human personality; it is the expression of an "existential situation" and not the acceptance of an objective assertion. Therefore, it is always subjective and objective in a strict interdependence. It is the beginning of a process of disintegration in theology if the objective side is isolated as a quasi-scientific assertion and the subjective side as an emotional "will to believe" in spite of a lack of evidence. The problem of truth in theology cannot be solved in terms of objective evidence. It can be solved only in terms of existential criteria. In the prophetic, as well as in the mystical, literature one criterion always appears: the unconditional character of the unconditional. Symbolically, it is called the "majesty of God"; or his exclusiveness against all finite claims (idols) or the unconditional dependence of every power on the divine power; or the "justification by grace alone." Every genuine heresy is an attack on the divinity of the divine. It gives to something finite infinite validity. It conditions the unconditional, for instance, by human morality or rationality. The "truth" of the Reformation theology against the canons of the Council of Trent is its emphasis on the ultimacy of the ultimate concern; it is not a "scientific" superiority of the Protestant over the Catholic propositions. It is an "existential," not an "objective," truth. This is the reason why the struggle of theologians is significant. They discuss, at least in principle, questions of "to be or not to be."

The method of correlation is especially the method of apologetic theology. Question and answer must be correlated in such a way that the religious symbol is interpreted as the adequate answer to a question, implied in man's existence, and asked in primitive, pre-philosophical, or elaborated philosophical terms. For instance, the question implied in human finitude is answered in the symbols which constitute the idea of God; or the symbol of revelation answers the questions which drive reason to its own boundary; or the question implied in man's existential disruption and despair is answered in the symbol of the Christ and his appearance under the conditions of existence; or the idea of the divine Spirit is interpreted as the answer to the question implied in the tragic ambiguities of life, especially man's spiritual life; or the problems of the meaning of history are answered in the symbol of the Kingdom of God. In all these cases the method of correlation establishes a mutual interdependence between questions and answers. The questions implied in human existence determine the meaning and the theological interpretation of the answers as they appear in the classical religious concepts. The form of the questions, whether primitive or philosophical, is decisive for the theological form in which the answer is given. And, conversely, the substance of the question is determined by the substance of the answer. Nobody is able to ask questions concerning God, revelation, Christ, etc., who has not already received some answer. So we can say: With respect to man's ultimate concern the questions contain the substance of the answers, and the answers are shaped by the form of the questions. Here the rational element in theological method has a determining influence on theological propositions—not on their substance but on their form. But there is no way of saying a priori how much substance is hidden in the form. This can be said only in the process of theological work, and never fully. The reception of the "new reality," is always conditioned by the "old reality," which is conquered and fulfilled by it. This is the reason why early Christianity formulated the doctrine of the Logos, who has appeared in a unique way in Jesus as the Christ and is, at the same time, the universal principle of revelation in religion and culture. In this way the old reality can be considered as preparation for the new one; and the philosophical form is ultimately related to the substance of the theological answer instead of being alien to it. It seems to me that, without some form of a Logos doctrine (even if the term "Logos" is not used), no theology—certainly no apologetic theology—is possible.

A few examples may suffice to give a concrete impression of the method of correlation. If the question implied in human finitude is the question of God and the idea of God is the answer to this question, then modern existential analysis of human finitude becomes extremely valuable for the theological treatment of the idea of God. God becomes the correlate to human anxiety and contingency. He becomes the symbol of a "transcendent courage," in which the characteristics of finitude, as essential insecurity, loneliness, having to die, etc., are overcome. In this way the idea of God receives existential significance. The meaningless and self-contradictory question about the "existence of God" is replaced by an intensely meaningful question concerning our participation in an infinite communion, security, power, and meaning in the divine life.

In the same way the question implied in the self-destructive trends of man's personal and social life is to be understood as the question to which the central Christian statement that Jesus is the Christ gives the answer. If Christology is treated on the basis of this correlation, it interprets the picture of Jesus Christ as the ultimate manifestation of saving power in life and history, as the appearance of a "new reality," a power of wholeness and reconciliation conquering the "demonic" mechanisms in personal and social existence. Then our recent rediscovery of the contradictory structures in soul and community determines the form of our christological answer and makes this answer existential for our time. The method of correlation liberates Christology from a historism which tries to base the Christian faith in the new reality on doubtful historical probabilities, and it also liberates Christology from the "alchemy" of the doctrine of two natures, interpreting its meaning as a statement of the paradox of the victorious maintenance of the divine-human unity in a personal life against all the disruptive attacks of man's existential situation.

The method of correlation, as these examples show, is at no point forced into the vicious debate between naturalism and supra-naturalism. It describes things as they show themselves to the religious consciousness in the light of the human situation, the questions implied in it, and the answers given to it by the Christian message. Theology has rediscovered its correlative and existential character. It has overcome a theology of objective statements and subjective emotions. It has become again a way of giving answers to the questions which are our ultimate concern.

The Actuality of God

3. GOD AS BEING

a) God as being and finite being.—The being of God is being-itself. The being of God cannot be understood as the existence of a being alongside others or above others. If God is *a* being, he is subject to the categories of finitude, especially to space and substance. Even if he is called the "highest being" in the sense of the "most perfect" and the "most powerful" being, this situation is not changed. When applied to God, superlatives become diminutives. They place him on the level of other beings while elevating him above all of them. Many theologians who have used the term "highest being" have known better. Actually they have described the highest as the absolute, as that which is on a level qualitatively different from the level of any being—even the highest being. Whenever infinite or unconditional power and meaning are attributed to the highest being, it has ceased to be *a* being and has become being-itself. Many confusions in the doctrine of God and many apologetic weaknesses could be avoided if God were understood first of all as being-itself or as the ground of being. The power of being is another way of expressing the same

(From Paul Tillich, *Systematic Theology*, Vol. I [University of Chicago Press, 1951], Part II, Chap. II, section B, pp. 235–52.)

thing in a circumscribing phrase. Ever since the time of Plato it has been known—although it often has been disregarded, especially by the nominalists and their modern followers—that the concept of being as being, or being-itself, points to the power inherent in everything, the power of resisting nonbeing. Therefore, instead of saying that God is first of all being-itself, it is possible to say that he is the power of being in everything and above everything, the infinite power of being. A theology which does not dare to identify God and the power of being as the first step toward a doctrine of God relapses into monarchic monotheism, for if God is not being-itself, he is subordinate to it, just as Zeus is subordinate to fate in Greek religion. The structure of being-itself is his fate, as it is the fate of all other beings. But God is his own fate; he is "by himself"; he possesses "aseity." This can be said of him only if he is the power of being, if he is being-itself.

As being-itself God is beyond the contrast of essential and existential being. We have spoken of the transition of being into existence, which involves the possibility that being will contradict and lose itself. This transition is excluded from being-itself (except in terms of the christological paradox), for being-itself does not participate in nonbeing. In this it stands in contrast to every being. As classical theology has emphasized, God is beyond essence and existence. Logically, being-itself is "before," "prior to," the split which characterizes finite being.

For this reason it is as wrong to speak of God as the universal essence as it is to speak of him as existing. If God is understood as universal essence, as the form of all forms, he is identified with the unity and totality of finite potentialities; but he has ceased to be the power of the ground in all of them, and therefore he has ceased to transcend them. He has poured all his creative power into a system of forms, and he is bound to these forms. This is what pantheism means.

On the other hand, grave difficulties attend the attempt to speak of God as existing. In order to maintain the truth that God is beyond essence and existence while simultaneously arguing for the existence of God, Thomas Aquinas is forced to distinguish between two kinds of divine existence: that which is identical with essence and that which is not. But an existence of God which is not united with its essence is a contradiction in terms. It makes God a being whose existence does not fulfil his essential potentialities; being and not-yet-being are "mixed" in him, as they are in everything finite. God ceases to be God, the ground of being and meaning. What really has happened is that Thomas has had to unite two different traditions: the Augustinian, in which the divine existence is included in his essence, and the Aristotelian, which derives the existence of God from the existence of the world and which then asserts, in a second step, that his existence is identical with his essence. Thus the question of the existence of God can be neither asked nor answered. If asked, it is a question about that which by its very nature is above existence, and therefore the answer —whether negative or affirmative—implicitly denies the nature of God. It is as atheistic to affirm the existence of God as it is to deny it. God is being-itself, not *a* being. On this basis a first step can be taken toward the solution of the problem which usually is discussed as the immanence and the transcendence of God. As the power of being, God transcends every being and also the totality of beings—the world. Being-itself is beyond finitude and infinity; otherwise it would be conditioned by something other than itself, and the real power of being would lie beyond both it and that which conditioned it. Being-itself infinitely transcends every finite being. There is no proportion or gradation between the finite and the infinite. There is an absolute break, an infinite "jump." On the other hand, everything finite participates in being-itself and in its infinity. Otherwise it would not have the power of being. It would be swallowed by nonbeing, or it never would have emerged out of nonbeing. This double relation of all beings to being-itself gives being-itself a double characteristic. In calling it creative, we point to the fact that everything participates in the infinite power of being. In calling it abysmal, we point to the fact that everything participates in the power of being in a finite way, that all beings are infinitely transcended by their creative ground.

Man is bound to the categories of finitude. He uses the two categories of relation—causality and substance—to express the relation of being-itself to finite beings. The "ground" can be interpreted in both ways, as the cause of finite beings and as their substance. The former has been elaborated by Leibniz in the line of the Thomistic tradition, and the latter has been elaborated by Spinoza in the line of the mystical tradition. Both ways are impossible. Spinoza establishes a naturalistic pantheism, in contrast to the idealistic type which identifies God with the universal essence of being, which denies finite freedom and in so doing denies the freedom of God. By necessity God is merged into the finite beings, and their being is his being. Here again it must be emphasized that pantheism does not say that God is everything. It says that God is the substance of everything and that there is no substantial independence and freedom in anything finite.

Therefore, Christianity, which asserts finite freedom in man and spontaneity in the nonhuman realm, has rejected the category of substance in favor of the category of causality in attempting to express the relation of the power of being to the beings who participate in it. Causality seems to make the world dependent on God, and, at the same time, to separate God from the world in the way a cause is separated from its effect. But the category of causality cannot "fill the bill," for cause and effect are not separate; they include each other and form a series which is endless in both directions. What is cause at one point in this series is effect at another point and conversely. God as cause is drawn into this series, which drives even him beyond himself. In order to disengage the divine cause from the series of causes and effects, it is called the first cause, the absolute beginning. What this means is that the category of causality is being denied while it is being used. In other words, causality is being used not as a category but as a symbol. And if this is done and is understood, the difference between substance and causality disappears, for if God is the cause of the entire series of causes and effects, he is the substance underlying the whole process of becoming. But this "underlying" does not have the character of a substance which underlies its accidents and which is completely expressed by them. It is an underlying in which substance and accidents preserve their freedom. In other words, it is substance not as a category but as a symbol. And, if taken symbolically, there is no difference between *prima causa* and *ultima substantia*. Both mean, what can be called in a more directly symbolic term, "the creative and abysmal ground of being." In this term both naturalistic pantheism, based on the category of substance, and rationalistic theism, based on the category of causality, are overcome.

Since God is the ground of being, he is the ground of the structure of being. He is not subject to this structure; the structure is grounded in him. He *is* this structure, and it is impossible to speak about him except in terms of this structure. God must be approached cognitively through the structural elements of being-itself. These elements make him a living God, a God who can be man's concrete concern. They enable us to use symbols which we are certain point to the ground of reality.

b) *God as being and the knowledge of God.*—The statement that God is being-itself is a nonsymbolic statement. It does not point beyond itself. It means what is says directly and properly; if we speak of the actuality of God, we first assert that he is not God if he is not being-itself.

Other assertions about God can be made theologically only on this basis. Of course, religious assertions do not require such a foundation for what they say about God; the foundation is implicit in every religious thought concerning God. Theologians must make explicit what is implicit in religious thought and expression; and, in order to do this, they must begin with the most abstract and completely unsymbolic statement which is possible, namely, that God is being-itself or the absolute.

However, after this has been said, nothing else can be said about God as God which is not symbolic. As we already have seen, God as being-itself is the ground of the ontological structure of being without being subject to this structure himself. He *is* the structure; that is, he has the power of determining the structure of everything that has being. Therefore, if anything beyond this bare assertion is said about God, it no longer is a direct and proper statement, no longer a concept. It is indirect, and it points to something beyond itself. In a word, it is symbolic.

The general character of the symbol has been described. Special emphasis must be laid on the insight that symbol and sign are different; that, while the sign bears no necessary relation to that to which it points, the symbol participates in the reality of that for which it stands. The sign can be changed arbitrarily according to the demands of expediency, but the symbol grows and dies according to the correlation between that which is symbolized and the persons who receive it as a symbol. Therefore, the religious symbol, the symbol which points to the divine, can be a true symbol only if it participates in the power of the divine to which it points.

There can be no doubt that any concrete assertion about God must be symbolic, for a concrete assertion is one which uses a segment of finite experience in order to say something about him. It transcends the content of this segment, although it also includes it. The segment of finite reality which becomes the vehicle of a concrete assertion about God is affirmed and negated at the same time. It becomes a symbol, for a symbolic expression is one whose proper meaning is negated by that to which it points. And yet it also is affirmed by it, and this affirmation gives the symbolic expression an adequate basis for pointing beyond itself.

The crucial question must now be faced. Can a segment of finite reality become the basis for an assertion about that which is infinite? The answer is that it can, because that which is infinite is being-itself and because everything participates in being-itself. The *analogia entis* is not the property of a questionable natural theology which attempts to gain knowledge of God by drawing conclusions about the infinite from the finite. The *analogia entis* gives us our only justification of speaking at all about God. It is based on the fact that God must be understood as being-itself.

The truth of a religious symbol has nothing to do with the truth of the empirical assertions involved in it, be they physical, psychological, or historical. A religious symbol possesses some truth if it adequately expresses the correlation of revelation in which some person stands. A religious symbol *is* true if it adequately expresses the correlation of some person with final revelation. A religious symbol can die only if the correlation of which it is an adequate expression dies. This occurs whenever the revelatory situation changes and former symbols become obsolete. The history of religion, right up to our own time, is full of dead symbols which have been killed not by a scientific criticism of assumed superstitions but by a religious criticism of religion. The judgment that a religious symbol *is* true is identical with the judgment that the revelation of which it is the adequate expression is true. This double meaning of the truth of a symbol must be kept in mind. A symbol *has* truth: it is adequate to the revelation it expresses. A symbol *is* true: it is the expression of a true revelation.

Theology as such has neither the duty nor the power to confirm or to negate religious symbols. Its task is to interpret them according to theological principles and methods. In the process of interpretation, however, two things may happen: theology may discover contradictions between symbols within the theological circle and theology may speak not only as theology but also as religion. In the first case, theology can point out the religious dangers and the theological errors which follow from the use of certain symbols; in the second case, theology can become prophecy, and in this role it may contribute to a change in the revelatory situation.

Religious symbols are double-edged. They are directed toward the infinite which they symbolize *and* toward the finite through which they symbolize it. They force the infinite down to finitude and the finite up to infinity. They open the divine for the human and the human for the divine. For instance, if God is symbolized as "Father," he is brought down to the human relationship of father and child. But at the same time this human relationship is consecrated into a pattern of the divine-human relationship. If "Father" is employed as a symbol for God, fatherhood is seen in its theonomous, sacramental depth. One cannot arbitrarily "make" a religious symbol out of a segment of secular reality. Not even the collective unconscious, the great symbol-creating source, can do this. If a segment of reality is used as a symbol for God, the realm of reality from which it is taken is, so to speak, elevated into the realm of the holy. It no longer is secular. It is theonomous. If God is called the "king," something is said not only about God but also about the holy character of kinghood. If God's work is called "making whole" or "healing," this not only says something about God but also emphasizes the theonomous character of all healing. If God's self-manifestation is called "the word," this not only symbolizes God's relation to man but also emphasizes the holiness of all words as an expression of the spirit. The list could be continued. Therefore, it is not surprising that in a secular culture both the symbols for God and the theonomous character of the material from which the symbols are taken disappear.

A final word of warning must be added in view of the fact that for many people the very term "symbolic" carries the connotation of nonreal. This is partially the result of confusion between sign and symbol and partially due to the identification of reality with empirical reality, with the entire realm of objective things and events. Both reasons have been undercut explicitly and implicitly in the foregoing chapters. But one reason remains, namely, the fact that some theological movements, such as Protestant Hegelianism and Catholic modernism, have interpreted religious language symbolically in order to dissolve its realistic meaning and to weaken its seriousness, its power, and its spiritual impact. This was not the purpose of the classical essays on the "divine names," in which the symbolic character of all affirmations about God was strongly emphasized and explained in religious terms, nor was it a consequence of these essays. Their intention and their result was to give to God and to all his relations to man more reality and power than a nonsymbolic and therefore easily superstitious interpretation could give them. In this sense symbolic interpretation is proper and necessary; it enhances rather than diminishes the reality and power of religious language, and in so doing it performs an important function.

4. GOD AS LIVING

a) *God as being and God as living.*—Life is the process in which potential being becomes actual being. It is the actualization of the structural elements of being in their unity and in their tension. These elements move divergently and convergently in every life-process; they separate and reunite simultaneously. Life ceases in the moment of separation without union or of union without separation. Both complete identity and complete separation negate life. If we call God the "living God," we deny that he is a pure identity of being as being; and we also deny that there is a definite separation of being from being in him. We assert that he is the eternal process in which separation is posited and is overcome by reunion. In this sense, God lives. Few things about God are more emphasized in the Bible, especially in the Old Testament, than the truth that God is a living God. Most of the so-called anthropomorphisms of the biblical picture of God are expressions of his character as living. His actions, his passions, his remembrances and anticipations, his suffering and joy, his personal relations and his plans—all these make him a living God and distinguish him from the pure absolute, from being-itself.

Life is the actuality of being, or, more exactly, it is the process in which potential being becomes actual being. But in God as God there is no distinction between potentiality and actuality. Therefore, we cannot speak of God as living in the proper or nonsymbolic sense of the word "life." We must speak of God as living in symbolic terms. Yet every true symbol participates in the reality which it symbolizes. God lives in so far as he is the ground of life. Anthropomorphic symbols are adequate for speaking of God religiously. Only in this way can he be the living God for man. But even in the most primitive intuition of the divine a feeling should be, and usually is, present that there is a mystery about divine names which makes them improper, self-transcending, symbolic. Religious instruction should deepen this feeling without depriving the divine names of their reality and power. One of the most surprising qualities of the prophetic utterances in the Old Testament is that, on the one hand, they always appear concrete and anthropomorphic and that, on the other hand, they preserve the mystery of the divine ground. They never deal with being as being or with the absolute as the absolute; nevertheless, they never make God a being alongside others, into something conditioned by something else which also is conditioned. Nothing is more inadequate and disgusting than the attempt to translate the concrete symbols of the Bible into less concrete and less powerful symbols. Theology should not weaken the concrete symbols, but it must analyze them and interpret them in abstract ontological terms. Nothing is more inadequate and confusing than the attempt to restrict theological work to half-abstract, half-concrete terms which do justice neither to existential intuition nor to cognitive analysis.

The ontological structure of being supplies the material for the symbols which point to the divine life. However, this does not mean that a doctrine of God can be derived from an ontological system. The character of the divine life is made manifest in revelation. Theology can only explain and systematize the existential knowledge of revelation in theoretical terms, interpreting the symbolic significance of the ontological elements and categories.

While the symbolic power of the categories appears in the relation of God to the creature, the elements give symbolic expression to the nature of the divine life itself. The polar character of the ontological elements is rooted in the divine life, but the divine life is not subject to this polarity. Within the divine life, every ontological element includes its polar element completely, without tension and without the threat of dissolution, for God is being-itself. However, there is a difference between the first and the second elements in each polarity with regard to their power of symbolizing the divine life. The elements of individualization, dynamics, and freedom represent the self or subject side of the basic ontological structure within the polarity to which they belong. The elements of participation, form, and destiny represent the world or object side of the basic ontological structure within the polarity to which they belong. Both sides are rooted in the divine life. But the first side determines the existential relationship between God and man, which is the source of all symbolization. Man is a self who has a world. As a self he is an individual person who participates universally, he is a dynamic self-transcending agent within a special and a general form, and he is freedom which has a special destiny and which participates in a general destiny. Therefore, man symbolizes that which is his ultimate concern in terms taken from his own being. From the subjective side of the polarities he takes—or more exactly, receives—the material with which he symbolizes the divine life. He sees the divine life as personal, dynamic, and free. He cannot see it in any other way, for God is man's ultimate concern, and therefore he stands in analogy to that which man himself is. But the religious mind—theologically speaking, man in the correlation of revelation—always realizes implicitly, if not explicitly, that the other side of the polarities also is completely present in the side he uses as symbolic material. God is called a person, but he is a person not in finite separation but in an absolute and unconditional participation in everything. God is called dynamic, but he is dynamic not in tension with form but in an absolute and unconditional unity with form, so that his self-transcendence never is in tension with his self-preservation, so that he always remains God. God is called "free," but he is free not in arbitrariness but in an absolute and unconditional identity with his destiny, so that he himself is his destiny, so that the essential structures of being are not strange to his freedom but are the actuality of his freedom. In this way, although the symbols used for the divine life are taken from the concrete situation of man's relationship to God, they imply God's ultimacy, the ultimacy in which the polarities of being disappear in the ground of being, in being-itself.

The basic ontological structure of self and world is transcended in the divine life without providing symbolic material. God cannot be called a self, because the concept "self" implies separation from and contrast to everything which is not self. God cannot be called the world even by implication. Both self and world are rooted in the divine life, but they cannot become symbols for it. But the elements which constitute the basic ontological structure can become symbols because they do not speak of kinds of being (self and world) but of qualities of being which are valid in their proper sense when applied to all beings and which are valid in their symbolic sense when applied to being-itself.

b) *The divine life and the ontological elements.*—The symbols provided by the ontological elements present a great number of problems for the doctrine of God. In every special case it is necessary to distinguish between the proper sense of the concepts and their symbolic sense. And it is equally necessary to balance one side of the ontological polarity against the other without reducing the symbolic power of either of them. The history of theological thought is a continuous proof of the difficulty, the creativeness, and the danger of this situation. This is obvious if we consider the symbolic power of the polarity of individualization and participation. The symbol "personal God" is absolutely fundamental because an existential relation is a person-to-person relation. Man cannot be ultimately concerned about anything that is less than personal, but since personality (*persona, prosopon*) includes individuality, the question arises in what sense God can be called an individual. Is it meaningful to call him the "absolute individual"? The answer must be that it is meaningful only in the sense that he can be called the "absolute participant." The one term cannot be applied without the other. This can only mean that both individualization and participation are rooted in the ground of the divine life and that God is equally "near" to each of them while transcending them both.

The solution of the difficulties in the phrase "personal God" follows from this. "Personal God" does not mean that God is *a* person. It means that God is the ground of everything personal and that he carries within himself the ontological power of personality. He is not a person, but he is not less than personal. It should not be forgotten that classical theology employed the term *persona* for the trinitarian hypostases but not for God himself. God became "a person" only in the nineteenth century, in connection with the Kantian separation of nature ruled by physical law from personality ruled by moral law. Ordinary theism has made God a heavenly, completely perfect person who resides above the world and mankind. The protest of atheism against such a highest person is correct. There is no evidence for his existence, nor is he a matter of ultimate concern. God is not God without universal participation. "Personal God" is a confusing symbol.

God is the principle of participation as well as the principle of individualization. The divine life participates in every life as its ground and aim. God participates in everything that is; he has community with it; he shares in its destiny. Certainly such statements are highly symbolic. They can have the unfortunate logical implication that there is something alongside God in which he participates from the outside. But the divine participation creates that in which it participates. Plato uses the word *parousia* for the presence of the essences in temporal existence. This word later becomes the name for the preliminary and final presence of the transcendent Christ in the church and in the world. *Par-ousia* means "being by," "being with"—but on the basis of being absent, of being separated. In the same way God's participation is not a spatial or temporal presence. It is meant not categorically but symbolically. It is the parousia, the "being with" of that which is neither here nor there. If applied to God, participation and community are not less symbolic than individualization and personality. While active religious communication between God and man depends on the symbol of the personal God, the symbol of universal participation expresses the passive experi-

ence of the divine parousia in terms of the divine omnipresence.

The polarity of dynamics and form supplies the material
basis for a group of symbols which are central for any
present-day doctrine of God. Potentiality, vitality, and self-
transcendence are indicated in the term "dynamics," while
the term "form" embraces actuality, intentionality, and self-
preservation.

Potentiality and actuality appear in classical theology in
the famous formula that God is *actus purus,* the pure form
in which everything potential is actual, and which is the
eternal self-intuition of the divine fulness (*pleroma*). In
this formula the dynamic side in the dynamics-form polarity
is swallowed by the form side. Pure actuality, that is, actuality free from any element of potentiality, is a fixed result; it is not alive. Life includes the separation of potentiality and actuality. The nature of life is actualization, not
actuality. The God who is *actus purus* is not the living God.
It is interesting that even those theologians who have used
the concept of *actus purus* normally speak of God in the
dynamic symbols of the Old Testament and of Christian experience. This situation has induced some thinkers—partly
under the influence of Luther's dynamic conception of God
and partly under the impact of the problem of evil—to emphasize the dynamics in God and to depreciate the stabili-
zation of dynamics in pure actuality. They try to distinguish
between two elements in God, and they assert that, in so far
as God is a living God, these two elements must remain in
tension. Whether the first element is called the *Ungrund*
or the "nature in God" (Böhme), or the first potency
(Schelling), or the will (Schopenhauer), or the "given" in
God (Brightman), or *me-onic* freedom (Berdyaev), or the
contingent (Hartshorne)—in all these cases it is an expression of what we have called "dynamics," and it is an attempt to prevent the dynamics in God from being transformed into pure actuality.

Theological criticism of these attempts is easy if the concepts are taken in their proper sense, for then they make God finite, dependent on a fate or an accident which is not himself. The finite God, if taken literally, is a finite god, a polytheistic god. But this is not the way in which these concepts should be interpreted. They point symbolically to a quality of the divine life which is analogous to what appears as dynamics in the ontological structure. The divine creativity, God's participation in history, his outgoing character, are based on this dynamic element. It includes a "not yet" which is, however, always balanced by an "already" within the divine life. It is not an absolute "not yet," which would make it a divine-demonic power, nor is the "already" an absolute already. It also can be expressed as the negative element in the ground of being which is overcome as negative in the process of being-itself. As such it is the basis of the negative element in the creature, in which it is not overcome but is effective as a threat and a potential disruption.

These assertions include a rejection of a nonsymbolic, ontological doctrine of God as becoming. If we say that being is actual as life, the element of self-transcendence is obviously and emphatically included. But it is included as a symbolic element in balance with form. Being is not in balance with becoming. Being comprises becoming and rest, becoming as an implication of dynamics and rest as an implication of form. If we say that God is being-itself, this includes both rest and becoming, both the static and the dynamic elements. However, to speak of a "becoming" God disrupts the balance between dynamics and form and subjects God to a process which has the character of a fate or which is completely open to the future and has the character of an absolute accident. In both cases the divinity of God is undercut. The basic error of these doctrines is their metaphysical-constructive character. They apply the ontological elements to God in a nonsymbolic manner and are driven to religiously offensive and theologically untenable consequences.

If the element of form in the dynamics-form polarity is applied symbolically to the divine life, it expresses the actualization of its potentialities. The divine life inescapably unites possibility with fulfilment. Neither side threatens the other, nor is there a threat of disruption. In terms of self-preservation one could say that God cannot cease to be God. His going-out from himself does not diminish or destroy his divinity. It is united with the eternal "resting in himself."

The divine form must be conceived in analogy with what we have called "intentionality" on the human level. It is balanced with vitality, the dynamic side on the human level. The polarity in this formulation appears in classical theology as the polarity of will and intellect in God. It is consistent that Thomas Aquinas had to subordinate the will in God to the intellect when he accepted the Aristotelian *actus purus* as the basic character of God. And it must be remembered that the line of theological thought which tries to preserve the element of dynamics in God actually begins with Duns Scotus, who elevated the will in God over the intellect. Of course, both will and intellect in their application to God express infinitely more than the mental acts of willing and understanding as these appear in human experience. They are symbols for dynamics in all its ramifications and for form as the meaningful structure of being-itself. Therefore, it is not a question of metaphysical psychology, whether Aquinas or Duns Scotus is right. It is a question of the way in which psychological concepts should be employed as symbols for the divine life. And with respect to this question it is obvious that for more than a century a decision has been made in favor of the dynamic element. The philosophy of life, existential philosophy, and process philosophy agree on this point. Protestantism has contributed strong motives for this decision, but theology must balance the new with the old (predominantly Catholic) emphasis on the form character of the divine life.

If we consider the polarity of freedom and destiny in its symbolic value, we find that there hardly is a word said about God in the Bible which does not point directly or indirectly to his freedom. In freedom he creates, in freedom he deals with the world and man, in freedom he saves and fulfils. His freedom is freedom from anything prior to him or alongside him. Chaos cannot prevent him from speaking the word which makes light out of darkness; the evil deeds of men cannot prevent him from carrying through his plans; the good deeds of men cannot force him to reward them; the structure of being cannot prevent him from revealing himself; etc. Classical theology has spoken in more abstract terms of the aseity of God, of his being *a se*, self-derived. There is no ground prior to him which could condition his freedom; neither chaos nor nonbeing has power to limit or resist him. But aseity also means that there is nothing given in God which is not at the same time affirmed by his freedom. If taken nonsymbolically, this naturally leads to an unanswerable question, whether the structure of freedom, because it constitutes his freedom, is not itself something given in relation to which God has no freedom. The answer can only be that freedom, like the other ontological concepts, must be understood symbolically and in terms of the existential correlation of man and God. If taken in this way, freedom means that that which is man's ultimate concern is in no way dependent on man or on any finite being or on any finite concern. Only that which is unconditional can be the expression of unconditional concern. A conditioned God is no God.

Can the term "destiny" be applied symbolically to the divine life? The gods of polytheism have a destiny—or, more correctly, a fate—because they are not ultimate. But can one say that he who is unconditional and absolute has a destiny in the same manner in which he has freedom? Is it possible to attribute destiny to being-itself? It is possible, provided the connotation of a destiny-determining power above God is avoided and provided one adds that God is his own destiny and that in God freedom and destiny are one. It may be argued that this truth is more adequately expressed if destiny is replaced by necessity, not mechanical necessity, but structural necessity, of course, or if God is spoken of as being his own law. Such phrases are important as interpretations, but they lack two elements of meaning which are present in the word "destiny." They lack the mystery of that which precedes any structure and law, being-itself; and they lack the relation to history which is included in the term "destiny." If we say that God is his own destiny, we point both to the infinite mystery of being and to the participation of God in becoming and in history.

c) God as spirit and the trinitarian principles.—Spirit is the unity of the ontological elements and the *telos* of life. Actualized as life, being-itself is fulfilled as spirit. The word *telos* expresses the relation of life and spirit more precisely than the words "aim" or "goal." It expresses the inner directedness of life toward spirit, the urge of life to become spirit, to fulfil itself as spirit. *Telos* stands for an inner, essential, necessary aim, for that in which a being fulfils its own nature. God as living is God fulfilled in himself and therefore spirit. God *is* spirit. This is the most embracing, direct, and unrestricted symbol for the divine life. It does not need to be balanced with another symbol, because it includes all the ontological elements.

Some anticipatory remarks about spirit must be made at this point, although the doctrine of the spirit is the subject of a separate part of systematic theology. The word "spirit" (with a lower-case *s*) has almost disappeared from the English language as a significant philosophical term, in contrast to German, French, and Italian, in which the words *Geist, esprit,* and *spirito* have preserved their philosophical standing. Probably this is a result of the radical separation of the cognitive function of the mind from emotion and will, as typified in English empiricism. In any case, the word "spirit" appears predominantly in a religious context, and here it is spelled with a capital S. But it is impossible to understand the meaning of Spirit unless the meaning of spirit is understood, for Spirit is the symbolic application of spirit to the divine life.

The meaning of spirit is built up through the meaning of the ontological elements and their union. In terms of both sides of the three polarities one can say that spirit is the unity of power and meaning. On the side of power it includes centered personality, self-transcending vitality, and freedom of self-determination. On the side of meaning it includes universal participation, forms and structures of reality, and limiting and directing destiny. Life fulfilled as spirit embraces passion as much as truth, libido as much as surrender, will to power as much as justice. If one of these sides is absorbed by its correlate, either abstract law or chaotic movement remains. Spirit does not stand in contrast to body. Life as spirit transcends the duality of body and mind. It also transcends the triplicity of body, soul, and mind, in which soul is actual life-power and mind and body are its functions. Life as spirit is the life of the soul, which includes mind and body, but not as realities alongside the soul. Spirit is not a "part," nor is it a special function. It is the all-embracing function in which all elements of the structure of being participate. Life as spirit can be found by man only in man, for only in him is the structure of being completely realized.

The statement that God is Spirit means that life as spirit is the inclusive symbol for the divine life. It contains all the ontological elements. God is not nearer to one "part" of being or to a special function of being than he is to another. As Spirit he is as near to the creative darkness of the unconscious as he is to the critical light of cognitive reason. Spirit is the power through which meaning lives, and it is

the meaning which gives direction to power. God as Spirit
is the ultimate unity of both power and meaning. In contrast to Nietzsche, who identified the two assertions that
God is Spirit and that God is dead, we must say that God
is the living God because he is Spirit.

Any discussion of the *Christian* doctrine of the Trinity
must begin with the christological assertion that Jesus is the
Christ. The Christian doctrine of the Trinity is a corrobora-
tion of the christological dogma. The situation is different
if we do not ask the question of the Christian doctrines but
rather the question of the *presuppositions* of these doctrines
in an idea of God. Then we must speak about the trinitarian
principles, and we must begin with the Spirit rather than
with the Logos. God is Spirit, and any trinitarian statement
must be derived from this basic assertion.

God's life is life as spirit, and the trinitarian principles
are moments within the process of the divine life. Human
intuition of the divine always has distinguished between the
abyss of the divine (the element of power) and the fulness
of its content (the element of meaning), between the divine depth and the divine *logos*. The first principle is the
basis of Godhead, that which makes God God. It is the
root of his majesty, the unapproachable intensity of his being, the inexhaustible ground of being in which everything
has its origin. It is the power of being infinitely resisting
nonbeing, giving the power of being to everything that is.
During the past centuries theological and philosophical rationalism have deprived the idea of God of this first principle, and by doing so they have robbed God of his divinity.
He has become a hypostasized moral ideal or another name
for the structural unity of reality. The power of the Godhead has disappeared.

The classical term *logos* is most adequate for the second
principle, that of meaning and structure. It unites meaningful structure with creativity. Long before the Christian Era
—in a way already in Heraclitus—*logos* received connota-

tions of ultimacy as well as the meaning of being as being. According to Parmenides, being and the *logos* of being cannot be separated. The *logos* opens the divine ground, its infinity and its darkness, and it makes its fulness distinguishable, definite, finite. The *logos* has been called the mirror of the divine depth, the principle of God's self-objectification. In the *logos* God speaks his "word," both in himself and beyond himself. Without the second principle the first principle would be chaos, burning fire, but it would not be the creative ground. Without the second principle God is demonic, is characterized by absolute seclusion, is the "naked absolute" (Luther).

As the actualization of the other two principles, the Spirit is the third principle. Both power and meaning are contained in it and united in it. It makes them creative. The third principle is in a way the whole (God *is* Spirit), and in a way it is a special principle (God *has* the Spirit as he has the *logos*). It is the Spirit in whom God "goes out from" himself, the Spirit proceeds from the divine ground. He gives actuality to that which is potential in the divine ground and "outspoken" in the divine *logos*. Through the Spirit the divine fulness is posited in the divine life as something definite, and at the same time it is reunited in the divine ground. The finite is posited as finite within the process of the divine life, but it is reunited with the infinite within the same process. It is distinguished from the infinite, but it is not separated from it. The divine life is infinite mystery, but it is not infinite emptiness. It is the ground of all abundance, and it is abundant itself.

The consideration of the trinitarian principles is not the Christian doctrine of the Trinity. It is a preparation for it, nothing more. The dogma of the Trinity can be discussed only after the christological dogma has been elaborated. But the trinitarian principles appear whenever one speaks meaningfully of the living God.

The divine life is infinite, but in such a way that the

finite is posited in it in a manner which transcends potentiality and actuality. Therefore, it is not precise to identify God with the infinite. This can be done on some levels of analysis. If man and his world are described as finite, God is infinite in contrast to them. But the analysis must go beyond this level in both directions. Man is aware of his finitude because he has the power of transcending it and of looking at it. Without this awareness he could not call himself mortal. On the other hand, that which is infinite would not be infinite if it were limited by the finite. God is infinite because he has the finite (and with it that element of non-being which belongs to finitude) within himself united with his infinity. One of the functions of the symbol "divine life" is to point to this situation.

Existential Analyses and Religious Symbols

Existential analyses are older than existential philosophy. It is a familiar event in the history of philosophy that a special philosophy opens one's eyes to a special problem which was not unknown to former philosophers but which was not the center of their attention. If they or their followers then assert that this problem is nothing new for them, they are both right and wrong. They are right because most problems and perhaps even most types of solutions are as old as man's asking of the philosophical question. They are wrong because the movement of human thought is driven by the intensity with which old problems are seen in a new light and brought out of a peripheral significance into a central one. This is just what has happened to the existential problems. They were pushed into the background after the Renaissance and Reformation, definitely so following the victory of Cartesianism and theological rationalism. It was the function of the Existentialist movement to rediscover the significance of the existentialist questions and to reformulate them in the light of present-day experiences and insights.

(From Harold A. Basilius, ed., *Contemporary Problems in Religion* [Wayne University Press, 1956], Chap. II, pp. 37–55.)

The thesis of this paper is that in the period during which the existential questions were pushed aside or forgotten, the cognitive approach to religious symbolism was largely blocked, and that the turning of many representatives of twentieth-century philosophy, literature and art to existential questions has once again opened the approach to religious symbols. For religious symbols are partly a way of stating the same situation with which existential analyses are concerned; partly they are answers to the questions implied in the situation. They are the former when they speak of man and his predicament. They are the latter when they speak of God and his reaction to this predicament. In both cases, existential analysis makes the religious symbols understandable and a matter of possible concern for our contemporaries, including contemporary philosophers.

In order to define the nature of an existential analysis we must distinguish it from an essential analysis. The terms "existential" and "essential" analyses shall be used here as grammatical abbreviations for analyses of existential structures and analyses of essential structures, while the terms "essentialist" and "existentialist" shall be used for the movements and attitudes of the one or the other character.

Since the analysis of existential structures is predominantly an analysis of the human predicament, the best way of distinguishing existential and essential analyses is to do so with respect to their doctrines of man. There is a large group of problems concerning man which have been investigated and discussed throughout the history of philosophy in purely essentialist terms. They all deal with the question, What is the "nature" of man? What is his *ousia,* that which makes him what he is, in every exemplar who deserves the name man? Neither nominalism nor process philosophy, neither philosophical empiricism nor even existentialism can escape this question. Attempts to describe human nature in its essential structures, be it in more static or in more dynamic terms, can never cease to be a task of human thought.

The existentialist philosopher, for example, asks the question of the *differentia specifica* between man and non-human nature. If he answers the question with Aristotle, that man is *animal rationale,* this may not be specific enough, or the nature of the rational may not have been defined sufficiently, but the method itself is correct and clearly essentialist. There are theologians who react violently against the Aristotelian definition, not in order to amend it in this or that direction, but in order to deny the method in the name of an assumedly existentialist analysis of man's nature. They point to man's existential relation to God and consider this relation as the nature of man, misinterpreting for their purpose the Biblical phrase that man is the image of God. In the Biblical view, man is and always remains the image of God because of his bodily and spiritual qualities which give him control over nature in spite of his estrangement from his essential being. This is an important point because its negation was one of the ways by which neo-orthodox theology cut off all relations with essentialist philosophy and surrendered all rational criteria for theological thought.

The question of man's essential nature leads by itself to the mind-body problem. If we discuss the several monistic and dualistic answers given to this ever-present question and try to find a solution to it, we do an essentialist analysis. And we should reject theologians who interfere in this discussion out of an existential interest. They are aware of man's finitude and the question of the infinite which is implicit in his finitude. And they try to give an answer in terms of an essentialist psychology which includes an immortal part of man. This is the key to the failure of Thomas Aquinas when he tried to combine the essentialist Aristotelian doctrine of the soul as a form of the body with the Platonic-Christian dualism of the immortal soul and the mortal body. By this attempted combination, Aquinas injected existentialist analysis.

A third problem discussed in essentialist analyses of human nature is the relation of man as individuality and man as community. Again, the Aristotelian definition of man as a political animal is truly essentialist and remains valid, however it is enlarged upon or refined. Today the discussion of the problem is presented in Martin Buber's famous phrase, "the I-Thou relationship." This phrase *can* be understood in essentialist terms and can be used as a descriptive feature, showing how the ego becomes an ego only in the encounter with another ego in which it finds its limit and is thrown back upon itself. Therefore, man's ethical and cultural life is possible only in the community in which language is created. In this sense the ego-thou interdependence is a piece of essential analysis. Yet it was an existentialist invasion when Buber tried to remove the universals from the encounter between ego and thou, and to make both speechless, because there are no words for the absolute particular, the other ego. And it was a distortion of communal being when Heidegger referred to the problem as an escape into the non-authentic form of being, the being as a *"man"* (German), as an *"on"* (French), as a general "one." The political body of which Aristotle speaks is not the result of an escape into unauthentic being. Essentialism is right in rejecting this as an invasion.

A last example is man's ethical structure. Essentialist analysis has described it either in terms of the formal categories which constitute the ethical realm, as, for example, Kant did, or in terms of the ethical character and its virtues, as, for example, in the manner of Aquinas, or in terms of the embracing social structures, as, for example, according to Hegel. Kierkegaard has accused Hegel of neglecting man's ethical situation, namely, that of the individual who has to make the ethical decision. But although Hegel obviously neglects the structures which make the singular person as such a moral subject, he cannot be accused of excluding in his essentialist analyses the existentialist question, the question of the anxiety of decision to which Kierkegaard refers. If neo-orthodox theologians deny that the Bible has essentialist ethical material in the manner of Aristotle and the Stoics, they can be refuted not only by the partly Stoic elements of the Pauline letters, but also by the fact that the content of the ethical law never has been denied in the New Testament. Only its character as law is denied for those who are reconciled unto themselves. There can be no ethics without an essentialist analysis of man's ethical nature and its structures.

We have given examples of essentialist analyses of man's nature as they have been performed in all periods of philosophical thought. At the same time, we have drawn attention to existentialist attacks on this kind of philosophizing and to the necessity on our part of rejecting these attacks. In doing so, we have given first indications of what an existentialist analysis is, namely, a description of man's antiessential or estranged predicament. We have also indicated that the existentialist attacks to which we have referred have continuously interfered with the essentialist task.

If we now turn to a more direct characterization of existential analyses, we find that in contrast to essentialism they concentrate on the human situation and that their point of departure is the immediate awareness man has of his situation. Both characteristics follow from what an existential analysis is supposed to do, namely, to describe those elements within experience which express being in contrast to what it essentially is. This experience is not a matter of objectifying observation from outside the situation. It can be understood only as an immediate awareness from inside the situation. It has, for example, the character of finitude itself in contrast to a finitude which I see objectively if something comes to an end. One may think here of the difference between the observed death of someone else and the anticipation of one's own death. In the first experience, the material of an essential analysis is given; in the second experience, one's existential situation is manifested in anxiety. Another example is the experience of guilt. It is an essentialist analysis if types of law-breakers are described or the degree of guilt in a criminal action is discussed. But guilt becomes an existentialist concept if it is the expression of one's own deviation from what one essentially is and therefore ought to be. Guilt in this sense is connected with the anxiety of losing one's true being.

A third example is provided by the experience of meaninglessness. We often have the more or less adequate impression that somebody lives an empty and meaningless life, without being fully aware of his doing so. Quite different from such an essential description is the experience of feeling oneself cut off from any meaning of life, of being lost in a desert of meaninglessness and of feeling the anxiety implicit in this situation.

In each of these examples, to which others will be added later on, I alluded to what I suggest calling "existential anxiety." This points to the fact that the concept of anxiety has played a decisive role in all existentialist thinking since Augustine and Pascal. I assume that the frequently discussed distinction between anxiety and fear is known and largely accepted. The main point is that fear has a definite object and is, as such, an object of essentialist philosophy, while anxiety has no definite object and is a matter of existential analysis. With this thought in mind, I want to draw your attention to some symbols of anxiety in literature. Dante's descriptions of the Inferno must be understood as structures of destruction in man's existential experience of estrangement, guilt and despair. They symbolize modes of despair as external punishments. Taken literally, they are absurd as are the symbols in Kafka's novels *The Castle* and *The Trial*. In the first instance, symbols of the anxiety of meaninglessness are given; in the second case, symbols of the anxiety of guilt. Conceptualized or symbolized, the description of anxiety is central for the existential attitude.

In order to give further examples of existential analyses, I want to reverse the procedure which I first used: that is, I shall cite essentialist criticisms of existential analyses and then the existential defense against the criticisms.

Essentialism criticizes the existentialist emphasis on anxiety and related concepts by denying that there is a qualitative difference between them and other internal experiences. The so-called existential analyses, are, so it is said, essential analyses of a predominantly psychological character. Experienced anxiety is like experienced anger or sadness or joy, an object of the psychology of emotions, a part of the general description of human nature. It is claimed that nothing verifiable in existential analyses is included in any essentialist description. If these arguments are valid, the existentialist claim has been refuted. But they are not valid. For there is a sharp qualitative difference between two kinds of affections (in the Cartesian-Spinozistic sense of affections). The one kind belongs to man's essential nature and embraces the totality of those affections which respond to stimuli coming from the universe of objects in the temporal-spatial continuum. Most of the affections discussed in ancient and modern philosophy have this character. They are objects of essentialist psychological descriptions.

But there is another kind, namely, those which respond to man's existence as existence and not to any stimuli coming from the contents man encounters within existence. Being aware of existence, experiencing it as existence, means being in anxiety. For existence includes finitude, and anxiety is the awareness of one's own finitude.

I have already pointed to the difference between fear and anxiety, the first having an object, the second not having one. But we must go one step further. Anxiety is the more fundamental affection because the fear of something special is ultimately rooted in the fact that as finite beings we are exposed to annihilation, to the victory of non-being in us. In this sense, anxiety is the foundation of fear. Their ontological relation is different; for anxiety has an ontological precedence; it reveals the human predicament in its fundamental quality, as finitude.

The relation of anxiety to fear is representative of similar relations in which two partly synonymous concepts point to something qualitatively different, the one to an essential structure, the other to an existential characteristic.

Since a comprehensive treatment of existential analysis is obviously impossible on this occasion, I shall restrict myself to those aspects of it which are especially useful as keys to the meaning of religious symbols.

Man in his existential anxiety feels estranged from that to which he properly belongs. Although created by Hegel in order to make the fact of nature understandable from the point of view of the absolute mind, the term soon acquired an existentialist meaning and has, since then, been used against Hegel. Man feels estranged from what he essentially is; he experiences a permanent conflict within himself and a hostility towards the world. This must be distinguished, though not separated, from the feeling of strangeness which every living being, animal as well as man, has for most of the other beings and often for himself. The emotions of strangeness and its opposite, familiarity, belong to the realm of essential relationships between finite beings. But estrangement is a negation of essential belongingness. It has an existential character.

Existential estrangement expresses itself in loneliness, which should be clearly distinguished from essential solitude, the correlate of which is essential community. Loneliness is an expression of anti-essential separation from that to which one belongs. This loneliness can express itself in the flight from solitude into the *"on,"* the *"man."*

Finitude includes insecurity. There is essential insecurity, the correlate to essential security, in the biological, social, and psychological realm. In all these spheres risk and chance are at work, but also law and certainty. The contrast to that is the ultimate insecurity of existence which is experienced in anxiety and described as being homeless and lost in one's world, and as being anxious about tomorrow, in German, *sorgen*. The distinction between being anxious and taking care, between *Sorge* and *Vorsorge,* is again linguistic support for the distinction between an essentialist and an existentialist concept. Essential insecurity may provoke the feeling of ultimate insecurity; but conversely, in an externally secure situation, existential insecurity may come as a sudden shock as it breaks into the world of finite relations.

The anxiety of estrangement has the color of existential guilt. We have already spoken of "guilt" as an example of the difference between an essential and an existential analysis. This distinction must be carried through in several directions. The first is the establishment of the existentialist concept of risk or of daring decision. In every decision a risk is implied; the risk to win or to lose something or someone. This belongs to man's essential character or finite freedom. He deliberates and then risks a decision. He may even risk his life. But there is another risk which belongs to man which is the cause of guilt and estrangement, namely, the risk of actualizing or non-actualizing himself, and in doing so to lose himself, namely, his essential being. This situation can be observed in every moment in which innocence is put before the decision either to remain in a state of non-actualized potentialities or to trespass the state of innocence and to actualize them. In both cases, something is lost; in the first, a fully actualized humanity; in the second, the innocent resting in mere potentiality. The classical example is the sexual anxiety of the adolescent.

As myth and experience tell, mankind as a whole risks its self-actualization and is consequently in the state of universal, existential estrangement. This produces the situation of tragic guilt in which everyone, in spite of his personal responsibility, participates. An early philosophical expression of this experience of being involved by destiny in a universal situation for which one is at the same time responsible seems to be the fragment of Anaximander, which, however one interprets particulars, combines separation, finitude, and guilt in a cosmic vision. This certainty transcends an essentialist analysis of responsible or irresponsible actions between persons. It judges the predicament of man and his world as such.

The last confrontation of an essentialist and an existentialist concept concerns man's cognitive estrangement from his essential being, as it is manifest in the situation of doubt. Doubt in the form of finite freedom is an essential element in the cognitive task of man. Essential doubt is the condition of all knowledge. The methodological doubt of Descartes was the entering door for the modern scientific consciousness. Quite different from it is the existential doubt, the doubt about the meaning of one's being in man's existential situation. Essential doubt is an expression of courage; existential doubt is a cause and an expression of despair. It is doubt neither of special assertions nor of all possible assertions, but it is the doubt about the meaning of being. It is the doubt concerning the being of him who doubts. It turns against itself and against the doubter and his world. And since it wrestles with the threat of meaninglessness, it cannot be answered by any of those assertions which have methodological certainty, probability, or improbability.

These are examples of existential analyses which seem to me sufficient to show the qualitative difference and independent standing of existential concepts and which may also be used as keys for the interpretation of religious symbols.

The examples we have given to show the difference between existential and essential analyses have provided us with the material necessary to interpret the basic religious symbols. It is almost a truism to assert that religious language is symbolic. But it is less of a truism to assert that for this reason religious language expresses the truth, the truth which cannot be expressed and communicated in any other language. And it is far from a truism to say that most errors in religion and most attacks on religion are due to the confusion between symbolic and literal language. This confusion, which must remain a chief concern of everyone who takes religion seriously, is not only a failure of the intellect, but also a symptom of the idolatrous distortion which is found in all religions and which makes the divine an object amongst objects to be handled by man as subject, cognitively and practically.

Once this fact is understood, one can easily see the relation between existential analyses and religious symbols. Existential analyses express conceptually what the religious myth has always said about the human predicament. And in doing so they make all of those symbols understandable in which the answer to the question implied in the human predicament is given: the symbols and myths which center around the idea of God.

Existential analysis deals with man's finitude as it is experienced in anxiety. The mythological symbol for this experience is man as a creature. Man and his world are creatures. Some forms of this symbol can be found in every religion. Man is not by himself. He has not what God has in classical theology, *aseitas*. He is a mixture of contrasting elements, divine and demonic, spiritual and material, heavenly and earthly, being and non-being. This is true of Eastern as well as Western religions, although the difference between the two appears immediately if one asks for the meaning of creaturely existence. The answer given in the East is negative and non-historical. Creaturely existence is something which should not be and from which one desires to be saved. In the West, the answer is positive and historical. There should be creaturely existence, but it must be saved not from itself as creature, but from its self-estrangement.

The consequence of the Western attitude is that creation has a positive side, answering the question implied in the experience of creatureliness. The answer is not a story according to which once upon a time a divine or half-divine being decided to produce other things. But creation expresses symbolically the participation of the finite in its own infinite ground; or, more existentially expressed, the symbol of creation shows the source of the courage to affirm one's own being in terms of power and meaning in spite of the ever-present threat of non-being. In this courage, the anxiety of creatureliness is not removed but taken into the courage. And in it, the loneliness of the estranged individual is taken into a unity which does not remove the threat of loneliness and its correlate, the flight into the *"man,"* the *"on,"* but which instead is able to create genuine solitude and genuine communion. And in the symbol of creation, existential insecurity is taken into a certitude which does not remove the insecurity of having no definite time and no definite space but which instead gives the security of participation in the ultimate power of being. Symbols like omnipotence, omnipresence, and providence corroborate this meaning. They become absurdities and contradictions if taken literally. They radiate existential truth if opened up with the key of existential analysis.

In the center of the symbolism of many religions we find the contrast of the fall and salvation together with a large group of corroborating symbols. The key to existential analysis is able to open them up even for those who have a special strong resistance against this kind of symbolism.

The symbolism of temptation has already been mentioned in connection with the analysis of the anxiety of existential decisions. Temptation is possibility, and the anxiety of having to decide is the awareness of possibility. There are many myths and legends of temptation of which probably the most profound is the Biblical story in which the situation of man, symbolized by Adam and Eve, is clearly the decision between remaining in the dreaming innocence of Paradise and achieving self-realization in knowledge, power, and sex. Man chooses self-realization and falls into the state of estrangement, and with him his world also falls. Understood in this way, the myth of the fall, for which there are analogies in most religions, represents a very particular case of the transition from the innocence of potentiality to the tragic guilt of self-actualization. It is a genuine description of man's predicament here and now and should not be vitiated by the absurdities of literalism.

The traditional term for man's status of estrangement is "sin," a term whose meaning has undergone more distortions and has consequently been the object of more protest than almost any other religious notion. Sin, in the light of existential analysis, is man's estrangement from his essential being, an estrangement which is both tragic necessity and personal guilt. The extremely questionable terms "original sin" and "hereditary sin" express the tragic and actual sin, the personal element. I suggest that we drop the terms "original sin" and "hereditary sin" completely. They seem to be beyond salvation. And certainly some words, especially theological and philosophical ones, need salvation. The term "original sin" should be replaced by existential descriptions of the universal and tragic character of man's estrangement. But the term can and should be saved by being reinterpreted as the stage of estrangement for which, in spite of its tragic character, we are personally responsible and out of which the concrete acts of estrangement from ourselves, from others, and from the meaning of our being, follow. If we use the term "sin," it should not be used in the plural but in the singular, without the article, as Paul does: sin, the power of estrangement.

The state of estrangement is the state in which the anxiety of guilt is amalgamated with the anxiety of finitude. The predominant religious symbols of this anxiety are, as already indicated in relation to Dante's poem, judgment, condemnation, punishment, and hell. They usually appear in a dramatic framework with a divine being as judge, demonic powers as executors, and a special place reserved for long-lasting or everlasting punishment. Although this imagery is largely recognized as such even in the average membership of the Christian churches, it is good to apply here also the keys of existential and depth-psychological analyses. It seems that in people like Peter Brueghel this was already a conscious situation. His highly existential pictures of the demonic realm are understandable only in the light of an existential analysis of the anxiety of guilt. Seen in this light, the divine law, according to which judgment is executed, is obviously the law of one's essential being, judging us because of the estrangement from ourselves. Only because of this situation has the law as law an unconditional character, however the content of the law may change. Seen in this light, condemnation and punishment are obviously not things which judge us from above, but symbols of the judgment we inescapably make against ourselves, of the painful split within ourselves, of the moments of despair in which we want to get rid of ourselves without being able to, of the feeling of being possessed by structures of self-destruction, in short, of all of that which the myth calls demonic.

The question and perhaps the passionate quest included in this situation is mythologically expressed in symbols such as salvation, redemption, regeneration, and justification, or in personal symbols such as savior, mediator, Messiah, Christ. Such symbols are common to most of the great religions, although the description of the way of salvation is immensely different.

Existential analyses have given decisive keys for the understanding of this symbolism, the dramatic frame of which corresponds to the dramatic frame of the symbols of estrangement. Some of these keys merit special mention. The first is connected with a semantic reflection by means of which salvation makes a whole of something which is split. *Salvus* and *saos* mean whole and healed. Salvation is the act in which the cleavage between man's essential being and his existential situation is overcome. It is the religious answer to the innumerable analyses which can be summed up in the title of Menninger's book, *Man Against Himself*. The second key is equally prepared by existential analysis, namely, the insight that the situation of existence cannot be overcome in the power of this situation. Every attempt to do so strengthens this situation, which can be summed up in the title of Sartre's play, *No Exit*. That is how the religious symbols which point to saving powers in nonpersonal and personal embodiments must be understood. The tragic bondage of estranged existence produces the quest for that which transcends existence although it appears within it, creating a new being. This and this alone is the religious paradox and not simply a logically "nonsense-ical" statement. The third key which has been successfully used is the understanding of reconciliation in the light of the experience of methodological as well as poetic-intuitive psychology. It is the idea that the most difficult thing for a human being is to accept himself and that the basic step in the process of healing is to give man the feeling that he *is* accepted and therefore can accept himself. Nobody understands today what justification by faith means. Everyone understands what it means to accept oneself as accepted.

In the analysis of existential doubt, in contrast to essential doubt, we touched on the concept of despair, literally, of hopelessness. Existentialist thinking, especially at one period of its development, devoted a great deal of work to the problem of nihilism, meaninglessness, nothingness, etc. The wide spread of this feeling is confirmed by many witnesses in this country as well as in Europe. Its analysis gives a key to a long neglected part of religious symbolism, the symbols of hope. Most religions are full of mythological, usually very fanciful, images of hope. Taken literally in any sense, they appear as pale but beautified images of our daily experienced world. Taken as highly symbolical, they express the conviction that in the realities of our daily experience, in spite of their seemingly meaningless transitoriness and ultimate emptiness, there is a dimension of meaning which points to an ultimate or external meaning in which they participate here and now. This is the key to the symbol of eternal life which can be more easily used in such an interpretation because it is less open to literalism than more dramatic but dangerously inadequate symbols such as life after death, immortality, reincarnation, heaven. Eternal life means that the joy of today has a dimension which gives it trans-temporal meaning.

In each of our attempts to open up a religious symbol with the help of an existential analysis, we open up implicitly the basic and all-embracing symbol of religion, namely the symbol of God. In relation to creation, He is creator; in relation to salvation, He is savior; in relation to fulfillment, He is the eternal. We lead from different points and with different keys to the central symbol. But we do not start with it. This is an implication of the existential method, which, I believe, is adequate to religion, because religion is a matter of man's existential situation. We must start from below and not from above. We must start with man's experienced predicament and the questions implied in it; and we must proceed to the symbols which claim to contain the answer. But we must not start with the question of the being of God, which, if discussed in terms of the existence or non-existence of God, is in itself a lapse into a disastrous literalism.

Following the method which goes from below to above, we reach an idea of God which avoids literalism and which,

just for this reason, establishes the reality of that which answers the questions implied in human existence. God, in
the light of this question, is the power of being itself, prevailing over against non-being, overcoming estrangement,
providing us the courage to take the anxiety of finitude,
guilt, and doubt upon ourselves. This experience is expressed in innumerable largely personal symbols describing
the idea of God. Symbols are not signs. They participate in
the power of what they symbolize. They are not true or
false in the sense of cognitive judgments. But they are authentic or inauthentic with respect to their rise; they are
adequate or inadequate with respect to their expressive
power; they are divine or demonic with respect to their relation to the ultimate power of being.

The vast problem of symbols, however, lies beyond the
scope of the present discussion. My task was to show that
existential analysis has made it more difficult for the modern
mind to dispose of religious symbols by first taking them
literally and then properly rejecting them as absurd. Any
attack on symbolism must be conducted on a much deeper
level, namely that of symbolism itself. Genuine symbols can
be overcome only by other genuine symbols, not by criticism of their literalistic distortions.

The Ontological Problems
Implied in the Objective
Side of Biblical Religion

1. THE DIVINE MANIFESTATIONS AND THE SEARCH
FOR ULTIMATE REALITY

We have confronted three symbols of the divine self-manifestation (creation, the Christ, the *eschaton*) with some ontological concepts and have found seemingly insuperable contradictions between them. Again I want to show that such contradictions are not necessary and that each of these symbols demands and has received ontological interpretation.

Creation by the Word out of nothing describes the absolute independence of God as creator, the absolute dependence of creation, and the infinite gap between them. The ontological question arises immediately at several points. One must ask how the eternal Logos, the principle of God's self-manifestation, is related to the contents of the world process. The classical answer, that the essences or potentialities of the world are eternal in the divine "mind," must either be accepted or be replaced by another one—and every answer is necessarily ontological.

(From Paul Tillich, *Biblical Religion and the Search for Ultimate Reality* [University of Chicago Press, 1955], Chap. VIII, pp. 73–85.)

Theology has rightly insisted that the "nothing" out of which the world is created is not the *me on* of the Greeks, that is, the matter which receives and resists the creative act. But, if the answer of a dualistic ontology is rejected, one must seek for another answer to the question: What does this "nothing" mean? How is it related to the divine, which as life presupposes nonbeing? Can one perhaps say in a highly symbolic phrase that the divine life is the eternal conquest of the nonbeing which belongs to him? Whatever the answer may be, it is ontological.

If we ask about the relation of the divine creation to the divine preservation and answer with Augustine that preservation is the permanent creativity of God in everything that is, we have reached the ontological metaphor "ground of being." And if we ask about the meaning of the ever-repeated assertion that God is both *in* and *above* the world and question the use of the spatial metaphors "in" and "above," we have asked an ontological question. If we then answer that the relation of God and the world is not spatial but must be expressed in terms of creative freedom, an ontological answer is given, but an answer in terms of freedom. The freedom of the creature to act against its essential unity with God makes God transcendent to the world.

Such ontology of freedom does not deprive existence of its sinful character, as an ontology of necessity would do. But, at the same time, it states the universality of the fall in terms of the concept of destiny which stands in an ontological polarity with the concept of freedom.

The christological confrontation has led to the question: Is there a necessary conflict between the universal Logos and the Logos who is present in the personal life of Jesus as the Christ? The early church and, following it, the church in most periods did not believe in such an unavoidable conflict. The Logos (i.e., the divine self-manifestation) is actively present in everything that exists, because everything is made through it. But only the ultimate divine self-manifestation shows what Luther has called the heart of divinity, God for man, eternal God-manhood in its very center. The Logos universal and the Logos as the power of a personal life are one and the same Logos. Only against the background of the universal Logos is the incarnate Logos a meaningful concept. Biblical religion has shown the ontological implications of one of its fundamental assertions in the prologue of the Fourth Gospel. Ontology is able to receive the christological question—the question of the place in which the universal Logos manifests itself existentially and unconditionally; the universal Logos appears in a concrete form. Every philosophy shows the traits of its birthplace. Every philosophy has concrete existential roots. To say that Jesus as the Christ is the concrete place where the Logos becomes visible is an assertion of faith and can be made only by him who is grasped by the Christ as the manifestation of his ultimate concern. But it is not an assertion which contradicts or is strange to the search for ultimate reality. The name "Jesus the Christ" implies an ontology.

The third manifestation of God which we have confronted with ontological categories is history, running toward an end, the historical-eschatological element in biblical religion.

Here again the first answer to the question is that only special kinds of ontology make the historically new impossible, for example, circular interpretation of the temporal processes. If time is symbolized as a circle, the new is excluded; everything repeats itself. The same is true of mechanical determinism in which a given state of things has necessary consequences, calculable in principle for all following states. But such ontologies do not represent ontology as such. The philosophies of life and process which have roots in men like Augustine and Duns Scotus have emphasized the openness of reality toward the future and have made a place for the contingent, the new, the unique, the irrepeatable. And no theologian who interprets the Bible through Greek terms like "history" can escape the profoundly ontological question: how history is related to nature; how all history is related to the small section of world historical events with which biblical religion deals; how the events in which man is involved are related to the events in the whole universe.

And there is another, even more difficult, question which demands an ontological answer implied in the historical-eschatological view of biblical religion. It is the meaning of the *eschaton* or the relation of the temporal and the eternal. If one identifies the eternal with the temporal continuation of life after death, one has made an ontological statement, and a very poor one, by confusing eternity with endless temporality. If one, in opposition to this, says that eternity is the simple negation of temporality, one has also made an ontological statement, also a very bad one, by confusing eternity with timelessness. There is, however, a third answer, also ontological, which does justice to the meaning both of time and of eternity. Eternity transcends and contains temporality, but a temporality which is not subject to the law of finite transitoriness, a temporality in which past and future are united, though not negated in the eternal presence. History then runs toward its end in the eternal, and the eternal participates in the moments of time, judging and elevating them to the eternal. Such statements are ontological in a half-symbolic gown. No theologian can escape them. And those who use a primitive-mythological language deceive themselves if they do not realize that the phrase "life after death" contains an ontology of a highly questionable character.

2. THE DIVINE-HUMAN RELATIONSHIP AND THE SEARCH FOR ULTIMATE REALITY

God speaks to man in biblical religion. The *word*, literally taken, is a spoken sound or a written sign, pointing to a meaning with which it is conventionally connected. But it is obvious that the God of the Bible does not speak or hear in this way. His Word is an event created by the divine Spirit in the human spirit. It is both driving power and infinite meaning. The Word of God is God's creative self-manifestation and not a conversation between two beings. Therefore, the Word is one of the aspects of God himself; it is God manifesting himself to himself. It is an expression of God as living and, as trinitarian thinking has always realized, an element in the power of being itself. It is ontological in its implications, although it is a genuinely religious symbol. This makes the doctrines of creation and salvation through the Logos possible and necessary, and it should make it impossible to confuse a theology of the Word with a theology of talk. The Word is an element in ultimate reality; it is the power of being, expressing itself in many forms, in nature and history, in symbols and sacraments, in silent and in spoken words. But it is not bound to spoken words. The nature of the word is a problem as old as ontology, and the divine Word is a symbol as old as religion. Without knowing something about the nature of the word, without an ontology of the Logos, theology cannot interpret the speaking of God, the divine Word. But, if theology uses this insight into the ontological nature of the word, it can teach meaningfully about the nature of the divine Word, the Logos who is with God.

The most devastating conflict between biblical religion and ontology appears to be the conflict between reciprocity and participation in the divine-human relationship. Ontology seems to remove the living interdependence between God and man, and it seems to remove the meaning of prayer, especially of the prayer of supplication.

The problem is present within biblical religion itself in the tensions between the unconditional emphasis on God's working in everything, even evil, sin, and death, and human responsibility for good and evil. A divine determinism often seems to conquer biblical personalism, and in men like Augustine, Thomas, Luther, and Calvin this determinism reaches sharpest expression. But at no point do these men and the biblical writers allow their emphasis on the divine activity to destroy the divine-human reciprocity. This can be understood only through the ontological polarity of freedom and destiny and through a distinction between the levels of being, namely, between the ground of being, which transcends all polarities, and finite being, which is subjected to them.

The divine determinism of biblical thought does not make the prayer of supplication impossible. No religious act expresses more obviously the reciprocity between God and man. Without the presupposition that the prayer changes the will of God in some respect, whether he hears or rejects the prayer, no prayer of supplication seems to be meaningful. But the early theologians, whose prayers underlie most of the Christian liturgies, emphasized the unchangeability of God against all paganism. God, the immovable, the transcendent One, was the first object of their theology. They were thoroughly ontological, and their relation to God was thoroughly reciprocal and full of prayer, including the prayer of supplication. This was and is possible because every serious prayer includes surrender to the will of God. It is aware of the ultimate inadequacy of words, the literal meaning of which is the attempt to move the divine will into the direction of one's own will. In every true prayer God is both he to whom we pray and he who prays through us. For it is the divine Spirit who creates the right prayer. At this point the ontological structure which makes God an object of us as subjects is infinitely transcended. God stands in the divine-human reciprocity, but only as he who transcends it and comprises both sides of the reciprocity. He reacts, but he reacts to that which is his own act working through our finite freedom. He never can become a mere object. This is the limit of the symbols of reciprocity. This makes the ontological question necessary.

3. GOD AS THE GROUND OF BEING IN ONTOLOGY AND BIBLICAL RELIGION

Our confrontation of biblical religion and the search for ultimate reality started with the doctrine of God. And our attempts to show the ultimate unity of ontology and biblical personalism must return to the doctrine of God. It is the beginning and the end of all theological thought. There is an element in the biblical and ecclesiastical idea of God which makes the ontological question necessary. It is the assertion that God *is*. Of course not everyone asks what this word "is" in relation to God means. Most people, including the biblical writers, take the word in its popular sense: something "is" if it can be found in the whole of potential experience. That which can be encountered within the whole of reality is real. Even the more sophisticated discussions about the existence or nonexistence of God often have this popular tinge. But, if God can be found within the whole of reality, then the whole of reality is the basic and dominant concept. God, then, is subject to the structure of reality. As in Greek religion, fate was above Zeus, determining him and his decisions, so God would be subject to the polarities and categories of reality as constituting his fate. The fight against this dangerous consequence of biblical personalism started in the Bible itself and continued in all periods of church history. The God who is *a* being is transcended by the God who is Being itself, the ground and abyss of every being. And the God who is *a* person is transcended by the God who is the Personal-Itself, the ground and abyss of every person. In statements like these, religion and ontology meet. Without philosophies in which the ontological question we have raised appears, Christian theology would have been unable to interpret the nature of the being of God to those who wanted to know in what sense one can say that God *is*. And the question is asked in prephilosophical, as well as in philosophical, terms by very primitive and very sophisticated people.

This means that *being* and *person* are not contradictory concepts. Being includes personal being; it does not deny it. The ground of being is the ground of personal being, not its negation. The ontological question of being creates not a conflict but a necessary basis for any theoretical dealing with the biblical concept of the personal God. If one starts to think about the meaning of biblical symbols, one is already in the midst of ontological problems.

Religiously speaking, this means that our encounter with the God who is a person includes the encounter with the God who is the ground of everything personal and as such not *a* person. Religious experience, particularly as expressed in the great religions, exhibits a deep feeling for the tension between the personal and the nonpersonal element in the encounter between God and man. The Old as well as the New Testament has the astonishing power to speak of the presence of the divine in such a way that the I-thou character of the relation never darkens the transpersonal power and mystery of the divine, and vice versa. Examples of this can be found in the seemingly simple words of Jesus about the hairs on our head, all of which are counted, and the birds which do not fall without the will of God. These words imply that no single event among the infinite number of events that happen in every infinitely small moment of time happens without the participation of God. If anything transcends primitive personalism, it is such a saying. And it is only a continuation of this line of biblical religion when Luther, who was very suspicious of philosophy, speaks of God as being nearer to all creatures than they are to themselves, or of God being totally present in a grain of sand and at the same time not being comprehended by the totality of all things, or of God giving the power to the arm of the murderer to drive home the murderous knife. Here Luther's sometimes unreflective biblical personalism is transcended, and God as the power of Being in everything is ontologically affirmed.

The correlation of ontology and biblical religion is an infinite task. There is no special ontology which we have to accept in the name of the biblical message, neither that of Plato nor that of Aristotle, neither that of Cusanus nor that of Spinoza, neither that of Kant nor that of Hegel, neither that of Laotze nor that of Whitehead. There is no saving ontology, but the ontological question is implied in the question of salvation. To ask the ontological question is a necessary task. *Against* Pascal I say: The God of Abraham, Isaac, and Jacob and the God of the philosophers is the same God. He is a person and the negation of himself as a person.

Faith comprises both itself and the doubt of itself. The Christ is Jesus and the negation of Jesus. Biblical religion is the negation and the affirmation of ontology. To live serenely and courageously in these tensions and to discover finally their ultimate unity in the depths of our own souls and in the depth of the divine life is the task and the dignity of human thought.

Being and Love

1. Ontology is the rational explanation of the structure of Being itself. Philosophy always was and always will be in the first place ontology, whether the philosophers admit it or not. The classical philosophers never were in doubt about this fact. Those who pretend not to presuppose an ontology deceive themselves. Even a skeptical epistemology such as present-day logical positivism is based on a hidden interpretation of the structure of Being itself.

2. Ontology deals with the structure of Being itself, not with the nature of a special being or a special realm of beings. Ontology asks the question: What does it mean that something *is* and is not *not?* Which characteristics show everything that participates in Being? The ontological question presupposes the attitude of a man who has experienced the tremendous shock of the possibility that there is nothing, or—more practically speaking—who has looked into the threatening abyss of nothingness. Such a man is called a philosopher.

3. If we speak of the ontology of Love we indicate that Love belongs to the structure of Being itself, that every

(From Ruth Nanda Anshen, ed., *Moral Principles of Action* [Harper, 1952], Chap. XXIII, pp. 661–72.)

special being with its special nature participates in the nature of Love since it participates in Being itself. The participation of a being in the nature of Love can happen even as the negation of love, as indifference, or as hate.

4. The thesis that Love is in the nature of Being itself must be tested by its adequacy to interpret life in all its aspects. Especially, it must be able to give a uniting ground to the different forms of what is called love. It must be shown that without the ontological approach the other approaches remain without a foundation.

5. Every ontology is fragmentary because of the finiteness of the human mind. So the ontology of Love cannot reach the form of a closed system. Hegel distorted his ontology of Love as expressed in his early fragments and in his *Phenomenology of the Mind* when he transformed the fragments into a closed system. It became a loveless mechanism —which has hidden some of his significant insights into the ontology of Love.

I. GOD AS LOVE

1. Theology as far as it uses the *logos* is philosophical. Consequently it includes an ontology, an interpretation of Being itself. This is expressed in the basic statement of every doctrine of God, that God is Being-Itself. God is not *a* being, not even the highest one. The atheistic protest against such an assertion is justified and must be a permanent tool of theological thought. God as *a* being is below Being itself; He has something above Himself, He is an idol. The fight against this idol is the theological truth of atheism.

2. Classical theology has affirmed that God is Being-Itself beyond any special form of being. It has not affirmed that this is the full concept of God but that it is *that* element in the idea of God which establishes His divinity. The fullness of the idea of God is based on the revelatory manifestation of Being-Itself. The rational transformation of the

manifestations of Being-Itself is the task of ontology. Ontology is based on the universal, although fragmentary, process of revelation.

3. The ontology of Love is classically expressed in John 4:8 and 16: "God is Love." It is not said that God is first something else and then *has* Love, but that He *is* Love, that Love is his very nature. Therefore he who remains in Love remains in God. And knowledge of God is impossible except through participation in Love. Loving God means "*loving Love*" as the ultimate, as Being-Itself.

4. Being-Itself is Love, this statement is implicit in the statement that God is Love. But besides this ontological statement there is the ontic statement, describing a special act of God, namely that He loves us, me, the world, the Christ. God as Being-Itself *is* Love. God as Being-For-Us *has* Love. The statement that He *is* Love is dependent on the act in which he manifests himself to *us* as Love.

5. The distinction of God *being* Love and God *having* Love is a key to the trinitarian idea and its symbolism. He who loves must have an independent being in relation to him who is loved. Love is real only if there is a "serious otherness" as Hegel has called it. But in the trinitarian process, going on between Father and Son in the medium of the Spirit, is no serious otherness. Therefore it is a play of the divine with itself, playing love, but not serious love. In less romantic terms this means that the Ground-of-Being is the principle of Love but that Love is actual or serious only in relation to the beings. For the beings are separated from their Ground by their freedom. The historical Christ is the seriously beloved son, not the eternal *logos*, except if seen eternally in unity with the historical Christ.

6. The importance of the trinitarian idea is that it points to the roots of life and love in Being-Itself. It points to the principles of otherness and reunion which since Parmenides and Plato have moved the ontological thought. "Being-

Itself has the nature of Love." This means that Being-Itself has trinitarian structure.

7. The Love structure of Being-Itself presupposes differentiation. The idea of otherness is spread all over the realm of ideas, Plato says. Everything which *is* shows this character. Being drives toward individualization. The individual thing is, according to Aristotle, the *telos* (aim) of nature. It is the really real, namely, that which has reality in itself or hypostatic, substantial reality.

8. Real is what has the power to resist non-being and what cannot be resolved into something else. According to this criterion the self-related being is the most real being. A completely self-related being has complete reality in itself. It resists absolutely the dissolution into something else. It cannot be divided, it cannot be made a mere part of something else. This is the reason why the logical solipsist can dissolve everything into a perception but not the other Ego. All genuine "realism" is based on the Ego-Thou relation. This is further the reason why we discover our own Ego only through the demanding resistance of the other Ego which makes us personal because it claims personal dignity for itself.

9. But the serious "otherness" does not deny the essential identity in the Ground of Being. The difference actualizes the identity and transforms identity into Love. The Love structure of Being is secondly the structure of reunion. *Tat twam asi* (This is Thou) is the classical expression of the moment of identity. But in India the difference is not taken seriously. Therefore Love is not understood, the otherness is only half real. If, on the other hand, separation is not balanced by the principle of identity, the separation becomes absolute as, for instance, in the two historically related ideas, the idea of a double predestination and the principle of unlimited competition. In both cases separation and not participation is the last word. Love as an ultimate principle is denied.

II. LOVE, POWER, AND JUSTICE

1. Reality is the power of resistance against dissolution into nothingness. Consequently, Being can be described (not defined) as the power of resistance against non-Being, or simply as the power of Being, whereby power means the chance of carrying through one's own self-realization. The power of Being is not a static possibility but it is the dynamic process in which a being actualizes itself by providing time and space to itself. This process and its limits cannot be determined a priori. It is a continuous venture, a pushing forward and encountering other beings, constellations, and laws, a being thrown back and starting again. In this process the principle of identity and differentiation are united. It is the source of all conflicts and of all creativity.

2. Love is possible only within the process of self-realization which is the process of reality itself. Therefore Love is real only as the power of Being. It is not the negation but the affirmation of power. The powerful being is the bearer of the powerful love. Love is not weakness, not resignation of power but the perfect power of Being. This is symbolically expressed in the statement that in God, Love and Power are identical. Ontologically this means that Being-Itself, the power in every power, is, at the same time, Love.

3. If Love is not the negation of power, self-denial cannot mean the denial of the power of Being, self-sacrifice cannot mean the sacrifice of self-realization. It can only mean that the resignation of a special time and a special space in the ecstatic experience of Love is the fulfillment of the self-realization. It is meaningless to say that I sacrifice my life for the sake of another life or my power for the sake of a strange power, if nothing else than this is implied. In reality all self-denial and sacrifice are accomplished for the sake of Love, which realizes its uniting power in a special moment by the surrender of special forms of self-realization. Not

even the individual who dies for the future of the many
(namely each single one within the many) dies for each
single one as such, but for the realization of the power of
Love in him and the many. If the individual has infinite
value and infinite depth he cannot surrender his meaning.
But he can surrender finite elements including the future
existence for the sake of his infinite value. This implies, of
course, the participation of the individual in Love itself, in
the eternal ground of Being (but it does not imply the
symbols of immortality and of a transcendent reward).

4. Love as the power of reunion of the independent elements of reality judges every process of self-realization and
demands venturing self-affirmation as much as venturing
self-negation. This judgment of Love is the justice immanent
in Being and therefore identical with the power of Being.
It is the just judgment which gives and denies space and
time to each being. It is the *diké* of the Greeks and the
divine righteousness of the Jews. But it is not something
strange to Love. It is the one element of Love; the other is
Power. The fact that both are rooted in Love gives them
their content, their limits and their interdependence. This
is the reason why Love can be called supreme law because
it is the criterion of the demands of justice. Justice is the
form of the uniting Love. Justice which destroys for the
sake of justice is injustice.

5. Love, justice, and power are inseparable in Being-Itself.
But they are separable in finite existence. Every self-
realization is partially unjust, because it is a *partial* self-
realization. Its power of being conflicts with other powers
of being. Higher units should be higher realizations of
power on the basis of uniting love and the form of justice.
Their higher power restricts the more partial powers in the
name of Love and in the form of justice. But they themselves may become unjust and lower units may represent a
higher, more universal justice. From this does not follow the
negation of power and justice for the sake of love, as re-

ligious anarchism and religious pacifism demand. Much more profound is Luther when he says that power breaking unjust power is Love's strange work, while Love's proper work is the mutual self-surrender to Love itself.

6. The judging side of Love demands justice in the self-realization and destroys injustice, but subjects it forcefully to a higher unity. The emotional attitude in the act of judging is the wrath which is directed against the evil and its bearers, not only against the evil but also against those who do it. Wrath is often understood as the opposite of Love. A whole theological school tried to find the balance between the divine Love and the divine wrath. But wrath is the negative side of Love, excluding the elements, subpersonal, personal and suprapersonal which prevent or dissolve the unity of Love. The divine wrath is the reaction of Love against the forces which are opposed to Love. Wrath is an implicit element of Love.

7. Wrath is not hate. The word hate has the connotation of the ultimate exclusion of somebody from the community of Love. It can even become the negation of Love-Itself, as the hate against God indicates. Therefore hate is not the other side of Love but the negation of it. There is a just wrath, but there is not a just hate. He who hates is not in a process of self-realization. He has not reached the stage of forgiving Love or *agape*. He sticks to his unjust self-realization and wants to preserve it by removing the other one from the universal unity of Love. (The fact that hate is often the expression of frustrated love confirms the ontological interpretation of love.)

III. TYPES OF LOVE AND THEIR ECSTATIC CHARACTER

1. Love in all its forms is ecstatic. The moment of love is a moment of self-transcendence. This implies the ecstatic character of Being in the sense of our transcending into the other Self while remaining within our own self. This ecstatic

self-transcendence is as original as the self-relatedness. Life is originally ecstatic. This is the basic refutation of the pain-pleasure psychology which is an expression of loveless self-centeredness.

2. This is true of the different types of love. We distinguish four types of love: The *libido* type, culminating in sex; the *eros* type, culminating in mystical union; the *philia* type, culminating in friendship; the *agape* type culminating in *caritas*. In each of these types the culmination is, at the same time, the culmination of the ecstasy.

3. The sex ecstasy is prepared in the ecstatic form of uniting oneself with material realities. The joy of eating and drinking, its intoxicating character is a part of the ecstasy of *libido*. The total union is reached in the sex experience.— The estranged form of eating and drinking as a physiological means of bodily self-preservation and the estranged form of sex as the physiological means of propagation are sins of Puritanism against Love. The opposite sin is the denial of the ecstatic character of Love by the pleasure principle (Hedonism). One necessarily follows the other. Vital ecstasy is self-surrender not to the other being as such but to the other being as far as it is the other side of the love-unity. The aggressive and destructive element in sex-ecstasy is not the denial of Love but the distorted expression of the self-transcendence of both partners. The Heraclitean identity of Dionysos and Hades, of love and death, is deeper than Freud's death-desire which is the result of the unfulfilled pleasure principle. Already in the vital sphere the deepest quality of Love appears: Love is loving the Love, it is *amor amoris*. If God is Love and the vital Love is real Love, the Dionysian element must belong to the divine Love. The danger is the limitlessness of the Dionysian love (*concupiscentia*), the lack of measure and form.

4. The second or *eros* type of love unites "Apollo" with "Dionysos." The classical expression of this type of love is Plato's *Symposium*. It starts with the sex ecstasy but ele-

vates it beyond the vital self-transcendence. While in the biological union beauty is present as a servant, in *eros* beauty becomes dominant, without destroying the vital basis, the *libido* element. *Eros* also produces knowledge, namely the intuition of Being in its logical form. The *eros* of knowledge is the ecstasy which is never disinterested, though it always keeps away from prejudiced judgments— for the sake of a union of subject and object. According to Plato and all mystics *eros* drives finally beyond any special form to the principle of form, the true and the beautiful itself. But the principle of form is not form itself. It is the highest ecstasy and the fulfillment of the *eros* type. Its danger is the confusion with the vital type. The ecstasy above the forms can become an ecstasy below the forms: chaos! The character of the *eros* type of love is also the love of love but it is not disinterested love. It participates in the ultimate. And in this participation the self is affirmed and denied at the same time.

5. The third or *philia* type of love is bound to personality. It is the self-transcendence toward the equal. But the equal of a different Self. Not consuming, not self-surrendering, but creating the third, the community which becomes an independent reality. The ecstatic element in the *philia* type of love is the participation in the self-realization of the friend in his changes and negativities. The representative couples of friends are ontologically bound together. The disciples of Jesus participate in his mystery and his task. This makes them his friends. In this respect they are equals, not servants. Friendship depends on the participation of both sides as equals in an embracing unity.

6. The *agape* type of love is ecstatic, by transcending the given self of the loving and the loved toward the unity of fulfillment. It is self-sacrificing not for the sake of the other Self as such, but for the sake of the ultimate destiny of the other Self. The union of *agape* is the union with the other Self in the realm of the ultimate meaning. The clearest ex-

pression is the charity character which sees in the other his potential fulfillment and makes the union not dependent on the judging wrath or the lack of *philia*. In this sense *agape* has always the forgiving element in itself. It is an ecstatic anticipation which is creative in the anticipated direction. Therefore God's love toward us is basically *agape*.

7. The love toward God is the love of love, but neither *agape* nor *philia* nor *eros* nor *libido* alone, but all of them united. The love toward God is the life finding itself and its substantial love-character and the affirmation of this character.

IV. SELF-LOVE AND SELF-HATE

1. The use of both words is analogous and not proper. By analogy you can consider the self-relatedness as a duality of a related subject and a related object. But if analogies are used their limitations and dangers must be realized. Which is the Self that loves its-Self? Is the loving Self a real Self, self-related in the sense of the accompanying self-awareness? And is it actually related to another Self of the same character? But it is not the same. And the whole play of thought is nonsense. Or is the loving Self only the awareness of the self-actualization of its being Self and the happiness connected with it. Then the word self-love without a loving Self and a loved Self is not a description, but a *façon de parler*, the old age of which does not improve its inadequacy. In Hegel's early writings we read: "Love your neighbour as yourself does *not* mean loving him as much as one loves oneself. For loving oneself is a word without meaning. But love him as him who is you, a feeling of the same life, not stronger, not weaker." The relation to the other Ego is measured by the value of self-realization in every Self. The equal value of the other's self-realization shall be acknowledged emotionally and by participation.

2. The same is true of self-hate. It may be said analogously,

it cannot be said properly. The emotional will to remove oneself can only mean the inability to participate in the love unity or to find the life which is reconciled with itself. But enthusiastic satisfaction is not self-love and desperate dissatisfaction about the lack of self-realization is not self-hate in the proper sense of the word.

3. Self-love does not show the characteristic of the real love: ecstatic self-transcendence in all its forms. The poverty of sexual satisfaction shows the contrast between love and self-relatedness in the realm of vital love. There is no good self-love in the sexual realm. The same is true of the *eros* realm. The attempt to create into oneself the forms of beauty and truth must lead to what Kierkegaard calls the aesthetic type, the detachment, the attitude of the spectator. There is no good self-love in the *eros* type of love. The same is true of the *philia* type. Sayings as: "I am the best friend to myself; I prefer to be alone with myself, to talk to myself, to embrace myself, and to agree with myself" are possible if taken in a metaphorical sense, but not in a proper one. In the realm of friendship there is no genuine self-love. The nearest to a meaningful idea of self-love seems to be in the *agape* type, because it points to one's own ultimate fulfillment. But the love of the *agape* type includes forgiveness and charity. And we can neither forgive ourselves nor can we be charitable toward ourselves. What then can self-love mean if it is neither charity nor friendship nor *eros* nor *libido* of oneself? Nothing! The same is true of hate. If in a great physical pain we wish to get rid of ourselves—this is not hate, even analogously. If in a psychological pain produced from outside we want to die—this is not hate either. If in a psychological (and perhaps consequently physical) pain produced from inside we want to die—this is split consciousness, the knowledge of being judged, the inability to stand the shame of forgiveness, the emptiness of the separation from uniting love. But it is not self-hate. We

do not want to remove ourselves and to prevent ourselves
from reaching the unity of love.

4. Selfishness or evil self-love or egocentrism or egoism are
all together words for self-realization which is lacking the
ecstatic self-transcendence. Here the use of the word self-
love is not admissible at all because the uniting, self-
transcending character of love is lacking and just the opposite, separation, seclusion takes place. If Love is what is
described in I Cor. 1, then the prefix "self" cannot turn the
meaning of the word into just the opposite.

5. The danger of inadequate words is inadequate connotations and practical consequences derived from them. The
words self-love and self-hate favor an attention upon ourselves which hampers the ecstatic self-transcendence of
love. The right attitude toward oneself is the right self-
transcending ecstasy of love which unites with other selves,
or substances or forms. The love of love, not the self-love,
is grace.

V. LOVE AND KNOWLEDGE

1. They are united in this that they overcome the strange
objectivity. The whole process of consciousness is the overcoming of the estrangement which we call the objective
world, according to Hegel. This self-estrangement of life is
the condition of love. It is based on reflection or self-
relatedness. "In love life finds itself as duplication of itself
and unity with itself." Love takes away the strange character of the object, the opposite. "In love the separated still
exists but no more as separated, but as united, and the living feels the living."

2. If love dissolves the fixed objectivity or strange opposition, knowledge is an act of love, because this is just its
function. The other self or resisting reality becomes united
in understanding, it comes home to us. This is the impulse
of the "phenomenology of spirit." Gnosis is loving "recogni-

tion," it is "cognized again," as what it is: an estranged part of the life process to which we belong. Love is the creative power of knowledge. Therefore knowledge follows the different types of love: the *libido* type of knowledge, the *eros* type of knowledge, the *philia* type of knowledge and the *agape* type of knowledge. They are attitudes, not methodological differences. The empirical attitude is, so to speak, the eating and drinking of the object and the possibility of using it for subjective purposes. It leads to "controlling" knowledge, the creator of the technical age. The intuitive attitude rests in the essences of things and is the foundation of sacramental thinking. The community attitude understands knowledge as a dynamic correlation between subject and object in which both are transformed. It is the foundation of the revolutionary thinking. The *agape* type of knowledge is the existential, self-determining knowledge, the knowledge of faith and revelation.

3. If knowledge is an act of love, is not self-knowledge an act of self-love? This seems to destroy all the arguments against self-love. But self-knowledge is not the uniting knowledge of an estranged object by a self which is estranged from it. Our knowing self-consciousness is never estranged from our Self. It is the awareness of our self-realization. The subject is only a logical, not a living, subject. Self-knowledge is like self-love an analogous term. The *gnothi sauton* demands the awareness of our situation as a finite, individual Self. Not the walls of objectivity must be penetrated, but the will which is afraid of self-awareness must be broken. The prayer of the psalmist that God may search his heart is the expression of the need for self-awareness.

CONCLUSION: THE UNITY OF LOVE

1. I close with the answer to the first question: If God is Love and consequently Being-Itself is Love, what does this

mean? The answer to this question cannot be an emptying of the mystery of Being. The real answer is the ecstasy of Love in the moments in which we experience the Ground of Being. The abstract answer points to experiences for those who are able to feel the power of reality which is behind an ontological concept.

2. The answer to the question, what does it mean that God is Love, is this: The Ground of Being from which every being takes its power of being has the character of self-separating and self-returning life. Self-separating is the abbreviation for complete individualization. Self-returning is the abbreviation of the return of life to itself in the power of reuniting love.

3. The difference between the pagan and the Christian interpretation of this process is the following: The pagan doctrine interprets the separation as an accident which happens to Being and contradicts its essence. With the exception of some Platonic words this is the Greek and Indian attitude. Therefore Love is the desire to return and the measure of Love is the measure of the nearness to the unity. In Christianity, Love is the meaning of the separation as well as of the return. Therefore Love is directly related to the lowest as well as the highest. This is the difference between the *agape* and the *eros* type of Love.

5. But this difference is no ultimate. If God is Love and Being is Love, the whole process of self-realization and reunion has a divine character: *libido*, for instance, eating, drinking, sex are sacramental; *eros,* the creations of the spirit are holy; *philia,* the communities of persons are consecrated. But all this has in itself the tragic perversion and frustration, the self-centeredness which contradicts the return to the unity. Only *agape* can overcome it. The ultimate meaning of our being can only be fulfilled in the paradoxical leap beyond the tragic-demonic frustration. It is a leap from our side, but it is the self-surrendering presence of the Ground of Being from the other side. The sym-

bol of God sending his Son to the Cross, the symbol of the suffering God, is the expression of the *agape* type of love. This is the foundation and the corrective of the other types. Without it they end in tragedy, frustration and despair. *Agape* does not remove the other types of love, but it makes them possible. Faith is the acceptance of the paradox of *agape* as the innermost center of Being-Itself.